Researching Local History

Approaches to Local History

General Editor: David Hey

Local history has been a spectacularly successful growth area in recent years, among professional historians and enthusiastic amateurs alike. In this new series, Longman will be publishing books on particular themes and aspects of the subject, written by experts for a student and lay readership. It will include practical volumes that explore the methodology of local research, and volumes that themselves illuminate the hidden lives of ordinary people in times past.

Already published:

A History of British Surnames   Richard McKinley

A History of English Field-Names   John Field

Oral History and the Local Historian   Stephen Caunce

Researching Local History   Michael A. Williams

Researching Local History

The Human Journey

Michael A. Williams

Longman
London and New York

Addison Wesley Longman Limited,
Edinburgh Gate,
Harlow, Essex CM20 2JE, United Kingdom
and Associated Companies throughout the world.

Published in the United States of America
by Addison Wesley Longman, New York

© Addison Wesley Longman Limited 1996

First published 1996

ISBN 0 582 04289 5 CSD
ISBN 0 582 04288 7 PPR

British Library Cataloguing-in-Publication Data

A catalogue record for this book is available from the British Library

Library of Congress Cataloging-in-Publication Data

Williams, Michael A. (Michael Arnold), 1936-
    Researching local history: the human journey/Michael A. Williams.
        p. cm. – (Approaches to local history)
    Includes bibliographical references and index.
    ISBN 0-582-04289-5 (casebound). – ISBN 0-582-04288-7 (pbk.)
    1. Great Britain – History, Local – Research – Methodology.   2. Great Britain – History,
    Local – Historiography. 3. Wales – History, Local – Research – Methodology.
    4. Wales – History, Local – Historiography. I. Title. II. Series.
DA1.W54   1996
941'.0072 – dc20   95-45476
                                                                                             CIP

Set by 3TT in 10/12pt Times

Produced by Longman Singapore Publishers (Pte) Ltd.
Printed in Singapore

Contents

Contents

Contents

Contents

Contents

List of Illustrations

List of Tables

Author's Preface

It is seventeen years since my 'need to know' first drove me to enter the Public Record Office. By the time I caught the train home that day I was probably already committed to a personal research theme. Indeed, one close friend, even then, said that I would write a book on local history. As years went by, I found that my major problem lay in deciding which of the possible books to write. The brief I finally received was to write a how-to-do-it local history book concentrating on the past 100–150 years.

Many people have encouraged me. My wife Dominique Simon-Williams told me a thousand times (at least) how important the task was. Sue Turton never failed to be interested in aspects of local history over coffee. Michael Turton, on our many travels together, so often produced the negative that was just a bit better than mine. He also printed all of the illustrations, and did the *CorelDraw* work. I had lots of help and information over the years from the Sheffield University Names Group.

I am especially grateful to David Hey, the editor of the series, and to the staff of Longman for their advice and kindness. They have been especially patient in dealing with a scientist setting off to write about history, and have saved me from many embarrassments. Any faults that remain are entirely of my own making.

Michael Arnold Williams
Riverdale Park, Sheffield

Editorial Preface

There are many ways of approaching local history. The earlier books in this series have dealt with surnames, field names, and oral history. Other books have concentrated on showing the reader where to find documentary records, how to read them, and how to use their information. The widespread interest in landscape history is catered for by numerous attractive books which show the local historian how to interpret the visual evidence of his or her everyday surroundings. And in recent years the enormous growth in the popularity of family history has given fresh impetus to the local historian's desire to relate people to places.

Michael Williams's book is about ways and means of investigating the people of particular places. He is interested in their origins, their networks of neighbours and families, their connections with local and national events, and with organised groups. He concentrates on the lives of ordinary people, their movements and mixing. The dynamics of the communities that he is interested in are revealed through a series of family histories. Indeed, an interest in the various branches of his own family led him to wider studies of the places where they lived.

His book is intended as a methodological guide for amateurs. It differs from most guides to local history in concentrating on the last two or three centuries. In practice, most local and family historians are concerned with this later period, and are even turning to the twentieth century now that it is drawing to a close! One of the strengths of the book is the way that it describes the impact of the First World War on local communities and the suggested ways of researching this topic. Another strength is the advice it gives on the use of computers for studying local history. Now that computers are 'user-friendly' and are installed in numerous homes, this guidance is invaluable.

Michael Williams has written a 'how to do it' book, based on his own

Editorial Preface

experiences. He has long been interested in local and family history, but this has been an amateur interest, in the best sense of the word. He is Professor of Anatomical Science in the Department of Biomedical Science at the University of Sheffield. It is fascinating to see how someone who has a distinguished reputation for writing books on the scientific method approaches the study of local history. Like all good teachers, he wishes to encourage others and uses his own studies to illuminate matters of general interest. The reader will immediately sense that the author's suggestions are stimulating and practical. These are avenues of exploration that any local or family historian can follow.

DAVID HEY

The publishers would like to thank Carmen Balcells, Agencia Literaria Carmen Balcells, S.A. for granting permission to reproduce an excerpt from *Cien Años de Soledad* (*One Hundred Years of Solitude*) © Gabriel García Márquez, 1967.

*'We will not leave,' she said. 'We will stay here,
because we have had a son here.'*

*'We have still not had a death,' he said. 'A person
does not belong to a place until there is someone dead
under the ground.'*

Ursula replied with a soft firmness:

*'If I have to die for the rest of you to stay here,
I will die.'*

*José Arcadio Buendia had not thought that his wife's will was so firm. He
tried to seduce her with the charm of his fantasy, with the promise of a
prodigious world where all one had to do was sprinkle some magic liquid
on the ground and the plants would bear fruit whenever a man wished,
and where all manner of instruments against pain were sold at bargain
prices. But Ursula was insensible to his clairvoyance.*

Gabriel García Márquez, *One Hundred Years of Solitude*, translated from
the Spanish by Gregory Rabassa

Peter Llewellyn Williams
1926–94
who also marched upon
the ridges of the sunset
but who saw there an other
truth

CHAPTER ONE

The Why and How of Studying History

For a scientist like myself brought up on experiments, measurements and coefficients, as someone who thought in terms of statistical tests, the study of history has seemed strange and difficult to take in hand. It is broad and diffuse, and stretches to unreachable horizons, and yet is crammed also with minute pieces of factual information. How on earth does anyone evaluate the material of a subject that is so lacking in means of experiment for disproving theories? How can any factors be identified as causing things if there are no opportunities for isolating variables?

Indeed, the whole matter of the nature of 'history' has seemed to me problematical. Just what is the history of an event, or of a country? What information qualifies to be part of it? How do you get that relevant information? What do you leave out? Such dilemmas were not mentioned during the (apparently) very factual history lessons that children of my generation received at school.

But of course, I am far from being the first person to notice that writing the history of a place, or the story of the events during a particular period of time, poses some awkward problems. However, it was only when I became interested in the past of some particular places that I found myself confronted by these problems: how do you research a history? How do you write the story of a place?

No doubt all the authors who laboured to compile the huge number of existing published 'histories' of all sorts – of places, of events and of times – have met these questions. Really, at the beginning, there are three issues: how do you decide what to study; how do you study it, and how do you report the results? To create a discussion, it is easiest to start by thinking first about written histories.

WRITTEN HISTORY

Putting aside the matter of how historians have chosen their research topics, and their tasks in finding and processing the data that the research throws up, the way that they most usually dealt with the matter of compiling a historical account has been one or another of the following.

First, they have concentrated on certain major features of the past time in question, on generalities, on some broad relation such as that between nation states or between other large bodies of people. They have written then what is sometimes called a macrohistory.

Second, they have focused on certain personalities that flourished at the time of their interest – their lives and their influences: kings, generals, ministers of state, preachers, teachers or perhaps even renowned demagogues.

Third, they may not have concentrated on people at all, but on things which do not move or talk, the products of trade or industry, or the fabric – the buildings, and the site and the growth of a place.

Finally, they may have chosen to concentrate upon specialities, slivers and fragments of special information within the whole: perhaps the origins and developments of institutions and their proceedings. Examples of this last way might be the rise and workings of a political party, the beginnings of a trade union or a religious sect, or the development of a body such as the Royal Society. All of these ways solve the 'history writing problem' by narrowing it down. Science works like that too. It is a very successful strategy.

Many of the products of this sort of work inevitably point up the role of the people who wielded power – monarchs, princes and rulers, and others who governed. These accounts offer little detail of deed, thought or choice among the people who were governed. The histories tell much of owners and generals, but little about labourers and common soldiers. And of course, since the great and powerful have more often than not been male, the histories have often told much about powerful men; but much less about women. Perhaps some issues of real substance are: how to contrive to deal with manageable quantities of material, yet how also to refine it, presenting the reader of a resultant 'history' with a product that they can relate to. For even though the mass action events of continents and nations did affect the lives of millions, and although many striking personalities did influence great events, one must ask if ordinary people even heard tell of the famous names. And surely, few ordinary folk set eyes upon palaces or on the great chambers of government?

Certainly, the value of the many distillations of the past lies not at all in showing detail at a human scale, but rather in offering important generalities or conclusions. It rests too, in the provision of short abstracts, texts suitable for easy transmission, for sharing and repeating. The transmission of history in this form has very important social roles and implications. Material at the scale of the individual has to be sought and found elsewhere.

GETTING AT THE ORDINARY

We each know that, inside ourselves, we have a unique set of experiences. Indeed, even when we attend an event with other people, we do not all see it the same way. Great events are always made up of lots of tiny ones. Inevitably individuals, from their own vantage point, see their own proportion of them, and on top of that have their own selective recall. Every individual can generate a unique account that is personally truthful. The total of details they all remember is often impossibly large. Even for one ninety-minute football match, no one would have time or space to note down all the tiny events that the members of the 30,000 crowd recalled seeing. Of the match a macrohistory may simply and reasonably state that the final score was 3–0, and that it was an untidy game. This report will be all most of us will need. After all, we are much more likely to need the complete set of Saturday football scores, each with its attached brief report, than we are a multi-volume work written about one match. Macro versions of events ('macros') are essential components of a sane life.

There may be no problem at all in accepting the macros of last week's soccer programme, yet perhaps we have reservations about being provided only with the twenty-line or even the five-line versions of huge events such as the Second World War. In highly abridged versions, even great personages may be omitted, and the account may very well mislead. But even if it does not misinform in that way, it inevitably overlooks very many ordinary lives. Those whose words are included are selected to speak as the contribution of the people of power. As readers of histories, we may well feel and conclude differently, when we are offered writing about or from the common people. At any time, how close were the great personalities in experience and thought to the main body of people? Usually, not very.

Nevertheless, macros which distil the mass action of events, or which build a story around the lives of politicians or thought leaders, offer at least one other social essential: disseminated they make that glue that binds people to other people. Communities, races and nations need shared views of their collective pasts. The schoolroom and kitchen repetitions of gists of history ensure the existence of a shared reference material. Its potency is quite undiminished by its over-simplifications and by any inaccuracies that it propagates. The myth provision in society is so important that if something digestible and containing some skeleton of truth is not available, human nature will ensure that some truthless folklore will arise. Myths can fulfil their essential purpose even without resort to truth.

But there is widespread dissatisfaction with global accounts. For some people the accepted wisdom about events is simply not enough. And they need to ask 'how true are the myths?', or 'what relation did the well-known events have to the lives of my people?' Irrespective of what they read, some people want to know 'just what were the lives of ordinary people really like in past times?'

Somehow the challenge of these sorts of questions has to be met. There has to be some other way of examining the past; or perhaps even some other sort of history. And if there is another way of looking back, one question that must live there is: 'how do I and other folk fit to the past of our people?' For somehow we, the living, have to place ourselves in context, and bridge a ravine that lies between us and national or global events. But we can talk of another way of looking only if we think about research as an activity, and address the process – the actual way of doing it.

CHANGING HOW WE SEE

Imagine a busy, sunny, daytime city. You view it from the roof of a sky-scraper. Here is a thing of great flux. People and vehicles move one way and another way. Some move quickly, some pause. Others seem always static. The main shopping street is full and remains so, despite the comings and the goings. We cannot doubt the activity of the place. The volume of the traffic remains undiminished.

Our description, though, mentions only a part of what there is to see. By concentrating upon the fullness of the street we have restricted ourselves to one type of information, and in consequence have obtained a very incomplete picture of how the city works.

So suppose we change our way of looking; imagine we decide not to stare at the mass of people and vehicles, but at particular individuals. We will follow them from when and where they come into view to wherever it is they go. Doing this we may soon realise that although the street remains approximately as full for several hours at a time, the individual people in it are regularly exchanged. Many of them are only passing through, or pausing there briefly. Some occupy particular buildings. A few travel in company rather than alone. Some have come a very long way to the city; others have far to go when they leave. By looking at the individuals, the way the live city works is illuminated. In historical studies, if we turn the eye of our research from gross events, to a study of some individual places, a selection from the many, the history of the nation may be also illuminated, just as the organic city is traced by its active citizens.

The study of people and change in selected localities, at once, then, shows a potential for satisfying our need of relating ordinary lives to larger events, and for simultaneously gaining a view of the process of change as it happened to the common people. And in the course of this study, we would not put out of sight the major factors in the nation's past, even though we reduce a large lake of information to a drinkable glassful. We won't stop being conscious of great events. There is a prospect here of much minute labour. This makes the different sort of history we spoke of earlier.

BEING A STAKEHOLDER

As far as most of us are concerned, the time and effort needed to reveal details of the lives of past individuals might not be forthcoming, had we not a personal stake in the business. A personal connection drives us on. For instance, my own route to studying British history has been via local history. But my first steps into local history were upon the carpet of my own family's past.

I had naturally chosen to study first the places where I and my ancestors had lived. Later I commenced a study of the city in which I live now. The results of this work, and especially that which started with my own ancestors, to some extent colours my view of great events in British history. It has also beaten a path for me into a story of two nations. Sometimes it has offered a feel of some currents that pass among 58 million people.

Like myself, most local historians are motivated by personal curiosity. Often, though not always, this commences with a need to clarify things about their own roots, or their own surroundings. On the trail of their own forebears, individuals will invest hours without number seeking out and studying documents. They will incur uncalculated personal expense, on the road to a clearer view of their own background, and in the hope of explaining that in themselves which they so far have found unexplainable.

While many searchers do seem well satisfied with some names written on a genealogical chart, others, once they have named great-grandfather, must locate his house. They find themselves deeply curious about his neighbours. For these people, a study in local history has been entered on, almost without a conscious decision.

As a result of this sort of sequence, I have come to know several Somerset villages, the tenancy of the farms in them and the lineage of many of the long-established families. I have identified people who left them for America. Some years ago, when certain very old people were still alive, I could hold conversations with them about farming methods and about families that had long since disappeared. My family's history had, without my noticing it, grown up into local history.

But the growth process does not stop there. The past of those same villages includes and illustrates many, many other phenomena: the eighteenth-century draining and enclosure of the Levels, the depth of nineteenth-century rural poverty, commercial turf cutting, the growing of cider apples. The list is very long. Some, at least, of these matters lead directly to considerations of topics of general importance in British rural history.

There is, then, a 'hot line' from family history, through local history to national history. Not that one should imagine for a moment that genealogy is the only starting point for local history. After all, had I gone to live on King's Sedgemoor, even with no knowledge of my own roots there, I may still have been fascinated enough by that watery landscape to begin to ask questions about the locality. Curiosity about one's current surroundings is often quite sufficient to provoke the beginnings of a local study. That too has happened to me, though I had lived in this city quite some years (two decades in fact), before I finally felt sufficient of a Sheffielder to begin to formulate questions about Sheffield history. I saw the place. I even went to lectures about the place. But I did not formulate research questions until much later. Perhaps it is true that before one actively poses local questions, one has to feel some local connection. Certainly you have to have some experience of the place. It can thus be argued that the questions always begin with our own selves, and hence always start with our own time.

MICROHISTORIES

If potted histories and myths serve the needs of nations and act as binding forces within communities, they must also have some role in securely establishing new children within their own people. Local histories, though, are 'microhistories' – accounts in which the historian attempts to understand the past and possibly, therefore, the present, by a study of fine detail. The historian is taking first, not the global, but the parochial view. The concerns of the research are not immediately those of nations and their great events, but those of named people, of families, villages, employers, homes and landlords. In this prospect of affairs, compilers are likely to place themselves close to the questions asked, and to look thereby for the generation of a history, in which their own face can be reflected. It will, they hope, also be a history in which the past of their people can be viewed in a personal perspective. As compilers build a history with their own tiny place implied, they may find themselves disabling handed down myths. They may claim their personal line in the story, exchanging for it the insignificance assigned to them in the formal macro versions.

DIRECTIONS

Starting points for local studies can naturally range very widely. The seed can be of the sort: 'I've often wondered about that piece of empty land I go past on the way to work. What was it once used for?' Alternatively, it might be something like: 'Why did my family come to live here?' or 'Why was I brought up with these particular beliefs?' It can originate too in curiosity about a name, or in people or buildings seen in photographs. Whatever the original questions, though, they will certainly possess two particular important characteristics. The first is that they are likely to expand and branch out, when one tries to find answers to them. The second is that attempting to answer them commits one to making a journey backwards through time.

Take the first of the three questions that I have just mentioned, the one concerning a piece of land. This might be approached by looking for the current large-scale (say 1:2500) Ordnance Survey map, and then following up study of that with examination of an earlier edition. If you find on the map the name of a works that once stood on that site, a next move might be to look for old editions of local trade directories.

The second question, about family movement, is a much more complicated affair. Pursuing it must necessitate finding out *when* your people arrived. That might well involve finding out not only what trades they had, but also what other people were coming to the town at that time, what trades they were in, and where they *all* came from.

Of the three, the third question, the one about beliefs, is much the hardest. It implies the need to find out about the life experience of earlier members of your family, and the churches and other institutions they were connected with. It also implies that an attempt may have to be made to find out the value systems of their local society. But were the beliefs and attitudes that your family held also shared by their neighbours?

JOURNEYING BACK

History teaching texts are often compiled histories (tales, almost), which start with the earliest time under consideration and work their way story-like forward, frequently stopping well before they reach the present date. But reasonable as this is as a way of presenting an analysis, this arrangement does not reflect the way one pursues a question in practice. The process of research is not equivalent to the written story. The three questions mentioned above are all posed in and approached from the 1990s. However, as each question is clarified and some answers are generated, fresh questions are born. The likelihood is high that each of these new questions will reach further back in time than its parent question. After all, the reasons for events lie previous to them, not after them. So you may study increasingly earlier maps; you might search earlier and earlier censuses for a family's geographical roots; you could proceed backwards through directories until you identify the earliest reference to a certain trade. The process goes from now, the edge of newborn events, backwards to yesterday, to last year, a generation ago, the nineteenth century, the time before Waterloo, the years of the Commonwealth, and beyond.

SOURCES AND CHOICES

It is coining an aphorism to say that history is not that which happened, but is that which is told about what happened. But it has to be said. A history is created text; it is not the events themselves. Even when we choose to approach studies of the past by the route of a local study, there are still innumerable components within each small happening. Even dealing with small places, a process of selection is inevitably applied to the data, in order to create the final account. One simply cannot include everything!

It is worth reflecting, though, that not only are the obtained data selected for writing an account, but so also was the source for those data. Thus you can choose which aspects of a parish register to quote, but you can also choose in the first place which registers of which parish to take them from. You might take data from any of a huge variety of sources and hence obtain information of a vast array of types. You could talk to people and ask them questions; you could search newspapers and periodicals. You might take vital event data from national records, study censuses, peruse drawings, maps and photographs or consider the form of buildings, and the topography of the land. You are in charge here, and you make the choices.

In practice, for a retrospective journey starting in 1990, you are likely to choose different sorts of sources for your information at different stages. Partly this is because all possible sources are not available for all time periods. At some dates, one type of record was kept and another not, while some types of records have fared better than others in the survival stakes. Twentieth-century studies depend little on records such as church baptismal and burial registers, but on the other hand, many events are recorded in the minute books of elected local authorities, as well as in a host of print and picture ephemera.

Moving further back, many printed sources peter out before you reach 1840. Very many local newspapers for example, started after 1850. And going back previous to 1800, parochial, quarter sessional and manorial records assume major importance, as much because of the lack of some other records, as because of their intrinsic worth, though that is very considerable.

Progressively, as the past is penetrated, the various documentary sources fall away. Then, usually among the last sources that remain, one of the wealthiest is the form of the land surface itself. Both landscapes and townscapes owe their rich detail to the fact that Britain has been occupied to an appreciable population density by a sedentary people, for well upwards of 2000 years. Human usage is bitten deep into hills and valleys. Most low lands have been used and re-used many times, hardly a stone remaining in the place assigned to it by wind, ice and water. The reality of such ordering of the land is brought home to British visitors to North America. There, even in the states of New England, one of the parts of that continent longest lived upon by Europeans, homes seem to rest merely upon the surface of the soil, while in parts of western Canada, large tracts of hinterland remain quite free of any sign of human influence. Returning to the British Isles reminds travellers that detail of our land can be close read, like an artist's proof plate of human habit.

In Britain the list of sources concerning each small segment of the country is indeed long and varied. As a researcher, it is both your privilege and your responsibility to choose from among all the possible places for study, and then to choose again from among the sources, materials and methods that may cast a revealing light on your place. Of course, all aspects – historic landscape, buildings, artifacts, documents and people – can act as primary focus. But all these aspects interconnect. You can start working at a problem from any of many different points, yet you may approach similar conclusions.

THE PURPOSES OF THIS BOOK

My own personal preoccupation has been with the studying of the people of particular places. I am interested in from whom they descend, how and why they or their forebears came there, the nature of their personal, family and neighbourly connections, the groups and associations that they formed, and how those associations functioned. These are the aspects of local history that I want to promote. This book is not itself intended to be a history of anywhere, although it is illustrated with the results of actual studies. It is a method book, which naturally contains some fragments of place histories, compiled either as text or as other appropriate products.

The localities that the text is centred upon are very frequently (though not always) places with which I have a personal connection. I was born and brought up in the small town of Caerleon, an ancient place in the county of

Figure 1.1 Caerleon in the Lower Usk valley, Gwent. The town, which is now subsumed within Newport Borough, was previously an Urban District cut out from the ancient parishes of Llangattock juxta Caerleon and Christchurch. They are separated by the River Usk, which is tidal at this point. The photograph, taken in 1992, shows how house building of the past fifty years has reached out on to the hill to the north of the old town. [Photo M. Turton]

Gwent (Figures 1.1–1.3). I have drawn upon data about its past many times in this book. The city of Sheffield too is mentioned several times. It has been my home since 1963. Further examples are taken from studies of various places in Somerset and Wiltshire, and in addition, brief reference is made to many other districts around and about, and across England and Wales. Since my experience is almost entirely of research in Wales and England, it was appropriate to leave research in Scotland and Ireland to some other better qualified writers. However, Irish and Scots born people do feature in some accounts of English and Welsh districts.

Figure 1.2 A view of Caerleon, taken in 1911, showing ancient housing at Ultra Pontem in Christchurch parish. Local people have for many years referred to Ultra Pontem as The Village to distinguish it from The Town in Llangattock parish.

Figure 1.3 Some of the products of the building boom that took place in and around Caerleon Common between about 1890 and 1910. The photograph was taken about 1933.

My preference in research period has always been for what, in historians' terms, are modern times. Since I am talking of method, and of a retrospect and journey from the 1990s, I am concerned especially with available material about the last 100–150 years. I do think that insufficient attention is generally given by local historians to the twentieth century, so the weighting of the material here goes a little way towards putting something right. In a few places where this has been essential, I have sought sources from far further than 150 years into the past.

Recurring questions that have interested me very much and which have provided some foundations for the material of the book have been:

- Where did these people come from?
- When did they arrive?
- Why did they come here?
- How did incomers and long-established families behave towards each other?
- What interpersonal networks grew up?
- What were the influential events and institutions in the place at various previous dates?
- What employment and skills were available here?
- Why, how and when did industrial enterprises and social institutions arise?
- Did people emigrate from here?
- If so, when, why and to where?

These questions are all much to do with origins, movement and mixing, and the reasons for movement, the *dynamics* of the local people. This perspective on local history is in no way intended to dismiss the building and landscape aspects of places. Rather, it wishes to treat them as the physical context or sometimes the creations of the people. Many times buildings or institutions are referred to as the cause of personal meeting, or the focus of group activity.

The ebb and flow of the people, you might loosely call the population history of place. The strategies and protocols that I have applied, and which I describe in this book, are intended for establishing detail. They are methods of asking precise questions and procedures for verifying answers. What is being investigated and logged is not only origins and movement of past people, but also the past networks of connections between people: genetic, neighbourly and institutional, the sharing of experience and events.

RESEARCH METHODS

It will be clear from the list of English and Welsh places mentioned in the last two sections that the sort of research this book addresses might be applied to hamlets, villages or cities. Like place, local seems to be a very flexible word! It is worth briefly considering what is included, since to a degree this defines the area of play. Putting the question formally: what is an appropriate geographical unit of inquiry?

Before attempting to answer that, it is worth saying that most people set off to study a named place. Named places can range widely in population, and can occupy land area from a few tens of acres to several hundred square miles. Thus they may range from the very practical to the entirely impractical. Furthermore, although they do have a clear picture of what the place is now, the entity that went under that name 100 or 200 years ago was not the same in population, in fabric or in numerous other ways, even though the local hills and valleys remain. A place defined just by name is too complicated to use. To be clear, we have to define a study area by appropriate boundaries on the ground, and meet certain other requirements too.

Since our research usually starts in the present, we normally define what is local for us by reference to where we presently live or work. We do this using, as markers, familiar topographic features and buildings. The area we think of as our locality often roughly coincides with our usual area of frequent personal contact. It follows, then, that what is local to us when we are children is a very small patch, and our personal locale gets larger as our age and personal mobility increases.

Experience shows that as local historians we are much more likely to set off to research the area we feel is 'local' than we are to start off on another area. And since feelings of personal connection are often involved in our choice, the area chosen might well be what was local for us when we were a child. That area may have changed a great deal in recent years and it is the remembered image, rather than the present one, which is often our starting point. Despite this, the choice of geographical unit has to make sense on the ground in the 1990s.

So, bearing in mind that the ultimate units to which data refer are individual people or families, what is a reasonable geographical patch on which to begin?

Whatever the detailed nature of the research questions, choosing will probably have to be done on several rational bases:

1. There must survive written records and/or sources of oral evidence of types appropriate to the study.
2. The choice of area must have some geographic logic. Thus, the patch must be of sufficient area so that much of the very frequent, short-range movement of people is contained within it, for otherwise all data obtained will be very unstable. Furthermore, it must have unambiguous boundaries on the ground. Ideally, this might also mean that the chosen area is in some sense functionally or socially identifiable, and discrete.

3. The choice must be made, too, with a consciousness of how many people the area contains or did once contain. Remember that a village of population about 500 in the year 1900 may well have baptismal records alone, numbering 5,000–10,000, over a 300-year period. This is, of course, a considerable underestimate of the total number of persons who passed through the place within that same period. Naturally, a large town has records of very many more people – maybe far too many to be handled with any ease.

But having said these things, there have to be enough records of people to provide a coherent picture. This requirement can mean that in districts where parishes are small, the study of a patch of parishes is a much sounder proposition than a study on just one. And it is worth saying, even here, that a consideration of how the data you accumulate are going to be recorded and stored must to some extent determine how much data you are prepared to collect. Mindful of these issues, this book draws upon examples of study of various kinds, in places ranging in population from the very small to the very large indeed.

Depending on the questions being asked, the numbers of the relevant sorts of people may be the point, rather than the total population. You cannot reliably comment on the lifespan of farm workers from a sample of four or five.

DATA AND HANDLING THEM

While noting that there are still plenty of limitations, modern methods of data storage using desktop computers do make possible studies on a scale and of an efficiency such as could only be dreamed of even in the mid-1980s. Data recording, storage and handling by microcomputer are not obligatory practices for local historians. However, as a topic it is unavoidable in a book of this kind. I have sought to give a painless account of IBM clone machines, and of their advantages in recording and processing local study data.

HANDLING NUMBERS

At a few points, I have tried to show how certain simple quantitative procedures – such as counting and plotting data on graph paper (e.g. baptisms per year) – can be particularly rewarding. Procedures of that kind often reveal major local events of which there are no surviving explicit records.

The turning of events as shown by the change in slope of a graph may set off entirely new and important lines of documentary or oral research. Such data manipulation is perhaps the nearest that historical research comes to experimentation. Many people (and that includes some scientists) are tempted to disappear at the mention of numbers. But do stay and read on! There is no need to run for cover; no particular knowledge of mathematics is asked. Besides, the rewards may astonish you.

THE PRODUCTS OF RESEARCH

Although much local and family research is done simply for the pleasure of doing, most people do like to have a product. Undoubtedly, even if no particular product was in mind at the start, one is likely to come to mind during the course of the work. It would be true to say that in much research there is an imagined product from the outset, an idea that got remodelled as research proceeded. For many people, the product is, and remains, knowledge in the mind. But many studying local history do imagine writing a text – a historical story if you like. This is not the story of the research, but a story of unfolding events as revealed by the research. However, many other sorts of products are as appropriate, or even more so than historical stories. Film, audio tapes and collections of images (drawings, maps, photographs) are all true products. Some work may result in both printed accounts and reference collections. Electronic databases placed for reference in record offices, consolidated data on fiches and reference volumes are all possible valuable products of research. They may act as supports and stimulants to other workers, especially if placed in record offices. These are discussed in Chapter 10, which also refers to the creation of 'hypertexts', branched textural material through which readers can wander by choosing from menus of connected topics.

REFERENCES AND FURTHER READING

Braithwaite, L. (1986) *Exploring British Cities*. London: A & C Black [Guide with Victorian maps for exploring older parts of cities].

Darby, H.C. (1974) *The Medieval Fenland*. Newton Abbot: David & Charles [Classic account].

Field, J. (1993) *A History of English Field Names*. London and New York: Longman.

Finnegan, R. (1994) *Studying Family and Community History*. Cambridge: Cambridge University Press and the Open University, 4 volumes.

Hey, D. (1980) *Packmen, Carriers and Packhorse Roads*. Leicester: Leicester University Press [Trackways in the landscape].

Hoskins, W.G. (1973) *English Landscapes*. London: BBC [Pictorial].

Jenkins, K. (1991) *Re-thinking History*. London and New York: Routledge [About the nature of history].

Lewis, C. (1989) *Particular Places*. London: The British Library [Well illustrated brief introduction of the various aspects of local history].

Morris, R. (1989) *Churches in the Landscape*. London: Dent [Superbly illustrated].

Scarfe, N. (1987) *The Suffolk Landscape, Revised Edition*. Suffolk: Alistair Press [Beautiful account tying what we see now to far older times].

Williams, M. (1970) *The Draining of the Somerset Levels*. Cambridge: Cambridge University Press [Means and effects of draining in the late eighteenth century].

CHAPTER TWO

Given in Evidence

ASKING QUESTIONS

When I first became actively interested in history, I was very committed to document-based research. I suppose that, as a scientist, I imagined that only when I had found something actually written was I dealing with hard evidence. Yet I knew from experience that documents were not always factually correct. As time has gone by, experience has forced me to accept that very many important details about the past are not written down. Furthermore, I have been made to realise that inference on the part of the researcher is significant in historical research – as significant as it is in experimental science. One cannot somehow create a piece of 'crystal pure' historical research, independent of spoken evidence. Nor is it ever free of the researcher's own speculation and interpretation. Incidentally, experimental science, too, contains plenty of important knowledge that lives only in the minds of doers. And rather rarely is that laboratory lore freely published.

Actually, oral questioning is as natural as milk to babies. As children, we grow and learn, at least partly, by the process of questioning. If we are lucky enough to grow up in the same place as our parents, many of the questions they answer for us will be about local history and natural history, and about geography. When, as adults, we wish to know something about what existed or took place before we were born, we might start by reading a book, but what is more natural than asking someone older or more experienced than ourselves, about past people and old localities?

Then, as we did when we were small, we can take the responses to our questions, and match them with what we now see. Like the children, we will make our own syntheses from a combination of observation and story, and sometimes we will return to our storyteller for clarification or confirmation.

THE FOUR ROLES OF ORAL EVIDENCE

Since we are saying that valuable unwritten material is living in people's minds, it is necessary to ask just what character of material this might be, and what role it plays in inquiry into and presentation of the past. The material has four roles.

First, there is the uttering of the unrepeatable. Experience shows that, without question, oral inquiry elicits much information that would be irretrievably lost at the death of the speaker, for it resides nowhere but in their memories, or in that of one or two other people. When these few people die, much special knowledge perishes with them; making a record of their answers to a few questions rescues some pages from what is really a large book. Those readers who have lost one or both parents will know from experience how many times questions arise in their mind that Dad or Mum would probably have been able to answer. This is the information derived from taking part: the experiential knowledge of people now dead, the memory of places and events entered in no diary. This sort of material is literally the experience of their lives.

The second role performed by oral statements is giving directive information. If you spend days and hours in record repositories or on location, much of that time is spent in searching for and within sources. The essence of searching is that you do not know the location of the thing you seek. Sometimes, other people know well where to point you, and by their knowledge you can be saved a great deal of time. They may not know that they are pointing the way. But still, they are pointing.

The third role of spoken evidence is commenting on and illuminating material gained from documents. It may serve to explain the meanings of terms found there; perhaps make clear just what a written statement would have meant in practice. Oral evidence is thus both a platform for documentary research, and a stimulus for reflection upon it. The value of this sort of resource hits home when a stalwart informant dies.

Finally, there is the matter of providing colour. The value of spoken evidence lies not simply in its provision of a factbase. The voices of experience add an ingredient of resonance and richness to written histories. The importance of this colour stands out when written accounts of past events are examined. As the lapse of time lengthens, writers get more distant from the actual participants or eye-witnesses; their text becomes barer and drier. The flesh begins to disappear from the bones. Perhaps only in dramatised stage histories is this not seen. There is juice in a witness's account that seldom runs from documentary prose.

TALKING TO OLDER PEOPLE

Evidently, historically, the most recent eighty or ninety years are very special, since only for these years have we living witnesses. But time passes, even as we study, and much evidence that was collectible in 1990 will not be so in the year 2000. The matter is always urgent.

Who has things to tell? Almost everyone has things to tell; each person, of whatever age, has a unique collection of experiences. If you wish, you can demonstrate this by a deliberate test. Try asking questions of someone who was in your class at school, or who lived in the same street as you when you were children. They remember different things from you, or at least different details about the same things, people or places. You can learn a lot by questioning your own contemporaries.

It follows from this that almost anyone older than you will have much detail to offer about your place. And of course, if the place is not the one you were born in, almost any native will know more detail than you. An informant does not have to be over 75 in order to be a really valuable resource. But very old people are really special, though anything said in what follows about very old people may sometimes also apply to younger ones.

THE ELDERS

These days, life expectancy for Britons is distinctly over 70 years. However, the shape of the human survival graph means that past the age of 60, we do begin to notice a decrease in the number of our contemporaries. Despite the downward sweep of the mortality curve, those of us born after 1930 have rather good chances of seeing out the old millennium. Indeed, there is a fair chance that we will see some useful piece of the new one!

Of course, everything changes. When those of us who are middle aged were born, our apparent life expectancy was less than it has become. Around the year 1900 the life expectancy for new children was far less even than that of (say) people born in the 1930s. The very old people that we occasionally meet in the 1990s are thus very remarkable survivors. Each one is unique. Far along the mortality curve, they have scarcely any contemporaries left, and almost no one with whom to share talk of the old times.

They will very often be happy to talk to you. More so, because of their lack of contemporaries. A large proportion of very old people live upon the edge of poverty and of loneliness. Their life experience is almost the sum total of what they own. Yet you are wishing them to share it. If you are going to try to talk to them, it is important to be clear about the terms on which you do it.

First, you are not seeking their company out of a wish for something quaint or curious. You are not seeking entertainment. The persons you talk to will not thank you for any act or remark with a hint of patronage. You are not going visiting with exploitation in mind. Their experience is due your every respect. The following short story may clarify some aspects of the situation of questioner.

I knew a lady of nearly 90 who had, many years before, practised midwifery in the old iron towns of Ebbw Vale and Blaenavon. It was in the years before 1920. She had many recollections of family life and of medical practice within those communities, before the creation of formal nursing training. She had delivered babies in ancient iron works houses, where the floorboards were rotten enough for one's feet to fall through. She had worked in rooms where only brown paper existed as blankets on the birth bed. She had attended homes built of tin sheets upon old ash heaps, where the woman in labour would rather have died than call a doctor, whose fee she could not pay. I could choose to hear her factual accounts, only if I was also willing to hear her still active anger and grief at suffering in those times. Not only could her experience and her feelings not be dissociated, but also it was, if you like, my moral contract to listen to one along with the other.

It is always for us who ask questions to show appropriate respect. This we can do by understanding the pain that may be implicit in much of what we are being told. We can show respect too by making sure that we neither see nor present their stories to others as romantic or sensational. We must do our utmost to understand what it might have been like to have lived it. We must really try that, even though it is almost beyond us to imagine the life of another person who lived in another time. The more things we learn about that life, the more fragments we assemble, the clearer our view will get. The extent to which we can imagine the way we would have felt, had we been in their shoes, must play a central role in our understanding of the past they describe.

ORAL TESTIMONY

Before proceeding, I would like to clarify just what I mean, when I talk about the taking of oral evidence. This is particularly important because much has already been written about what is called oral history, and it is necessary to be clear. From the 1970s onwards, there has been a growing realisation of the value of the human experience that resides in living communities, and of knowledge, that will be erased with the passing on of those people. Encouraged by the writing and experience of Ronald Blythe,

George Ewart Evans and others, many local historians have set off to record the self-told stories of older people. The volume by Stephen Caunce in the present series, entitled *Oral History and the Local Historian,* gives fine examples of texts derived from tape-recorded interview material. He describes many details of method for recording oral histories. No useful purpose would be served by my writing about the same methods. In fact, what I have to write about has, I believe, a very different emphasis.

The way of work used and described by Caunce, Evans, Blythe and others is, I believe, justly described as 'person-centred' recording. It is ideal for the laying down of archives. By person-centred I mean that the speaker is remembering and in a sense going some considerable way towards determining the content of the tape. A point very much in the favour of this way of proceeding is that everything the person says is on record. This can be replayed, cut, or edited for typing, just as required.

An alternative approach, and one I have used a great deal, is much more interviewer-centred. Listeners are choosing the questions they want answered, returning to them if and when necessary, later in the talk; diverting the conversation to where they want it to be; referring to written or printed records or sometimes to another speaker, before returning to the interviewee. The process is closely steered by the interviewer.

It will be evident that this is not a process in which absolutely everything said is recorded, and it could be argued that material is sometimes lost by a failure to write down literally everything. This is occasionally so, though the proportion lost is very small. And the loss is compensated for by the whole interview being very sharply directed to chosen points. The process is cross-examination, not reminiscence. Later in this chapter, I describe some ways this can be done to best effect.

As the inquirers we make our own contribution to conversations, by thinking up and asking good questions. We can shape the interaction, and influence both the quality and quantity of the information that we receive. We can be far more effective and useful than simply eliciting reminiscence. While the latter may be centred on what the interviewee feels will please us, questions answered will take us down a chosen line of inquiry.

Tape-recorded recollections will not be what we primarily require, since they may not contain the sort of hard information we seek. Recordings do serve to yield an archive of a person's authentic voice, and hence the impression that that is likely to give of geographic origins, social circumstances, education and personal nature. Such recordings can be analysed very closely. But I am talking about looking for some well-focused statements, impressions and opinions given in response to accurately chosen questions. Although I am interested in hearing people, it may not be the person talking of themselves that I am seeking, but answers to specific questions about a place or local population, in a past time. I always hope that the answers will be directly revealing about individuals, the community, its social network, prominent people and its institutions, and that they will prove to be a sound platform for documentary research and re-interview.

I believe that, principally, there are two types of progress that can be made with this approach. First, you might build a picture of a society at a certain period such as 1900–10, during the First World War, 1920–30, etc. Second, you might penetrate more deeply but specifically into the past behind one person, and gain handed down memories of particular individuals. These may be about people whose lives ended before the end of the nineteenth century.

THE NATURE OF MEMORIES: LANDMARKS

To interview well, it is necessary to have a picture of how recall works. In order to remember information about events that took place a long time ago, it is first necessary to have landmarks or finger posts in one's mind. When first challenged with a question, our first response may be to shake our head and say that we know nothing at all of the matter. However, a prompt which locates us in the right time or place often yields an astonishing amount of detail.

When I asked an old friend of the family about the last days of my grandmother Agnes MacNaught Jarrett, who died in 1934, she responded by talking a great deal about houses that grandmother had once lived in, and about some of grandma's ways, including her phenomenal energy and her liking for parsnip wine. She, seemingly, had no recollection at all of Agnes' last months. Yet when it was mentioned, in the midst of conversation, that grandma had died at her eldest son's house (information in fact from the death certificate), my friend said with some animation that that indeed was so.

She went on to explain that when she died, grandmother was laid out in the front room, with all the associated inconvenience and anxiety that this might have caused. Another thing about it, she explained, was that when she was dying, '*they wouldn't let any of us in to see her, except for my Jack. Yes. Him with all the dirt on him from the works. He just walked in.*'

Once the people trying to do the remembering have got some landmarks, they can frequently recall detailed information about events, people and institutions at or near the time that has been 'flagged'. The choosing of landmarks to offer to the interviewee is one of the skills of the interviewer.

Offered landmarks may consist of documented statements about particular people. These may set off stories about those people, about the interviewee in relation to those people, or about the interviewee in relation to relatives or friends of the people. They may be the mention of a particular person, which may prompt memories of certain events in which they took a part, and these can be explored further by questions that fill out detail.

Other prompts that can be used are major national or local events (you could get them from the newspaper) and names from local lists of people of all kinds. Photographs, particularly, give excellent starting points, because they provide icons – visual rather than verbal or numerical cues. These can be offered to other persons too, and the responses collected and compared. The old people themselves may be a source of photographs for prompting purposes.

Time and again, questions may be found which at first give no positive result, but which, if placed in a new context, or simply re-asked later, are met with informative replies. These replies can be used in still later conversations, as anchor points for fresh, more precisely targeted questions.

CHECKING THE ANSWERS

When you have got answers, it is most important to be as clear as you can in your mind exactly what the answerer meant. For example, in asking who lived in which house, and to be as sure as possible about the meaning of the reply, it may be necessary to draw diagrams illustrating the street layout, then with them in front of you both, ask the interviewee again, just which house is meant. After this process, you will want to draw yourself an archival map, with the houses and occupants unmistakably marked. Remember, in the course of asking about streets and houses, the interviewee may be remembering the place as it was before certain buildings were demolished, and almost certainly, without recent building activity. He or she may know well the fairly recent changes, but may well speak to you still as if you the interviewer are familiar with things as they were many years ago, maybe before you were born. To be a satisfactory conversationalist, you will need to obtain the necessary familiarity with the area from the map, the newspaper or elsewhere, before you sit down to ask the questions.

There is the general matter of the oral checking of first answers to questions. This can be approached in two ways. One is re-asking the same person. A second is by finding a second informant. These ways are set out in Figure 2.1. Then as far as events are concerned you will want to find dates.

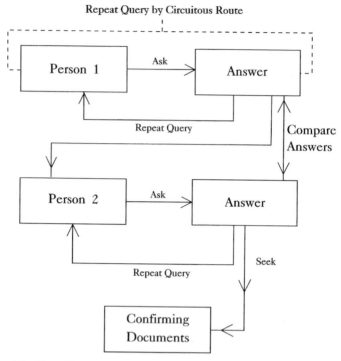

Figure 2.1 Flow diagram illustrating possible tactical paths in oral questioning.

BUT WHAT TIME ARE THEY TALKING ABOUT?

Putting dates and places to your own memories can be hard. Pinning down someone else's is no easier. But it is very important to try to establish dates of events that are being talked about: to often ask the interviewee 'When would that have been?', by posing other circumstantial questions, such as 'Was that when you lived at the old house?' or 'How old was your sister then?' Memories are not the material of history, until they have dates and locations, and perhaps occasions attached to them. It is a matter for regret that so often old people's recollections are recorded on tape without eliciting dates or precise locations, thereby creating some wonderfully compulsive listening and excellent material for novels, but hardly history.

At the time I commenced collecting the social material that I refer to in this book, the earliest times directly explorable via the memories of the living (as opposed to their memories of what their elders said they saw or heard even older people say) were near 1900. The work was based on the early memories of 90 to 95 year olds, i.e. persons born in the early 1890s.

Times have moved since then, of course, and more realisable possibilities in the mid-1990s are the clear memories and views of 1910–15 from people born 1900–05. When T, a dear friend of mine died in 1988, he was almost 95 years old. Over the last four years of his life, I learnt from him many facts about his contemporaries at Caerleon school, his early work experience, the practices at the local iron rolling mill, the training of the Territorial Force and the local styles in social matters, such as courting and dress, all in the period 1900–10. Many of the things he told me were corroborated in interviews with L, a precise female contemporary of his, though she, like him, had much unique information to offer. Both persons were born in 1893.

If you are lucky enough to be able to talk to several old people who have lived long lives in the same district, much information will coincide person to person. Some overlaps; some fits edge to edge. Thus it was at Caerleon I was able by additional input from W, a third interviewee who knew many of the same people, to gain pictures of the ways that local families, neighbours and organisations linked, especially in the period 1910–30.

Among the information obtained in the earliest years were details of habit, behaviour and appearance of some persons born well back in the nineteenth century. For instance, I heard from T many details of the life of his father (born 1863), who was a skinner, and of JTB, his maternal grandfather, a local fellmonger and malthouse keeper. He had been born in 1821, but did not die until 1905. By this and parallel routes, which commenced with other old people, hearsay evidence concerning my own great-grandparents' sayings and habits came to light. Great-grandfather and great-grandmother had died in 1884 and 1898, respectively. The latter type of information, what one might call handed down memory, is related to and merges with a body of local tradition. This is the collection of assertions and stories, concerning local people, events and institutions, that are generally believed, but which are without known authorship or provenance.

I believe that my access to some of this material, which could be clarified and extended by a networking process among much younger people, depended partly upon the privileges I have as a native of that town, as an inheritor of the traditions. The people concerned may not have revealed all of the same information to someone perceived by them as a stranger, and inappropriate.

THE LIMITS: JUST HOW EARLY DO PEOPLE'S MEMORIES GO?

If we want to know how far back a particular person might be taking us, we need to ask what is the likely limit of memory? How early in life do people's memories go? I decided to see if I could determine this for myself.

With a lot of effort, I have been able to remember and chronologically fix some of the events of my early childhood. The effort came not so much in the actual remembering (though many people do say they have no early memories at all), but more in putting a date or occasion to the memories. But many of the recollections that I believe I have can be confirmed or denied by asking other people. Mostly, the results of such queries have confirmed the happenings, though not necessarily adding any dates. More often than a date, they added an explanation of the occasion. In my family, photograph albums are almost non-existent, and any images that do survive carry no date or caption.

How early *are* my earliest memories? I was born in January 1936. I do remember clearly my first day at school. It was January, and frosty. The school admission book confirms that it was the week of my fourth birthday. I remember too that I was taken on holiday with a large group of children to Porthcawl in Glamorgan. (A recent interview yielded the information that there were sixty-six children! They were one of a number of groups of child refugees from the Spanish Civil War, dispersed to new homes in towns in England and Wales.) Sharing rooms with them was a vivid experience for me – one hard to forget. But suddenly, mysteriously, the noisy, boisterous holiday was cut short, and we left the sea and came home on a charabanc, travelling through the night. A few years ago I had an opportunity to talk to a woman who was a helper on that holiday. She confirmed that it was cut short – by the outbreak of war in 1939. So it is an earlier memory, from when I was 3 years and 8 months old.

Memories later than these times are numerous and can often be pinpointed in time: whistling bombs, the city of Bristol burning, my uncle's car laid up in his garage for lack of petrol, my small classmate who died of diphtheria, anti-aircraft fire from the local gun batteries. Later still, being taken to stand in the recently burned Coventry cathedral. But are there even earlier ones? I do remember several long journeys in the side-car of my father's motorbike. But that vehicle suffered a terminal breakdown in the spring of 1939, so they must have been journeys taken before that. There are even glimpses of things from when I was less than 3.

So it is sometimes *possible* to remember events from really quite early in life. But what are we to make of that? When reviewing verbal information given by old and not so old people, we are often dealing with their early memories. We need to take care in dating things they tell us. It would be quite easy to assume that the earliest events they relate are from the age of perhaps 8 or 10 years. Probably, for material outside their family this is so. But evidently, for family matters, memories can sometimes be from much earlier than that.

THE INTERPERSONAL CONNECTION

Even if you are a native of the locality, you will need to have active connections with it in order to be in a position to ask questions. To research interpersonal contact, you have yourself to make and keep contact. Visits have to be undertaken and, indeed, friendships created. The people who talk to you have to know you. For this to work, you have to be able to listen in a meaningful way. You may possibly find that the information you build is something you can give back. You may be able to fill people in on details of people that they lost touch with many years before.

The place as it is now, if not known by you, will have to be discovered, since the people you talk to probably live in it now and will need you to understand now. If the place you study is not your native place, you are still likely to be connected to it by some means, perhaps by many years of residence or of work there, or perhaps by descent from some residents of many years ago. In any of these cases, appropriate contemporary connections will have to be made and cultivated if you are to obtain any oral accounts.

IS ANYONE THERE?

It must be accepted that even being able to start this type of research entirely depends upon the existence of *anyone* of an appropriate age, who spent early life at that place. You cannot connect, if there is no one to connect to. Furthermore, studies which might reach far back must depend upon the maintenance of significant local continuity with the past generations. This can be hard to discover. You will need to find out if any such continuity exists.

My grandfather, Frank Emery, son of George Emery, was born in 1854 at Moorlinch in the county of Somerset, an ancient parish in the Polden Hill district, bordering on King's Sedgemoor. George was the sexton of Moorlinch church. The parish has several townships, including one that carries the name of the parish. Until about 1985, that had remained structurally very similar to when Frank left it around 1875. I had hoped to gain a picture of the social group of which great-grandfather had been part, and perhaps identify which houses various named people had lived in, and which farm each worked upon.

However, despite the life of three generations of Emerys there, and the fact that George lived until 1904 and his wife to 1912, five visits, including to church and pub, failed to locate among present residents anyone at all who recalled the Emery name. Neither were there any Emery gravestones that I could point to, to convince anyone that they had ever existed. No one could suggest anyone at all older that I could ask. Yet I knew from the parish registers that until about 1979 several old people did remain in the township. For instance between 1967 and 1979, no fewer than four members of the Coombes family passed on after reaching more than 85 years of age. It seemed that although George tended the churchyard for many years, and although one can almost retrace his daily footsteps, memory of him was entirely lost.

In 1990, quite serendipitously, I located, in another Sedgemoor parish, a lady just turned 98, who had lived almost all her life at Moorlinch and who could, and did, provide some parts of the picture I was seeking. She remembered not only him, but also his habits and family, and some of his peers. The information she gave was deep rather than broad. She recalled earlier people that George spoke of, especially the rector who died in the 1870s. It was, I think, not coincidental that the contacts by whom I got to know of her were closely and long connected to the present farming community in that area.

FACTORS THAT DETERMINE SUCCESS

While it is true that some connection to the old social networks have to remain for one to be able to make a study, and one has to be able to find them, it is fairly rare for there to be nothing left at all. While the possible connections in Moorlinch were not numerous, there were I believe particular contemporary reasons why connection by an outsider was difficult. Two general factors stand out as being relevant to success. The first is the size of the past population one is trying to connect to. The second is the heaviness of emigration in the past.

Undoubtedly, trying to make connections in some rural places in Somerset is made harder by the loss of people, first during the last twenty years before the First World War, and second, after the Second World War. Many people who might have provided the continuity of memory, and hence have answered visitors' questions, are now perhaps to be found in a distant English town, in South Wales, in British Columbia or Newfoundland or New Zealand.

The fate of George Emery's children was a common one. They were dispersed. Frank went to South Wales, his sister Selina moved to a farm at East Huntspill, where some old folk still remember her husband Tom Coombes. One sister, Emily, when old, lived in a Bristol workhouse. A brother also moved to Bristol, while a last remaining male sibling has proved so far untraceable.

Still in Somerset, and across the moor to the south of Moorlinch, lie the villages of Middlezoy and Othery, on the 'island' of Sowy. These two villages, and their neighbour Weston Zoyland, are on a rise in the ground that, until the creation of the great drainage scheme of the 1790s, was reached on land only by three causeways. Somewhat larger in population than Moorlinch, and occupying higher ground and perhaps better sites, loss by emigration from these villages has nevertheless been sustained long term. In 1861, the Revd E.A. Rouse, who was vicar of Othery parish, wrote in his Parish Register that so many families had left in the previous ten years that he could not remember them all. Emigration was still marked in the 1920s, and again in the 1940s, when many young men found Canada very attractive. However, despite the depredations of twentieth-century emigration, and perhaps due to the larger nineteenth-century population, some familial continuity has remained. When I made inquiries in the mid-1980s several people could be found, all female, who were born in the period 1895–1900, and who had memories going back to life in these villages before the First World War. They revealed the way of life of the families when cider orchards were more important, and when peat digging and osier growing were a bigger part of local life. These interviewees could not only describe the social impact of the Second World War Royal Air Force (RAF) base at Weston Zoyland, but also give descriptions of local persons who had been born in the 1830s and 1840s, and could point out their cottages. They were conscious too of the people who had left for Canada in the twentieth century, sometimes producing correspondence.

Some people they referred to were of families recorded in the parish back to before 1750, or who had arrived from Devonshire in a nineteenth-century move to look for work on the peat diggings. Families of some of the same names – Gullidge, Beake, Hucker, Moxey, Lovibond, Kierle, Kicke and Leaves – can be identified in Illinois (USA) and in Newfoundland. The clustering of the Sowy emigrants' descendants at Lake County, Illinois, is so marked that oral and documentary research there can reveal aspects of life in nineteenth-century Sedgemoor.

On the topic of out-migration, it is worth remembering that even in regions which have experienced long-term depopulation, some communities may have been foci of population growth. In central Somerset, at Bridgwater, many houses were built around the turn of the century, and in smaller places such as East Huntspill, there have been more recent accumulations of people. Housing built since the 1940s has been occupied in many cases by descendants of the families of other nearby parishes. In growing places of this kind, one may well find people holding information about the past life of the parishes nearby. I was several times recommended to seek out and talk to people in the local growth areas. It is perhaps also worth saying that some rural parishes contain houses which in the 1980s proved attractive to city incomers with money to invest. To a traveller, the presence of these very recent arrivals may at first obscure the extent to which the older population network has been eroded.

TACKLING LARGER PLACES

While researching villages, parishes or clusters of parishes can involve much work, it is not hard to envisage a meaningful outcome. It is possible to identify all the prominent people. It is possible to learn a great deal about networks – who related to whom, and in what ways. However, social networks, living conditions and types of employment are all likely to be of greater variety in larger places. Indeed, many more human institutions may be created in them. Churches, chapels, schools, workhouses, hospitals, clubs and courts of law are some of the institutions which people create as places grow. Evidently when considering bigger and bigger places, opportunities for study may increase, but so does the complexity of the situation, very rapidly. When a city the size of Liverpool, Leeds or Newcastle is reached, the complexity at an interpersonal level is quite immense. Approaches to research that may be plausible in villages cannot be considered for use in places were the individuals can have known only a small minority of their co-residents, and in which you are likely to be able to interview only a very tiny proportion.

Although some sort of sampling method has to be adopted, inter-person connections are unlikely to be revealed by a small sample spread widely in a such large space. It is easier to envisage a useful outcome emerging from either restricting oneself to a district of a city, since then chances of bringing out some aspects of connection are increased, or confining oneself to certain questions that may legitimately be posed to a sample of city people. This does raise the important general question of how many informants are needed for a fruitful study, and how that number in turn relates to the size of a place.

Looking though my records I see that in the study I made of Caerleon Urban District (Edwardian population roughly 2,000), I was preoccupied with identifying socially influential people, groups of members of chapels and clubs, school classmates, patterns of neighbours on streets, and the connections with people who appeared on the 1881 and earlier census books. I had not set myself a target number of interviewees. It is important to ask, though, did I have enough? Is there any way of knowing what enough is?

In fact, I used oral material from twenty-nine different people, ranging in age from 61 to 94. Some of these were interviewed three, four or five times, some only once. I did notice as I proceeded with my work, which consisted of asking a consistent range of starter questions about town notables, about the interviewee's birth place, family descent, residence when a child, neighbours, trades people that their parents used, school contacts, chapel and church membership and so on, that after a time, information repeated itself, person to person. A pattern emerged and stabilised. Naturally, I got less and less new local network information as I went on. (There was of course always new *personal* information.) From this experience, I could estimate how many people I needed to talk to in order, say, to get 90 per cent of the whole data set relating to the starter questions. As a result, I believe that there, about two people per hundred of population gave a reasonable coverage, provided that they were willing and able informants. Incidentally, follow-up questions were a different matter entirely, since there was a much great variety of answer. The detail produced from these tends to go on expanding with the number of interviewees.

Since it is possible to put a cost in time and maybe money on a single interview, estimates of this sort that can be used to indicate how much work there would be in studying places of various sizes, how long a thorough study might take or, indeed, whether one is feasible at all, or in what way. Feasibility does, of course, depend on other factors beside numbers, on the ground. The following paragraphs are examples of what happened when I went to try beginning oral inquiries in two towns and one city.

GOING TO TOWN: BRICKS, RUBBLE AND WORDS

Since 1983 I have tried to gain information on several towns of moderate size. One of them was Frome, a town of about 12,000 people that lies in Somerset, close to the border with Wiltshire. I had originally become interested because one of my grandparents had lived there. Her name was Alice Yerbury, though she was a stepdaughter in a family called Gifford. I had read that Yerbury had been a significant name in the history of the cloth trade. McGarvie's book on the history of Frome points out that many houses were built in the late seventeenth and early eighteenth centuries on land owned by a Yerbury family. I had looked too at various documents including the baptismal records of the ancient parish church, various census enumerators' books and modern telephone directories, and concluded that some surnames had persisted there over a long period. My first intention when I went to the town was to see if I could identify any of the old houses which I believed were in the Trinity District. My second objective was, if possible, to talk to people about the district and see if I could pick up any information about the network of families and memories of the trades. I took with me a copy of the 6 inch Ordnance Survey map from the late nineteenth-century to help me. I had mid- and late- nineteenth-century family addresses including house numbers.

I had quite a shock when I arrived. The Trinity District was not hard to find. But half of it was gone and in its place stood modern housing. Of the rest, much was empty; some was boarded up awaiting restoration by a trust; some awaited demolition. Who to ask? *How to ask?* I wandered about, took photographs, and retired hurt. I went home and wrote several letters, which produced nothing. Twice again I stopped off in the place, on my way else-where. I visited churchyards and the museum. The first good progress I made was when I discovered that the Royal Commission on Ancient Monuments had written a professional work about the history of Trinity houses. This helped me to understand the street pattern and to pinpoint the addresses and the ages of the houses. Seven years later, I returned once again. This time the remaining old houses had been reoccupied; the trust had finished its work, and was letting the refurbished products. But who to ask?

The lady at the museum in the town was helpful, but documentary help was not what I needed. I went in several local pubs and talked, but turned up no one who offered much of anything I wanted. However, later in the local shops I had success. At a local greengrocers I stood for some time talking to customers. One of them finally took pity and walked around the district with me. She had been born there and could tell much about the old houses and the way people made a living. We identified grandmother's home when a girl (a 1660 house, well restored), and I heard a great deal about the way that the place had changed in sixty years. She helped me talk to several other local people, who were living in council flats in that area. I got from them a very raw utilitarian view of the restoration of seventeeth-century houses. From all of this I had gained considerable insight into Trinity in the twentieth century. I had the suspicion that as far as connec-tions to grandma's time were concerned, I was really asking questions that my mother, had she been in a position to do so, might have gone there to ask forty years before.

DISTRICTS IN THE MEMORY

The current population of the Trinity district probably makes up 15–20 per cent of the town of Frome. It was not really the town overall that I was re-searching; it was only a specific and discrete district of it. In fact, in even moderate sized places, contact areas and knowledge of individuals can be quite small. If you talk to old people, they often can tell you only about what they see as their part of the town. They are often very specific indeed about what was and what was not 'foreign'.

I was once able to spend some time clarifying this a little. I gained access to some sheltered accommodation that housed old people principally from the head of the Sirhowy Valley in Gwent, which contains the old iron town of Tredegar. I wished to ask questions about memories of the First World War in that area. In the 1990s Tredegar has a population of about 18,000, though it was formerly larger than this, many people having left the area in the 1920s and 1930s. It is situated at the treeless head of the valley, at above 1,000 ft, a snaking, linear town, where, until postwar times, sundry rows of old cottages occupied a variety of steep hillsides.

The twenty or so old people that I met each tended to be able to tell me about one particular region of their town. One could tell me a lot about the district called Scrwfa, another about the south end of town, Georgetown, and the area there known as 'The Tip'. Some others spoke of the inhabitants of Dukestown, a northerly district, which was again separate in the mind. It seemed that each of these districts would reasonably be treated separately, if a study was to be developed, assembling a group of informants for each.

THE BIG CITY

One might well conclude from the foregoing that a thorough study via oral accounts of personal relations and networks within a large city would be feasible only through a huge long-term effort – the recording of the memories of hundreds of people. While this would indeed be a worthwhile way of proceeding, in time terms, much more geographically targeted interviewing with specific questions would be more realistic. Undoubtedly, there is much work to be done concentrating on certain city localities or workplaces.

Despite this, there is in a city population a body of memory that is shared by many, or even by most, older citizens. It concerns the features common to, or central in, everyone's experience of past life in their city. As a migrant to the city, I decided to see if I could establish what some of those aspects might be for Sheffield people. When I started, I had lived in the city for twenty-five years, but believed I was largely unsure of the way that locally born people saw its past.

Over a period of several years, I made a series of sixteen interviews with older Sheffield people. All the people were locally born, and aged between 71 and 85 years. I could not claim that they were a rigorously taken sample of the city, but they were contacted through a variety of sources: evening classes run under the auspices of the city, local churches, family and business networks and professional friends. Subsequently, I followed this work with a larger number of questioning conversations with younger local people – essentially a generation younger than the first set.

For the interviews I created myself a set of starting questions about life in Sheffield before 1939. Mostly the period remembered was 1920–39, though some memories were from before the First World War. The questions to the older people were about their origins, where they lived, the main features of the city centre (which was badly bombed in 1940), their workplaces and shopping habits. Questions to the younger people were essentially about their parents and family.

The information that emerged was not local in the sense of reflecting a small locality; rather it was civic information, about the city as a resource and as an environment. The result was also a picture of the feelings of the people of the recent past, about their place.

The most consistent and congruent things to emerge concerning the city centre of prewar Sheffield were descriptions of the Shambles, the market halls, of busy shops. It added up really to a picture of a market town, one to which one travelled from the outskirts – from your suburb. The suburbs had something of the nature of individual villages, the character of each partly made by its origin (maybe it *was* a village) or its topographic location. Some are valley-set places, some on hillsides. A few lie high on hills. From all these shoppers went, often by electric tram, along arterials or across contours, to a centre that was no grand civic design, but which was an essential shared resource.

Living conditions, and the quality of city housing, entered all conversations. Many Sheffield people lived in very poor houses, though life was grander for some. Considering how poor much of the housing was, I heard remarkably little complaint: there was wryness, resilience, laughter even, but no anger. I met more than one person who had lived seventy years in the same two-up and two-down house, with the front door opening on to the pavement. The older of these houses, built about 1870–90, were relatively good structures. Before the Second World War there had been numerous even smaller, older houses (some one-up and one-down), some of which were literally within 20–40 metres of active, smoke- and dust-generating hearths.

But it was not so much the living in these houses that surfaced in conversation, as the loss of them. Following a commissioned report made in 1924, tens of thousands of little houses, some of them built as early as 1730, were laid flat. In some cases this left bare patches in what were primarily industrial streets. In others it left only bare roods of brick-strewn space. There was no sadness at the loss of what were squalid eighteenth-century courts, but the memory of them – small-paned windows, below lintels of handmade brick – has remained vividly alive.

It was said to me several times, though I have not confirmed it with documents, that the families that were moved out of the last of the eighteenth-century 'crofts' were rehoused on one of Sheffield's council estates of semi-detached houses built at The Manor. This was one of a substantial series of housing projects carried through on high ground, above the (then) industrial smoke pall. I met several people who had lived on that estate from its start before 1930. I also met a man who had been living in the same council house on the earliest city estate since his parents moved there in 1909. The decade from 1985 to 1995 has seen the refurbishment and organisation of these estates, with the disturbance of strong cultures and communities that had grown up on what had been 'green field' sites.

I should have had no surprise that loss features so strongly in the Sheffield oral material. There was the Blitz in 1940. Then many houses fell to the bulldozers in the path of new ring roads. Furthermore, the processes of scheduled housing renewal and creation of zones intended only for industrial use have continued after the Second World War, and indeed through until the 1980s. As late as that date, terraces of substantial 1880s and 1890s houses were being swept away in the Lower Don area. This wide valley, Sheffield's East End, had for well over a hundred years been the city's rock of ages. It breathed, forge by rivet works, foundry by rolling mill, house by smoke stack. Here have been made axles, wheels, tubes, wire, armour plate, gun barrels, shells and fine shining steels.

The regret at the loss of those dusty, dense, smoke-stained communities is palpable. The demolitions were intended to leave heavy industry in its own ground, and to let homesteads live in clean air. The late outcome has, though, been both stark and unforeseen. The great recession of the 1980s brought down many of the works, which first lost their roofs. Then they too were bulldozed, leaving only huge tracts of dissembled bricks.

Among my sample of people, I had made no special effort to ask about the experience of work in those great mills. But I have been left with no doubt at all that the loss of a collective, dangerous, heavy employment took with it the belief in a place as a great enterprise of industry. The eclipse of this leaves a bigger mark than any other of the great losses of the century.

TAKING ORAL EVIDENCE IN PRACTICE

It is worth imagining how you would proceed in practice if you were given the chance to ask a lengthy set of questions of a recently located older person, whom we can suppose spent their early life in a locality of interest to you. First, you have to be prepared.

Preparation means having in your own mind the subjects you intend to pursue, and starter questions that you are going to pose. Before you even knock on the door, you have a list of topics and the starter questions about them, conveniently written in a large format notebook. As well as the latter, you have taken with you several pens. The things you write in your notebook are field notes. (There is more about field notes in Chapter 4.)

Using a notebook and pen

Since your notes themselves will form an archive, irrespective of your intended subject, make your start by writing down the date of the interview and the place. Follow this by recording the full name of the person you are talking to. It will almost certainly be useful to record interviewees' date and place of birth and, if possible, similar information about their parents and, if you can get it, about their grandparents. Then go on to your first starter. Almost certainly, there will be follow-up questions from this, either immediately or later. When you judge it appropriate, go on to a second starter.

To facilitate recording, learn a form of shorthand with which rapid compressed records can be made. I have found it useful to have standard abbreviations for many words, and to be able to record emerging information in tree form, showing by connections, how information descends, or relates. In many instances, lines with one-word labels will remove the need for sentences. However, ensure that crucial names, dates or words are spelled out in full.

Questions: subjects civic and personal

The subjects of questions are naturally yours to choose – from all the hundreds available. However, it is possible (and useful), theoretically at least, to distinguish in your mind between questions about the place, and questions about the interviewee, the person who lived there. In what follows, I shall make that distinction, even though the two sets of topics can never be entirely separate.

About the place

It is not difficult to imagine oneself deciding to question old people, if you have been seeking information about particular lost buildings or about certain past residents identifiable by name. The same might apply if you want details on a major local event, or on a change of circumstance. You may have been directed to people because they were formerly a member of a certain club or congregation, or had lived in the right street. Specific local questions of these kinds can really arise for you only when you already know quite a lot about the place. You have to know, to be able to ask. They are questions from a study that has already progressed.

When you are studying quite small places, people inevitably belong to several local organisations: one man can be, at the same time, a councillor, a sidesman at the church, a publican, member of the British Legion and former cricketer. Town institutions overlap and coincide. Questions about clubs or people can often give answers that run on naturally to other people and groupings. You cannot afford to be too specific, or you will lose a great deal. You might well conclude that you need to ask as many related questions as you can – to get everything you can. If they will let you, you will pose a spectrum of questions.

I have mentioned the topic of landmarks. You will want to have thought about these and have ideas ready in case there is a chance to use them. You may want to have photos with you – modern copies of old ones.

If buildings which have been demolished or otherwise lost are your concern, you may wish to know their appearance. Questions on this topic, though, tend to be very unsuccessful. It is amazingly difficult to remember details of buildings demolished only one year ago, let alone those that went sixty years ago. In any case, to many people, houses are just houses, and not objects of detailed interest. The appearances and details of buildings are matters that are ideal subjects for investigation via old photographs, sketches or paintings.

About the people

When you have people to question in front of you, remember that they, as individuals, are a wonderful resource. Their own life is, in a sense, distinct from the town you have been asking about. Centring the questions on them will reveal much about them, but also about the town.

You can try asking about who lived in the same street as them and who in the next house. You can go on to ask who else lived in the street, or in particular cottages. In reply to these questions you will certainly get some names, but these names will not necessarily correlate well with another set of names given by another informant, in answer to the same questions. Most people's memories work well as far as the streets that fellow residents lived in, but not necessarily so well for the particular houses, especially when all houses were similar. The matter is made more complicated by the frequency with which families in rented accommodation moved on, and by the uncertainty about just which years are being remembered. Events over a period as long as twenty years can sometimes get telescoped together in the memory.

If stumped for useful questions, ones such as 'Who delivered the milk to your house?', 'Who were your school friends?' or 'What was your first job when you left school?' are good starters. Also, 'Do you have a picture of yourself when you were little?'

Other valuable lines of inquiry are their workplace, if they had paid employment, who their work friends were, where these lived, details of what they made at work (if it was that sort of place); if it was a farm, who owned it, details of stock, milking, fruit picking, etc., and how they got to work, the hours they worked and the fun that they had there.

An important point

It will be apparent from the foregoing that your own knowledge is of pivotal importance in the interview process. Pre-existing knowledge is what determines the questions you ask and hence the limits to the information that you can gather. The more you know about the place at the time in question, the more chance there is of asking productive questions, and of setting up a free-flowing conversation, in the course of which almost any type of local information might emerge. It follows too that if you know nothing, you cannot know what to ask. Finally, the people you are talking too will prefer it if you are well informed. They can easily lose patience with someone who comes asking, but who knows nothing!

By correspondence: phone calls and letters

Sometimes it is not possible to travel to talk to the person that you would like to talk to, or there may be some other reason why you cannot meet. Naturally, the query arises: could I telephone or write, or ask some questions via an intermediary?

Telephoning old people who may be hard of hearing or worried by the phone is not always fruitful. Only with younger people, for whom the telephone plays a familiar, central role in life, can it be used really effectively. Even then, it is generally less productive than a face-to-face conversation, as some of the content of verbal evidence is in the facial expression, gestures and tone of the speaker. Written correspondence is also not as straightforward to exploit as might be expected. Old people often have arthritic hands, and in any case may be quite unused to or unable to afford writing letters. They may easily feel anxious about you writing and expecting a written reply, so do not be surprised if you get no answer. In any case, a single question is probably all that can be posed in one letter. It is thus a very slow method of progression. Personal correspondence, whoever it is directed to, is a very undependable method of getting information. Some people reply almost by return giving useful data, others may take a few weeks to send a vague and unhelpful reply, a surprising number insist months later that they could not answer because they had lost the letter! Occasionally though, after a delay, one gets a reply that is a real jewel. It is a most uncertain business. Stamped and addressed envelopes should always be enclosed as a matter of politeness and may help you in getting a reply, whatever the subject of the enquiry. It is always worth trying, and indeed keeping a steady trickle of letters going. As an aid in this, if researching a place at a distance the purchase of copies of the current telephone directory and Thompson directory for that area are useful investments. If you persist, sooner or later, some dark winter morning will be brightened by a letter of great interest.

On occasion, I have set off to get questions relayed to an inaccessible older person via a proxy. There are numerous hazards in this, not least of which is the possibility that the intermediary poses the wrong question. There is also the drawback that in the event of a perplexing or intriguing reply, the proxy may not know enough about the question to make a suitably agile response, and then an important chance has been lost. It is most important to make questions very clear and not too numerous (perhaps no more than six). Type them out leaving places for answers, and perhaps your proxy will fill them in.

ARCHIVING YOUR NOTES

Compressed notes taken as I have described are best decompressed within a few hours of taking the interview. My early decompressed notes were hand-written, with hand-drawn diagrams, where appropriate. Each set was dated and given a unique numerical identifying code, e.g. INT042 (interview number 42).

Subsequently I have moved to placing the material on computer record as a free text, first as a word processor file, lately as a file in a freeform database, using *Idealist* software (Chapter 4). As Chapter 4 discusses both paper- and computer-based records at some length, I will not say more here, other than that this and similar systems file interviews of almost any length and style, without the need to adjust a complicated record structure.

PREPARING TO BUILD ON ORAL EVIDENCE

To create evidence that may be relied upon, as far as possible, spoken words must be tied to written records. Ultimately the evidence may be used as a passage into written evidence. To do this, events and occurrences must be confirmed and may be dated. So how is it to be done? I have taxed myself trying to think of general comments about it. Is there any recommendation or instruction that always applies? What I concluded was the following.

First, *any verbal statement has first to be dissected to see if it is composed of more than one part.* I have been talking to Ada Chard, who is 89. Consider Ada's remark:

> 'Our George got a medal for carrying a message under fire.'

This comes in several testable parts. First, did George (her older brother) get a medal at all? If he did, did he get it for taking a message, or for some other reason?

Second, *the setting or context of the remark must be sought.* Consider her statement:

> 'Father was a coalman.'

When was he a coalman? Was he a coalman all his working life? Is she saying that she *remembers* him as a coalman? Perhaps neither of the latter two possibilities is correct. Maybe being a coalman was only for a few years, and he mostly worked at something else. It is time to consider the nature of written evidence and how it does or does not connect to oral testimony.

REFERENCES AND FURTHER READING

Baddeley, A. (1994) *Your Memory: A User's Guide*, England, USA and Australia: Penguin [Helps one to understand how we all remember].

Blythe, R. (1972) *Akenfield: Portrait of an English Village.* Harmondsworth: Penguin [Famous book based on interviews].

Blythe, R. (1979) *The View in Winter.* London: Allen Lane [A sobering insight into being old – based on interviews].

Buzan, T. (1993) *The Mind Map Book.* London: Woodland/BBC Books [Delightful book about making graphical connections in thinking].

Caunce, S. (1994) *Oral History and the Local Historian.* London and New York: Longman.

Coleman, A. (1985) *Utopia on Trial.* London: Hilary Shipman [Research report on postwar high-rise council estates].

Evans, G.E. (1987) *Spoken History.* London: Faber & Faber [One of a series of books by this author employing oral evidence].

Leech, R. (1981) *Early Industrial Housing: The Trinity Area of Frome.*

London: HMSO Royal Commission on Historical Monuments [Architectural analysis of very early housing plan].

McGarvie, M. (1980) *The Book of Frome*. Buckingham: Barracuda Books.

CHAPTER THREE

That Which is Written

Many historians regard documents as being the true material of their subject, and the evaluation and interpretation of them as the heart of their professional province. Indeed, it would be hard to have any established history of substance without written evidence. For what is written is potentially death-proof, a communication between the dead and the living.

As a local historian, documents may or may not be your chosen starting point, though for many people they are. However, even if you do not start by reading them, as you make your way they are likely to provide a large proportion of the total resource that you will be draw upon. Fascinating and irreplaceable as oral evidence is, the voices are really only blooms on the tree. Its trunk and boughs are of ink, paper and parchment. It is worth reflecting that most of us would imagine the products of our own research to at least include written material. Documents are where old information lives and where new information is consigned. Future historians will include among their study documents today's records on electronic media.

CHOOSING AND USING DOCUMENTS FOR STUDY

While there are so many general things to be said about documents, their types, and their uses, indeed, even their identity, that large volumes can be written about the subject, this chapter makes no attempt to cover the whole topic; it is intended only to introduce a few aspects. They are the general matter of what a document is, how one is evaluated, the ways of bridging from oral to written evidence, and the uses in local studies, of certain named categories of document derived from the last 100–150 years.

THE IDENTITY OF DOCUMENTS

It will be evident from Chapter 2 that though there may be scholars who would say that documents are the only valid historical resources, I am not one of them. Actually, some I know would take an even stronger stand. They would emphasise not only the supreme place of documents, but also the strictness they impose in defining one. They would assert that only 'unselfconscious' material qualifies to be called and treated as a true document, and that a historian's task, skill and privilege is the evaluation of the same; wheedling from it, if you like, its deepest secrets. Potentially, any information written on paper, or some equivalent medium including a computer disk, might be called a document. But what is a true document? And should *we* be making distinctions between true and not true?

A true, unselfconscious document is an 'objective residue' of the life of former times, a record compiled at the time, for use at the time, with no concern as to the impression likely to be created in later time. Imagine, as examples, the admission book of a hospital, an account book or minute book. Certainly many true documents are official records. Evidently though, they need not be official, though perhaps made under the law. Self-conscious documents could include memoirs and diaries, if they were made with any intention of their being read by others at a later date. We might also consider as self-conscious annotated photographs of individuals and of groups.

In local history, I would argue that, while it is necessary to be clear which documents are of which sort, it is not always going to be practicable to dismiss self-conscious documents. Often we cannot afford to throw away any sources of information. In any case, in the view of the fact that oral evidence is being accepted, we are in no position to turn away self-conscious documents, though we will have to use them with the utmost care.

DOCUMENT EVALUATION

Anyone who has spent hours taking data from a document in a record office has probably evaluated a document. When we meet a friend, we may tell them about it: the hand-writing, the paper, its completeness, the way it compared to other examples of the same sort of thing. Few of us set aside special pieces of time to evaluate documents. We do it in passing.

However, evaluating documents is an important part of studying history, since upon the evaluation depends the credence and weight to be given to any data which we may extract therefrom. There are professional skills, methodologies and technologies, even, that attach to the evaluation process; it is true that some of them are matters only for experts, for in some cases, evaluation can not only involve the information ostensibly offered, but also include the nature of the text, the script, and the materials used to create it. These things are a long way beyond the scope of this account. In this chapter we are concerned only with basics: good tactical use and some guidelines for best avoiding misleading ourselves.

SOURCES: PRIMARY AND SECONDARY

When it comes to getting questions answered, most of us are used to looking in books. Although we may value and enjoy oral questioning, the bookshop and the library are the resources to which we often turn for authoritative answers. Of course, some texts have more authority than others. Some subjects have works which are household names. Who has not heard of *Gray's Anatomy*? But even that famous reference text is founded upon the research of many, many other workers, primary observations interpreted and presented by the editors. Respected and relied upon as it is, it is not primary material. It is a wonderful example of what is called a secondary source. Most (though not all) non-fiction books are secondary sources. They are accounts distilled from many primary materials.

Most historical books analyse, interpret and review material and are thus far from being unselfconscious, though ultimately they derive from the study of objective residues and may well, and in detail, cite primary sources for their information. An obvious example would be a *Victoria County History,* or a book of essays about the family structures featuring on the 1881 census, containing summaries of some census data. A third would be a PhD thesis containing and analysing hard-won extracts from medieval manorial records, now put into modern English.

Essay books, textbooks and reference books are the natural places to answer queries; to obtain a summary of arguments, find the accepted wisdom, or the hard facts. They are both necessary and convenient starting points. However, if you are going to do some research yourself, you may well need to continue by digging into the material that hides behind them: research articles that lie nearer to the primary sources. Later, when you are clearer about your research questions, you will probably want to study the original, primary sources for yourself.

Put up in type: secondary copies of primary sources

Original documents are generally unique. As such, they are irreplaceable and sometimes fragile; often they are inaccessible. Microfilm or CD-ROM copies are now more frequently prepared and, provided they are well made, they are as useful as the originals. In some cases, versions printed in modern type have been published. Lately, typing on to a word processor has often taken the place of print. This allows convenient storage, and multiple copies to be made, including copy annotated or amended in various ways. These will all be far easier to read than the original manuscript, and may even be indexed.

Despite the convenience, and indeed the inevitable use of secondary copies, we must be aware that in quoting from such a copy we quote from the primary without reading it, and hence without checking its faithfulness. Serious errors can result in this way and they may get passed on from one uncritical use to another. Even careful, hardworking researchers can fall into holes! A friend of mine, with the aid of volunteer support and a typist, created a computerised copy of a local apprentice list running to 30,000 entries. A later close inspection revealed that the typist had omitted about 1 per cent of the entries and that she had applied an unbidden 'correction' to certain of them. Furthermore, the typist had been given the secondary printed version, published in the nineteenth century. Inspection of the primary documents revealed something that no one had suspected – that it too was both incomplete and unfaithful to the guild archive. With hindsight it is clear that it was unwise to lean so heavily upon the published secondary copy, particularly with so much work likely to be involved.

TERMS OF EVALUATION FOR DOCUMENTS

Having made the generally important point that we need to be always clear where all our sources stand in the ranking from primary, through unique research material, to secondary account, it is necessary next to consider the terms in which *all* documents have to be evaluated. John Scott (1990) in his excellent book *A Matter of Record* has pointed out that there are four operating criteria in evaluating a document. I give them in an adapted form below:

- *Authenticity* – is it what it seems to be? For instance, if it seems to be Hitler's diary, is it really that?
- *Credibility* – is the evidence in it free from distortion? If it is a typed copy how many errors have been put in?
- *Representance* – how typical is it of the whole genre? For example is this baptismal register typical of those of the period?
- *Meaning* – how understandable is it?

It is worth asking how things turn out when these criteria are applied to the commoner sorts of documents met in research on local history, and to learn to ask these questions afresh of each new document met with.

FROM THE SPOKEN WORD TO THE WRITTEN WORD

Had this book been primarily focused upon the eighteenth century or per-haps an earlier period, it would have been appropriate at this point to con-sider the evaluation, reading and research use of early documents in some depth. However, the book concentrates on the most recent century; it is a time for which living witnesses are still available. Furthermore, it is a period for which many much-relied-upon sources, such as census enumer-ators' books, are unavailable, and yet one dominated by a wealth of local governmental records. Accordingly, this chapter concentrates first on the way that oral accounts can be linked to written records, and second on the character and use of certain categories of record found in the twentieth cen-tury. Later in the book, some consideration is given to the way that twentieth-century records can be connected with certain types of nine-teenth-century documents.

DOCUMENTARY VERIFICATION OF ORAL STATEMENTS

Documentary verification can best be illustrated with some real examples: Ada Chard, a railway story and mother-in-law's story.

Ada Chard

Do you remember Ada Chard? She is 89, and was telling us that she had a brother George, who got a medal (p. 40). Her family came originally from Devon, and her father was a coalman. We do not disbelieve anything she says. On the other hand, although we have carefully dissected her state-ments, the information in them is very incomplete, and we are not entirely sure what some of it meant. So how might we proceed?

For each of the dissected parts of the statements there may be verifying documents. These may vary from none to lots. Take her father's origin. He *might* be found in Devon on an electoral roll, provided he lived there after 1918, and he was of appropriate age. (He would have to have been born before 1900.) As a child he may be there on the 1891 census return. And note that the various statements are linked up. She said that he was a coal-man. If he owned a business delivering coal or owned a house, it is very possible that he qualified to vote before 1918. Of course, if her father only *delivered* coal, and especially if he did that only at some particular period after the birth of his daughters, this piece of employment may be recorded nowhere, other than perhaps on the census enumerator's book for some date, which (like 1921), is not yet available for viewing.

It needs some very careful thought indeed to compile anything like a comprehensive list of the possible verifying sources for Ada's father's life events. But this is what has to be done. Similarly, a list of all possible verifying documents has to be made in relation to the medal gained by Ada's brother George.

A railway story

Both William Williams and his brother Arthur, two men of Caerleon, Monmouthshire, used to speak about events that they had witnessed 'when the railway was built'. The railway in question was a rather small affair known as 'the PCNR', the Pontypool, Caerleon and Newport Railway. This was apparently laid down as part of the ambitious expansion plans of the Great Western Railway (GWR), and it moved under the umbrella of that company name shortly after it was completed. The description given many times by William was of a period when many local forge and mill men were unemployed, and had been so for many months. Families were truly desperate for the means to buy food. The engineers constructing the PCNR advertised for labourers and large numbers of local men queued on the site seeking a job. Those that were lucky enough to be chosen soon found the going hard. Some proved too weak to continue and got stood off; others struggled on, with their soft-skinned hands raw and bleeding from unaccustomed use.

What period were the brothers talking about? More specifically, what date, and exactly what event did they refer to? What documents would be relevant for verifying or expanding the story? Table 3.1 lists six steps in choosing documents for the verification of statements. Table 3.2 lists some classes of document and their relevance to various categories of information.

I started a search by creating a short list of possible sources of information about the relevant railway history. This list included secondary sources (published histories of the PCNR and GWR) and primary sources (railway company archives). I found that both kinds of sources existed. I discovered that the formation of the PCNR was recounted in a detailed little book by Aubrey Byles (1982) *The History of the Monmouthshire Railway and Canal Company.* The history of the GWR had been written on more than one occasion, but of course it was a famous company.

Aubrey Byles's book was especially useful. It told me that the PCNR

Table 3.1   Confirming some oral evidence by means of documents

1 Which documents might confirm statement?	Answer: **a, b, c, d, e**
2 Which of these are accessible to me?	Answer: **a, b, e**
3 Which of these three can I most afford?	Answer: **a, e**
4 Which of these two will be easier to use?	Answer: **e**
5 Conclusion: Start work with **e**	
6 Second conclusion: Proceed to **a** if deemed necessary	

Six steps in the choosing of documents that might verify statements. They are taken in numerical order. In the exemplar offered, there seemed at the outset, to be five possible sorts of documents that could be used. It was a matter of choosing.

Table 3.2   Confirmation of oral evidence: sorts of documents

Category of information	Relevant documentary sources (examples)
Events	Newspapers, log books, minute books, diaries
Occurrences	Electoral rolls, census books, admission books, membership lists, rate books, directories
Family descent	General Register Office, local register office registers, parish vital records, monuments
Topography	Photographs, maps, deeds, tithe maps and schedules

was completed through Caerleon, and opened for goods traffic on the 18 September 1874. So did the events that William and Arthur speak of take place in 1873 or 1874? At first I thought so. But there was a possible alternative time. Although the line came into use in 1874, Caerleon railway station was not inaugurated until 1880. Of itself, the construction of a passenger station would have necessitated only a modest widening of the 1874 cutting, and the excavation of a driveway for horse traffic. However, a large new goods yard was also to be dug out at this time. This was very much larger in area than the station itself, and involved removing many thousands of tons of red earth and sandstone, a process which would undoubtedly have taken teams of men and horses many weeks. I considered looking in GWR archives – see the useful Federation of Family History Societies booklet by Tom Richards (1989) *Was your Grandfather a Railwayman?* – but decided that there may be other places which would be easier to reach and search.

My next step was to seek documents that might tell me if and when the two boys took work on the railway. Both boys attended Caerleon Endowed School. However, since they were both born in the 1860s neither featured in the admission book, which started after the Education Act 1870. Fortunately, the school governors' minute book of this school is deposited at Gwent County Record Office (CRO). This is helpful because it records all children joining and leaving the charity school between 1814 and 1879. William, it says, left school without permission, aged 12 in 1873; Arthur left (also aged 12) in 1877. The 1881 census enumerator's book described both young men as railway porters. Much later, I did find some details of William's career in GWR archives at the Public Record Office. He became a stationmaster. William seems to have joined the railway directly from school, for among his personal papers is one which was a reference he had received when he left the GWR in 1902. It pointed out that he had 'worked on the railway for 29 years, and left without giving notice', i.e. he started about 1873 (see Figures 3.1, 3.2 and 3.3).

Next, I wondered if I could find records referring to a local unemployment crisis. My list of possible sources included the local newspapers, and since Caerleon's major employer was a forge and rolling mill, general accounts of the history of the iron industry. Then there were also the possibilities of original records of Caerleon Works itself, and trade directory entries.

I noted from published industrial histories that there was a major national recession in iron making in the 1860s, but that by 1872 south-east Wales forge businesses were emerging from this. Evidently the year 1873 was by no means the worst of times. Inquiries at the CRO lead me to some original Caerleon works account books in Newport Reference Library, but these proved to largely relate to a much earlier period. In the local newspapers, I did find in the late 1870s several references to 'the great hardship lately ex-

Figure 3.1   Councillor William Williams of Caerleon, a portrait taken about 1900, which formerly hung in Caerleon council chamber.

Figure 3.2 The Revd Arthur Williams, younger brother of William, a portrait taken in 1921, which hangs in the vestry of St John's Burslem, Staffs.

Figure 3.3 Caerleon railway station in 1907. The goods yard spreads away to the right.

perienced at Caerleon', though I have not chanced upon a statement of the date of closure. A run of *John's Directory of Newport and District* did indicate a period of works closure, but I was not able to be sure of the dates, since sometimes directories of this sort contain entries to businesses after they have failed. The 25 inch Ordnance Survey map published in 1883 describes Caerleon Works as '*Tin and Wire (disused)*'.

After this, I decided to change tack. I turned to a study of the original parish records of baptisms, marriages and burials for St Cadoc's, the church in the town of Caerleon. These are held at the National Library of Wales, Aberystwyth. I plotted graphs of the numbers of births, marriages and deaths year on year, from 1850 to 1905. These analyses indicated that the highest mortality rates and the lowest marriage numbers, at any time in the latter half of the nineteenth century, were in the period 1876 to 1879. This suggested to me that the major local employer, Caerleon Forge, perhaps ceased production in the first of those years.

By this time I had got the picture in my mind of Caerleon Works closing in 1875 or 1876 and probably still being closed in 1883, though it evidently did reopen at some later date. The information I obtained after this was serendipitous. There were two separate components. First, I came upon a set of published Monmouthshire county biographies, quite uncommon items, two volumes devoted to literary figures of the county, compiled by W.J.T. Collins, a noted newspaper columnist. Copies of the books are rare. I found mine by chance in an antiquarian bookshop at Hay-on-Wye. Among the chapters in volume 2 (1948) is one on David W. Oates, a scholar and educationalist, who was son of the manager of Caerleon Works. It explains that Mr Oates senior came to Caerleon when the works reopened early in 1884. I was subsequently able to confirm his son David's attendance at Caerleon School. The second discovery was through correspondence with the Pennsylvania Historical Society, in which they pointed out that a tin plate tariff war with the United States broke out in 1875. Certain Welsh tin plate works were victims of it. Here I have halted in my search, the sum of the written evidence seeming to point to 1879–80, as being the period William and Arthur spoke of, and the event in question the digging of the new goods yard.

Mother-in-law's story

Another oral example concerns Madame Marie-Josée Simons (née Genart), my mother-in-law. She was born in 1912 in the ancient Belgian town of Namur, which lies at the confluence of the rivers Sambre and Meuse. Her stories of childhood during the First World War provide further examples of the rewards and frustrations of attempting to verify oral accounts.

M. Genart was an Avocat, and he lived with his wife and three daughters in a large villa in a town street that ran along the bank of the River Meuse (see Figure 3.4). Mme Simons said it was number 13 rue Adaquam, close

Figure 3.4 The Genart sisters, a posed photograph taken at Namur in 1918 or 1919. Left to right: Lucette, Manette and Marie-Josée.

to the Meuse bridge, a crucially important crossing point. She has re-counted how, during the First World War, she saw many hundreds of pris-oners of the German army, as they were often marched past their house. She described in detail the tactic her parents and the neighbours used to get food to the prisoners: first you had to offer the officer in charge something nice, to cause him to stop. Then you fed the guards. When they were all busy eating, you had a chance to distribute food among the prisoners. Troops of Frenchmen in blue, troops of English in khaki, were each ac-companied by one or two German guards.

She remembers the kisses of thanks from the French, the requests by the English soldiers for soap, and how the grateful men cut off embossed tunic buttons as gifts. She also remembered wondering just why the English sol-diers' 'Adam's apples' always stuck out so much. Was it, she had won-dered, a defining characteristic of all Englishmen?

On one occasion, by some means, the people of Namur learned that there was to be an unusual movement of Russian prisoners, and on this occasion she and her sisters were forbidden to watch. But they peeped out anyway, and saw well enough the guards driving the Russians along. She remem-bered vividly the prisoners snarling and fighting for bread thrown among them from the houses.

I felt bound to ask her in which year of the war she thought it had all hap-pened, since the date seemed to be the key to understanding the story. But she had been very young and she could not tell me. I wanted to know too, why so many prisoners were walking through Namur. Were there *really* Russians fighting on the Western Front? My questions, unanswered, prompted a further revelation from her – of ambulances full of wounded men, queuing up in their street, waiting to cross the Meuse bridge. Was this the same period, I wondered, as the forced marching of prisoners?

So how did I try to answer my queries? First, I took up the matter of the presence of Russian soldiers on the Western Front, by means of a search in periodicals of the war period. Contemporary English language newspaper and magazine war reports were numerous, several series such as those of *The Times* and the *Guardian* appearing in weekly or monthly parts. A second starting point was general war histories. A third possibility was a traveller's guide to the Western Front battlefields, since there would have been Russian casualties and hence graves.

Despite the profusion of contemporary newsprint, I found that reporting of the role of any troops other than those of Great Britain and the Empire was sketchy. Even French and Belgian actions were only briefly described, despite the crux of war being enacted on their soil. Although there was a great deal of illustrated material about the struggles of Russian and Serbian troops on the Eastern Front, I chanced on no mention at all of Russians on the Western Front. It was a similar story in concise histories of the war. The first positive report I found was in a 1970s battlefield guide which mentioned a Russian military cemetery east of Reims in France.

I turned my search to French periodicals, both newspapers and magazines, and there I had much more success. The weekly French magazine *L'Illustration* gave the Russians a good press, offering reports with photographs of the first Russians (reinforcements for the French army), arriving at Marseille on 21 April 1916, where they were received as heroes. Later articles reported that they first went into action near the north end of the French line, rather south of the river Somme.

I thought then that I could define the period of time the Russians spent on the Western Front and use this to narrow down the possible date of the events that Mme Simons reported. Because of the revolution at home, Russian troops stopped active participation in the war near the end of 1917. This seemed at first sight to define the window of time in which the events could have taken place, as between mid-1916 and late 1917. However, later I acquired some artifacts made by Russian prisoners. Some of these postdate the revolution and seem to indicate that the prisoners remained in German hands until the end of the war.

After this, I puzzled for some time about how to proceed with this matter. I consulted atlases, including among others the *Harmsworth Atlas* (Hammerton 1920), which contains details of the Front at various stages of the war. It was clear from this that Namur was a place which stood between the German lines of 1915–18 and their rail heads, roughly east of Mons and Cambrai. It was a natural place to bring prisoners through from west to east. But was that the way they walked?

I felt that I needed a chance to look at the site myself. In 1990 I took advantage of an opportunity to visit Namur and search for the Genart home. But this was not straightforward. There was no rue Adaquam in Namur. I went to the police station, then to the tourist office, and on to the town hall. The street name had been changed, they said, and the Genart house, which was still intact, was now known as 13 boulevard Baron Louis Huart. I went down to the river (Figure 3.5).

The house looked out at the Meuse, over a fine tree-clad boulevard. I took some photographs, got them rapidly processed, and returned with them to Mme Simons in Leuven. From the colour prints she was immediately able to describe to me the direction from which the soldiers came, and she then recalled also the time of year. It was summer. On this visit to Leuven she said to me that her sister Lucette had been 9 or 10 years old at the time. She had watched one day as Lucette had run to give hot milk to a sick French soldier who was being dragged along by his comrades. Lucette

Figure 3.5 Boulevard Baron Louis Huart, formerly rue Adaquam, Namur. The photograph, taken in 1994 across the Meuse, shows number 13, a large stone villa with a white door.

was knocked to the ground by a guard's rifle butt, smashing the cup of milk. From Lucette's age the year was probably 1918. The direction of marching was not west to east, it was north to south. The columns were arriving over the Sambre bridge, turning right along the Meuse bank on rue Adaquam, then left over the Meuse bridge. This fits well with the final German retreat in mid-summer 1918.

But are there any original local documents that confirm her story and support my interpretation of it? Though I do believe that there are local memoirs, I have set eyes on none so far, despite another visit (in which I was invited into number 13), an approach to the history department of the local university, and some local correspondence. There must also be other living witnesses of the war events at Namur, but it is documents that I am seeking.

USING DOCUMENTS

In the foregoing paragraphs I have tried to show by example some of the strategies by which oral evidence can be extended, pursued and verified in relevant documents. But documents themselves cannot be used uncritically. It is necessary not only to consider as far as you can the possible documentary sources for a study, but to think too about what character of material they will contain. The paragraphs that follow address certain chosen categories of source for local studies in the late nineteenth century or in the twentieth century. Some of them are true documents, others are definitely self-conscious. They can be classified also according to whether they are sources that may help in tracking named people, or sources that relate more to events or circumstances.

Local people: the need for nominal lists

Studies of the ways that people relate to each other and of social networks and processes are scarcely possible if you cannot put names to the individual people. Yet census enumerators' books are at present available only from 1891 back to 1841. The hundred-year rule in England and Wales ensures that one cannot gain from this source family, trade and address data on anyone who became adult after about 1910. In view of the need for nominal data, it is appropriate to talk about generally available sources that may give names, relationships and addresses. I have chosen four: twentieth-century electoral rolls, school admission and log books, local directories, and birth, marriage and burial registers.

Twentieth-century electoral rolls   One way in which oral history requires validation and pursuit is by formally identifying the persons mentioned. This may well mean moving from nicknames or familiar names to given names. For this process authentic manuscript or printed nominal lists are required. The lack of availability of census books in England and Wales (Scotland has only an eighty-year rule) means that some substitute nominal information has to be found. Modern electoral rolls are one possibility. They contain detail such as names and addresses, often, though not always, in cadastral (house by house) order. At chosen dates they are a useful place to start identifying people referred to in an interview. Used more generally, they provide material for studying population distribution and movement and the spread of urban streets. So what are the bare and essential facts about twentieth-century electoral rolls?

Although we like to think of Britain as being a 'birth place of modern democracy', most adults were still without a vote, locally or nationally, in 1900. Estimates suggest that even as late as 1913, only 60–70 per cent of men had any kind of vote, while the proportion of women with votes at that time was tiny. The few that went to the ballot box were business or property owners, since ownership, certain employment roles and university degrees conferred qualification. As far as men are concerned universal suffrage was achieved at the general election of 1919. Though the voters' lists compiled in 1918 and 1919, for the 1919 election, were in some ways odd (they contained some underage men as well as numerous errors of duplication), they were a foundation. From that point on, annual electoral rolls offered a largely comprehensive list of men aged over 21.

From 1918 they provided several details about each voter including given names, address, type of qualification to vote, and type of election qualified to vote in. Women came on to the registers in 1922 if over the age of 30 years, and then from the age of 21 starting in 1928. The rolls have continued to be prepared by regular survey and, except for the years of the Second World War, exist in long runs. Most county record offices carry extensive sequences of these. However, they may not prove to be complete for all the parliamentary constituencies in the county. Even a small county is likely to have as many as six constituencies, while larger counties have many more than that. The boundaries have been redefined by commission at intervals, those for the 1919 general election being set by a boundary commission which sat in 1917. The previous one was 1885. A very considerable (though by no means complete) post-1885 national collection of electoral rolls and much boundary information is held by the British Library (available to holders of reader's tickets).

Modern electoral rolls are not luxurious documents for the historian. No relationships among residents of the same address are given. No places of birth appear, since this was not relevant to voting rights. Naturally, no children appear. They are documents thin in content, but of huge value because of their regular yearly appearance. Attached to them too were lists of Absent Voters, sources which I shall discuss in Chapter 5.

As well as listing voters, the rolls effectively define rural voting districts or town wards, though when reading polling districts it is essential to have Ordnance Survey maps to hand. In rural areas the fine detail required necessitates use of the 6 inch series or its metric equivalent. In towns, maps with street names are required. The boundaries of polling districts in rural areas often coincide with those of much older civil parishes. They, in their turn, often derive from ancient ecclesiastical parishes. The boundaries of parliamentary constituencies at various dates, and hence the place in them of individual civil parishes or wards, appear in some atlases of appropriate date, and also upon the maps supplied with county directories.

But how does an electoral roll measure up to the sort of scrutiny we have outlined before? It is worth, as example, considering the four terms of reference we have for document evaluation.

First, the *authenticity*. of electoral rolls: the incidence of forged electoral rolls in the twentieth century must be very small indeed. (Does anyone know of one?) They are virtually all entirely authentic. A few turn up which are annotated and signed by the Returning Officer, verifying the use of that copy at an election. However, it is worth noting that the existence of a roll does not necessarily imply its use as a nominal list at a general election, though almost certainly it implies its use in a local election. Electoral use is an issue separate from authenticity.

Second, the *credibility* of rolls is generally very high. However, on the earliest rolls created during the First World War, one particular person's absence cannot be taken too seriously. Due to the pressures of war, men sometimes appeared in the wrong district, or were listed more than once.

Third, the *representation* of an individual roll, in the vast majority of instances (with the exception of 1918 and 1919, for the reason just stated), is unquestionable: one roll studied will prove to be representative of rolls in general of its date, and indeed very largely coincident in form and detail with the rolls of nearby date, for the same place.

Finally, the *meaning* of a modern electoral roll is in no doubt. It was intended to list those persons qualified to vote in a given district at the next election. The qualifications for being a voter are specified by law in the Representation of the People Acts.

It is worth pointing out that the constituencies adopted for parliamentary elections were usually made by the fusion of contiguous patches of rural or urban districts or of town wards. Rural and urban districts were administrative units with elected councils mostly dating from about 1894, and lasting until 1974. Many of these contained the land of several civil parishes. The parliamentary constituency boundaries were and still are set by boundary commissions, which, aided by the Registrar General's Office and the Ordnance Survey, report in government papers published by HMSO. Local ward boundaries are set by local commissions. More will be said about boundary commission reports in Chapter 5.

School admission and log books   Following the Elementary Education Act 1870, which set up elected school boards, many new schools were built. Some were 'board schools', others the products of denominations or charitable foundations. All schools had to meet certain requirements, one of which was the keeping of written process records as routine. These included a head teacher's daily log, and admission books. Others recorded matters such as pupil teacher training and the comments of Her Majesty's Schools Inspectorate. Naturally, since elementary schools were gender segregated, this process generated separate admission books for girls and boys and also for infants. There were separate log books too kept by the head teacher for girls and her opposite number for boys, and often a further one for the overall school head.

Log books can contain text reference to almost any subject that impinged upon school life: the weather, epidemics, local poverty, marriages of teachers, deaths of former teachers, public holidays, fairs, the harvest, absenteeism and irate parents. They regularly included certain financial details.

In contrast, admission books are structured records of pupils' full names and admission dates. Depending on the type of stationery used, the record might also contain the previous school (if any), parent or guardian's name, address at admission, date of birth, date of leaving and first destination.

From such admission lists one can easily identify the annual or termly clusters of new children, incomers to the town and families leaving or even emigrating.

Since these records have been kept ever since the acceptance of the authority of the Act in the 1870s, one school can have a large series of volumes. They are of particular use in identifying the proper names of persons, sometimes also their informal names. The entries can be cross-correlated with baptismal records, the census books for 1881 and 1891, and also with other twentieth-century local nominal lists. The latter could include sports club members, team sheets and electoral rolls. In the years immediately after 1870, it was particularly common for schools to get in photographers to take group pictures of classes; many photographs survive from the 1870s. Other periods when photographing of classes was popular were around 1902–13 and again about 1930. All too often these pictures survive without name captions, though the teachers are usually identifiable even when the pupils are not.

It is particularly unfortunate that the early formal school records are not required to be deposited in record offices, since they are of great social interest. Some are deposited, but others stay with schools, a situation which is now hazardous, as today's far-reaching programme of school closures gathers momentum.

The sets of school logs that I have examined have invariably shown evidence of being kept with the utmost meticulousness. They are rich in signed reports and comments. Totally authentic and credible, they leave little room for doubt about meanings. Although there is scope for variation in standard, all the ones that I have used have been exemplary.

Admission books vary in form more than log books. For instance, one can be lucky or unlucky with address detail. Address at admission is unlikely to coincide with address later on in childhood or in adulthood. However, a strength of these books is the lengths that head teachers went to, in order to unambiguously identify individual children.

Local directories   Most local and family historians will be familiar with directories as sources for family and business tracing. Directories range in date from the late eighteenth century to the present. Nineteenth-century directories are much sought after and highly valued, commonly being offered for sale in second-hand bookshops at £50–100. Late-nineteenth-century directories can be especially expensive. Fortunately, many record offices and libraries do carry at least some editions.

It is appropriate to confine what follows to twentieth-century directories. These too, are expensive if you purchase them second hand (£50 is not uncommon). The great majority that are met with are published by Kelly. This company absorbed many locally produced regional directories, eventually achieving a wide coverage of England and Wales.

There are three types of directories under the Kelly name that should be considered. These include city directories, for example the Birmingham directory that has run to over a hundred editions; smaller district directories such as Oxford and District (more than fifty editions) or Lincoln and District, which absorbed Ruddock's Directory; and county directories, which may address more than one county together and will have entries concerning towns and numerous small places.

Kelly's compilations offer information under five heads: a street directory, with cadastral listing of householders; an alphabetical listing of residents; a trade directory; a commercial directory; and an official directory. The city and district directories contain all five sorts of information. However, cadastral lists, which are invaluable, will not be found for the smaller places in a county directory, where only an alphabetical listing of residents is provided, along with trade and commercial lists. All directories are likely to give the names of officers, magistrates and members of councils.

It is not difficult to imagine how helpful a street list or alphabetical list can prove in searches for individuals, especially since long series of editions (though not necessarily annual) may be available. Many record offices and reference libraries have good local runs. There is also an outstanding collection at the Society of Genealogists' Library (37 Harrington Gardens, London). If a protracted study is in hand, though, there is no convenient substitute for owning a well-spaced set yourself. They do seem very expensive, but they are an excellent investment both research wise and financially!

Directories raise interesting issues of credibility and representation. Contemplating the huge size of county directories or some city directories, produced either every year or close to it, it is hard to understand how the job was done. There was an enormous amount of typesetting and proofreading required. How many errors crept in? I can answer only by impression. Odd spelling errors are quite easy to spot, but overall a remarkable product was achieved.

Representation is something else though. First, there is the matter of how well one volume represents a series. Often one year's book is very like the previous year's, though there are sudden changes that have to be looked out for. They presumably originate in changes of policy with regard to format. There can be a sharp change at the time a local directory is taken over.

Inside the directory there are issues with regard to the nominal and street lists. A short calculation shows that for a place of about 2,000 population, the names listed are roughly in the range 200–300, i.e. 10–15 per cent of the people. Assuming an average family size of four this suggests that at best only the householders will be listed. However, even among householders, in the poorest cases only about half are present. Compared to a 1930 electoral roll, a 1930 directory is likely to omit most of the women and a proportion of the men. The least well off men are more likely to be absent than the most well off. The women listed are likely to be widowed gentlewomen, tradeswomen or landladies. It is necessary to take great care if work is done on a series of years, since the percentage coverage may change over time. Particular care must be taken if bridging data extraction across a date where a local directory was replaced by the Kelly's series.

Birth, marriage and burial registers   Following through on verbal or published information about people is always likely to involve questions about their vital events: birth, marriage and death. Registers of these kinds of events do not of course offer true nominal lists, but despite that, they are essential resources, not least for identifying people by descent.

If you are studying a small district, the General Register Office in London will be no place to start a long series of searches for individuals. The indices at district register offices may be, provided you gain permission. However, the indices there are cryptic, and buying necessary certificates for an extensive piece of research would prove very expensive. The baptismal, burial and marriage records of the local churches and chapels are bound to offer a cheaper course. Fortunately these too have used standard form books since early in the nineteenth century.

Parochial vital event records raise interesting questions regarding authenticity, credibility, representation and meaning. They are in fact authenticated by signature for each year and each entry. The representation particularly can change markedly over long periods as can other parameters. In the eighteenth and nineteenth centuries occasionally records have been lost and redrafted from memory. Some books are found containing mixtures of entries from different townships or parishes. Often the bishop's copies (which may continue into the twentieth century) prove to be quite inferior in detail to the vicar's copy. Furthermore, sometimes the clerk's responsibility and discretion reached a long way. The clerk could leave things out purposely or inadvertently, lose pages, forget names, or distort entries for the sake of propriety. Books can vary a lot from parish to parish. From about 1870 onwards in many places the numbers of baptismal entries fall away for various reasons; after 1900, the record must be regarded as only a partial picture of children born in the parish.

It is probably true to say that working backwards as we are, remembered people are more reasonably first sought in burial registers, rather than in baptismal entries. We have evidence they were in this place as elderly people, and they may thus very well have died here. On the other hand, they could have been born or spent their childhood far away. In the twentieth century many burials have taken place in municipal graveyards or in burial grounds originated by cemetery companies rather than in churchyards. Many towns had large municipal graveyards before 1880. The cemetery records, which are not usually on open access, may prove an essential reference. Some city yards, which started as paupers' burial grounds, cholera grounds or cemetery company sites, go back to much earlier than 1880. It is worth noting that there must come a time before too long when researchers will need to refer regularly to crematorium records: since the 1960s this has begun to outstrip burial as a funerary practice.

Records of events

Sometimes it is not a person that you investigate as much as an event, or an institution. The latter are considered much later in the book (Chapter 9). The following pages consider the places you might use to seek information about local events. The possibilities include official true documents like district and county council and committee minutes, and more self-conscious records such as local newspapers. Also not to be overlooked are photographic records and the vast body of modern ephemera.

Local government papers   A characteristic of the past 100–120 years of local life has been the important role of an array of elected local govern-ment bodies in conducting local affairs. School boards and sanitary auth-orities were among the earliest bodies set up. However, local (rural and urban district), and county councils arose about 1894 and 1889 respec-tively, and gradually assumed various responsibilities, taking charge for in-stance, from sanitary authorities and school boards. County councils took over much new responsibility for elementary and secondary education (be-coming local education authorities), roads, planning, and some aspects of health. Boroughs assumed many tasks parallel to county councils.

The numbers of types of documents related to the activities of county, city and borough authorities is huge. Mostly these are unrelated to the pre-sent topic. However, moving to the other end of the scale, the meetings of small local councils for rural and urban districts do refer to small events and to the involvement of individual local people. The minute books of these councils are excellent places to search for references to events, to matters like the demolishing of certain buildings, closure of footpaths, to house building, including council houses, road mending and matters of local health. Often there are references to individuals involved in these matters.

The minute books, which will usually be deposited at the county record office, are very formal documents, often to the point of punctiliousness. They are signed and countersigned as true records of what transpired. The proceedings themselves were conducted according to protocol. These kinds of records are strong on authenticity, credibility and meaning. Each is likely also to be very much to type. Backing them up there are sometimes news-paper reports of meetings with verbal quotes, which can be matched to the minutes held at the county record office. Urban and rural district records run until 1974, when the small authorities were abolished.

Newsprint   Although in the examples I have discussed so far newspapers did not figure prominently, they are frequently the next place to turn to after oral evidence. Newspapers as objects are much nearer to oral sources in their character than are almost any other type of document. They really are rather special things: frequent, disposable, of richly diverse content, and minute. Yet they are self-conscious: sometimes written to give entertainment or for political motives; opinionated and undependable. With all their faults, they are indispensable in local studies of people and events in the nineteenth and twentieth centuries.

Although some local newspapers were in existence in the eighteenth century, those were not numerous. Many areas of the country had little or no newspaper coverage. By the middle of the nineteenth century, there had been a big change. There was a large increase in the number of newspaper titles, such that in a particular town, several local newspapers may well have begun to run in parallel. These newspapers underwent sequences of fusions and name changes, so that some titles lasted only a few years and others came into being that had incorporated two or three. By the end of the nineteenth century, things had become more settled and in most districts one or two local titles were well established. It follows that to look for all the newsprint on a particular local topic might involve studying many newspaper titles, especially when work is on a period before 1900. In the twentieth century, one to three major local publications would be a usual number. The volume of material can be huge, so big it can easily swallow you up.

Newspaper history   It is advisable before starting a search (and especially if a study spans a period) to become familiar with all the local newspapers there have been in the region, even the ones which had only a short life. The easiest way to do this is to consult the British Library Catalogue of the Newspaper Library, Colindale (this is a large book held by many reference libraries). In this the newspaper titles are listed by town or city. A large city will have many publications listed. Manchester, for instance, has more than 500 entries, which include well-known newspapers, such as the *Manchester Guardian* (from 1821), some eighteenth-century papers, the *Manchester City News* 1864–1936 (and then by other titles to 1960), and numerous specialised papers to do with textiles and cotton, or aspects of sport and social life. For comparison, Sheffield has over 100 entries, including the *Sheffield Daily Telegraph* from 1855 and, with variations of title, to the present time.

In a large city there is no shortage of choice of newspapers to read. When studying small places, the paper published in the nearest town is to be regarded as the 'local' one. For example, in the Sedgemoor villages, the *Bridgwater Independent* (1885–1933) or the *Langport and Somerton Herald* might be useful, or somewhat further afield, the *Somerset County Herald* (1888–1964), a paper published at Taunton.

While the collection of newspapers held at Colindale is the main national reference resource for newspapers, local libraries and county record offices are often very strong on local newsprint, and their collections will probably be easier to consult than the national one. Check always whether the title you are selecting has a weekly edition. This will be a better place to start than a daily one. Either way, be warned. Old newspapers are very addictive. You can find yourself spending absolutely weeks reading them.

The character of newspaper reports   If you were interested in some argument that a local or national politician had made in a speech this very week, you could look for the details of it in your local or national newspaper. Do you think you would find it though? Probably not. Newspapers in the 1990s no longer report speeches in detail as a routine, either at local or at national level. Currently almost every paper seems to feel that its readers ought to be interested in the newspaper's own comments on the news, while of the news itself the reader would want merely some gistings or highlights spiced with indications of interpersonal conflict. Many contemporary newspapers are not any longer detailed data and information sources so much as presentations of soap operas created out of current events.

The style of the local reporting was not always of this sort. Lasting until rather after the Second World War was a style far more sober, and full of details. Events of purely local interest, such as the unveiling of a cenotaph or the opening of a new church hall, were reported minutely, often with an accompanying photograph and usually with lists of the persons present. Funerals were reported with attached lists of mourners with their relationships to the departed (invaluable for family studies) and other persons present. Characteristic also were detailed accounts of what various persons said on public occasions. Political candidates' speeches were often reported in depth; sometimes there are reports of the life experience of the candidates and even remarks about their parents. (This practice continued until the 1950s.) Earlier in the century, many council meetings or other local authority committees were reported in detail, thus giving public insight into concerns about local health, weather and transport. Local courts have always contributed good newspaper copy; in old newspapers the rich wordiness of the advertisements should not be neglected either.

I have in front of me a Devon newspaper for a date in 1945, in which appear the adoption speeches of three local parliamentary candidates, who were to stand for parliament in the impending general election. They are all printed on one page. Despite the likely local strength of one view point or another, all three candidates have got equal column space (two whole columns each). Their photographs are all of the same size and all are placed at the same height on the page. Not only does the newspaper give no intrusive editorial, but also it apparently faithfully and fully reports each candidate's words. The reader is being given a balanced wealth of information, including some that was even then historical, such as the reference in one speech to Sir Richard Acland's victory in that constituency in 1935, and that parliamentarian's subsequent political career. This is, I believe, a far more factual resource than we would be offered in the 1990s.

It is worth reflecting that good as the coverage in that regional paper was, lots of vivid election-related events still evaded the eyes and pens of the reporters. I can vouch for some of them because, as a small boy, I was there! I spent much of spring and summer 1945 riding in poster-bedecked cars, playing in election offices and sitting on speakers' platforms. So far as I know, the papers did not notice or choose to report the stoning of a candidate's car in Lynmouth, nor did they cover well the occasion when hundreds of returned servicemen linked arms at Ilfracombe to sing the 'Red Flag'. One might speculate as to whether 1990s newspapers would have reported the latter incidents. I rather think that they might. The reporting in the past was more detailed with regard to formal matters, but this was balanced by the omission of some of the more disordered aspects of life, those which might be made much of today. Many kinds of documents are entirely unselfconscious. This is certainly not the case with modern newspapers.

Starting with a newspaper report: a hero's funeral   Here now is an excerpt from the funeral report of a man from Tredegar, Monmouthshire, published in the *South Wales Weekly Argus* in January 1920. Let us see how we get on in interpreting and evaluating this. It goes exactly as follows:

Although the late Regimental Sergt. Major G.A. Gravenor, D.C.M., C.G. had been connected with military pomp and ceremony from the days when he joined the Volunteers, he was modest and retiring in private life; and it was at his own wish that his funeral should be of a private nature. This was reverently observed – much as his comrades of his beloved 'Thirds' would like to have accorded full military honours to a colleague who had brought distinction to the Regiment. Not withstanding the wintery conditions (in a snow storm the coffin was borne on the shoulders of gallant men, who fought side by side with RSM Gravenor in France, to the hearse in Poplar Road). There was a large company present, the number of Officers testified to the respect in which he was held. Lt.Col. Bishop commanding 3rd Mons was at the head, and among those present were:- Capts. L.D. Whithead, W.P. Abbott, Dan Morgan, R.A. Lewis (Ebbw Vale), Lts. R.G. Davies, R. Bassett Spencer, Warren Jenkins, Basil Edwards, D.H. Angus, T. Thomas, Brinley Powell, H. Hopkins, MC, H. Davies, and Douglas Onions. Quartermasters Sergt. Cooke, Deveraux, Fraser, Shaw (Abergavenny), Elway; Sergt. Majs. Phillips, Coulson, (Ebbw Vale), T. Cary, Col.Sergt. Walters (Abergavenny), Sgts. Morgan, R. Davies, Frank Jones, G.O. Thomas, A.V. Jackson, J.Stewart, Restall, and Connelly, W. Coombes, Pickering, T. Northam and Price; Cpls. D. Roberts, c. Roberts; Trumpeter Bert Nash, Messrs. Amos Williams, Watkins, G. Powell (Abergavenny), W. Adam, Perrin, J.W. Price, Cliff Jones, M. Simmonds, Maloney and the following from Ebbw Vale:- Messrs. Baxter, French, Murphy, Gunter, Ross, Owen, and Hinton – all of whom had been associated with the deceased on military duty, either at home or abroad. The Officers and many N.C.O.s were in uniform and their presence in a semi-military capacity gave an impressive touch to the scene. Others present included:- Messrs. C Digby Watkins, A. Coombes, Stanley Harvey, J.B. Angus, D.A. Hughes, C. Bartlett, A.H. North, Tom Bosley, G.E. Golding, c.c., Rev. John Evans, Messrs A.J.P. Gough, C. Campbell, D.W. Davies, A. Phillips, H. Watkins, J.H. Davies, A. Saunders, Sam Filer, J. Jones, BA, C.L. Price, Ben George, C.E. Pettit, W. Jones; while there was a strong contingent from St Joseph's Young Mens Catholic Guild, of which the deceased was President. The coffin was covered with the Union Jack, upon which lay the deceased's cap, belt etc.

The mourners were three brothers:- Percy, Llewelyn and Ralph, and Mrs C.W. Morgan and Mr Reg. Crocker. As the cortege passed through the town, it was noticed that business premises were temporarily closed and that, at many private houses, the blinds were drawn. Father Vernacombe conducted the service at the residence and at the graveside. The floral tributes were very beautiful and were sent by widow and babies, sister and brothers, nephew and nieces at Bridgewater: nephews and nieces at St Fagans; nephews and nieces at Merriot; nephews and nieces at London; Aunt Lizzie and cousins; Connie and Ernest; all at home in Ireland; Staff at Bedwellty House; old comrades at Abergavenny; Discharged Soldiers & Sailors Tredegar; Capt & Mrs L.D. Whitehead; Mr H.J.C. Shepard; Mrs Power; Mr & Mrs Phillips (Drill Hall); Mr & Mrs C. Bartlett, Mr Richard Bartlett (Blackwood); Mrs Fear & Family; Mrs Lewis Bernstein and Family; St Joseph's Young men's Catholic Guild and Tredegar Football Club.

This is a document of whose authenticity there is no doubt. We have viewed the actual newspaper page on which it was printed. On the other hand, regarding its credibility, one can make several remarks. A number of pieces of otherwise obscure information are included. For instance, the remark on the Sgt Major's former membership of the 'old volunteers' is invaluable. Indeed the very unavailability of the information elsewhere makes it simultaneously valuable and unconfirmable. We have no cause to disbelieve it, but we can not confirm it.

His reported devotion to the Territorial Force lineal descendant of the volunteers is different. It can be read also from his DCM medal citation in the *London Gazette,* January 1916. That in its turn can be validated by obtaining from the Ministry of Defence a copy of the original. The award to him of the Croix de Guerre avec Palmes also appears in the *London Gazette* early in 1916.

The funeral notice gives a helpful hint that he may have been married into an Irish family. This is confirmed by his marriage lines which give his bride's name as Mary, daughter of Michael McCrink. The report indicates that he was himself a member of a large family. The extent of that family can be confirmed both from the 1881 census book and his parents' gravestone, which names many of the other Gravenor children, brothers and sisters of the Sgt Major.

It is worth noting that the newspaper report gives no indication of the real cause of his illness and death. His death certificate conspires with this. Neither on the certificate nor in the newspaper is it made clear that his death was promoted by the after effects of gassing with chlorine in May 1915. However, a much earlier edition of the same newspaper (June 1916) does report him being gassed in one of the very first gas attacks of the war. On this topic, the funeral report taken alone might well mislead the unwary.

The report does give several insights into the local community and its lifestyle. It seems to imply that not only were those attending the funeral almost exclusively male, but also his widow was not present in the funeral party. This seems at first sight very improbable, indeed can we believe it? Was it an oversight? Was it a convention of reporting at the time? It would be easy to assume that his widow must have gone to the funeral. However, verbal enquiries indicate that, as late as 1970, some funerals of South Wales men did indeed take place with their widows staying at home to see the funeral party off and to 'keep a warm house'. (The coffin of a widower was sometimes 'seen off' by a female neighbour.) A study of further funeral reports by the *South Wales Argus* might clarify this. It is possible that the report is entirely accurate, as far as it goes. Perhaps funerals really were men's work?

Still on the subject of credibility, the list of names of those present repays examination. It is clear that although the battalion's 'calling place' was the market town of Abergavenny, its catchment was wide and that part of the membership present on the day was principally persons from the valley head towns of Tredegar and Ebbw Vale. Were any of these his particular friends? Were any present on the occasion he won the medals? For all the riches of the report, our circumspection is required. We would even be unjustified in assuming that all the named persons were recent members of the battalion, the 1st/3rd Mons. In fact that battalion was dissolved on 31 August 1916 (for reference see E.A. James, *British Regiments, 1914–18*; see also Chapter 5). Furthermore, as the battalion war diary – at the Public Record Office (PRO) Kew in London – makes clear, as they stood on parade in preparation for leaving the Ypres Salient for the last time, a large shell from a German railway gun caused great carnage, killing among many others most of the non-commissioned officers (NCOs) then surviving from among those that had gone out with the Sgt Major in March 1915. In August 1916 the surviving personnel were dispersed to other units. This serves to make the point that newspaper reports, for all their richness, also set plenty of traps.

The text at its most self-conscious (deliberately making an impression) vividly captures the occasion. We seem from its words to imagine the local feeling towards the man, and something of the bleak climate and setting of the town of Tredegar. The town is set among bare hills at a valley head, more than 1,000 ft above sea level. I know the town well, so for me the report brings to mind images of the place. How much it helps a reader unfamiliar with the town, I do not know. But it seems to me a report full of local colour.

Interestingly, the report also offers some valuable unselfconscious information. It is unlikely that the report writer pondered on the surnames of the old battalion members that he listed. Yet they give one some insight into the geographic origin of the local communities. The Welsh patronymic surnames abound (Morgan, Davies, Jones, Powell, Price, Lewis – see Chapters 7 and 8), but they are augmented with several Irish names (Murphy, Maloney) and with occasional West Country ones as well (Coombes).

Images: photographs of groups and individuals   Having broached the subject of photographs, this is probably a good point at which to mention the problem of authenticating them. I referred in Chapter 2 to the use of photographs as prompts in conversation, and hence the matter of getting an elderly person to identify the figures and groups on them. But there are two other aspects to authenticating these images. The first is with regard to the nature of the photograph as an object – how it was made, by whom and where. The second is the date and occasion it records. On the subject of the first aspect, I can do no better than to refer the reader to the excellent book edited by Don Steel and Lawrence Taylor (1984) *Family History in Focus*, in which Chapters 3–6 discuss photograph dating and analysis. I have to point out how crucially important it can be to date the picture. If you do not know the date, you are unlikely to be able to place the event. It also decreases your chances of identifying the people portrayed. You may need to use every scrap of evidence on the picture, in order to infer the date, occasion and event.

Twentieth-century ephemera   Another way in which printed or pictorial record of the twentieth century differs from previous ones is the hugely increased number of ephemeral documents, many referring to events. Posters, brochures, sales and promotional leaflets are all among the printed material left in the drawers and wastepaper baskets of the century. Many of the older objects are bearers of valuable information and should be pounced upon when they show themselves. Posters, admission tickets and programmes particularly can be followed up in local newspapers. Postcards too can be used, in two separate ways. Images of buildings correlate with 25 inch maps while on the rear may be a date, a postmark and a signed message.

The latter part of the century has seen the rise of desktop publishing and countless small printing houses. Now almost any department of any organisation might produce its own newsletter. Any city council might seek to explain its local taxation; any group of football fans might produce their 'fanzine'. The last decades of the century are neck deep with paper ephemera, which are going to illuminate the view of our lives gained by local historians in 100 years' time.

The mix of paper objects from earlier in the century, though much different, is of great value since it all reveals detail of human activity that may not be easily gleaned elsewhere. One can give no good advice about finding it other than to keep your eye out. Then be sure when you have found something that you authenticate it as far as possible. Think out what questions you may want to ask about, for example, a local Liberal Party election address from 1950; the programme for a royal visit to the town in 1937; or a photograph of a Sunday school Whitsuntide procession of an unknown date, but early in the twentieth century.

Unique items: memoirs and diaries Mostly when we talk about documentary sources we mean items of which there are hundreds of examples – newspapers, workhouse admission books, burial registers, etc. Generally, although we do have some problems in understanding the content of these we rarely have to question their authenticity. But suppose that in searching for support to some story that I have been told, I come across something truly rare, a real 'one off' item. Imagine, for example, someone produced from a drawer a signed personal memoir compiled by an individual now deceased. Imagine also I was offered a wholly unique diary by another dead relative. I would certainly seize them with relish, but how would I evaluate them?

In both cases, the matter of authenticity would be the immediate issue. Are these things what they appear to be? Is the diary one really kept at the time? Was the memoir a contemporarily written document or a retrospective? Is the author intending to inform or just meaning to entertain, or maybe even to mislead? Can I tell?

If the diary and memoir are authentic, are the contents credible? (If not, they will still have a value, but mostly as a comment about the writer.) Are they representative? Of what should they be representative? If they are really unique, it is unclear what typicality might mean in their case, and is it important, since they contain crucial information? Finally, do I really know what they mean? It is possible that some of the contents will mystify me. If most of it proves mysterious, I will not know how to make use of the material.

If Mme Simons had died and left me a memoir in French, instead of telling me a verbal story about prisoners of war, how much of it would have seemed beyond my understanding? Without the opportunity to question her, how much of her written tale would I be right to take on trust?

REFERENCES AND FURTHER READING

Bingham, J.H. (1949) *The Sheffield School Board 1870–1903*. Sheffield: JW Northend [An example of a locally compiled education history].

Byles, A. (1982) *The History of the Monmouthshire Railway and Canal Company*. Cwmbran, Gwent: Village Publishing.

Collins, W.T.J. (1948) *More Monmouthshire Writers*. Newport: RH Johns.

Curtis, S.J. (1948 and later dates) *History of Education in Great Britain*. London: University Tutorial Press [A very full text giving details of all aspects].

Hammerton, J.A. (ed.) (1920) *The Harmsworth Atlas and World Pictorial Gazeteer*. London: Amalgamated Press.

James, E.A. (1978) *British Regiments, 1914–18*. London: Samson Books.

Northedge A. (1990) *The Good Study Guide*. Milton Keynes: The Open University [Has an excellent chapter on note taking, and another on reading].

Richards, T. (1989) *Was your Grandfather a Railwayman?* 2nd edn, Plymouth: Federation of Family History Societies.

Scott, John (1990) *A Matter of Record*. Cambridge: Polity Press and Basil Blackwell [Dissects the nature of written records].

Steel, D. and Taylor, L. (eds) (1984) *Family History in Focus*. Guildford: Lutterworth Press [Dating and interpreting photographs].

CHAPTER FOUR

Notes, Notebooks and Archives

DATA, INFORMATION AND KNOWLEDGE

It is in the nature of the process of microhistory that you work without knowing the final outcome. As in all research, the path of inquiry has to be chosen and then redefined, and perhaps redefined again. You seek knowledge without knowing what that knowledge is, for you travel from question to question. We can understand the whole process of gaining knowledge better, if the meanings of some of the words we use are set out.

We can conveniently think of three levels at which we work. At the first level, that of individual tiny fragments of sense, we find the very smallest events that can be separately recorded. These we call *data*.

However, though data evidently do have in them a content we can interpret, they make little or no impact without knowledge of their context. For example, when a lone *F* is written in a column on a document, it may mean female gender, but this is not clearly so, unless the column is labelled sex or gender, or the entry is at least stated to be describing the status of a person. The *F* is more understandable too, if we know it applies to a particular person: our mother, ourselves or some other identified human being. A collection of data in a known context makes *information*.

But is information *knowledge*? It is certainly true that the acquisition of information ('facts') is commonly taken to be the acquiring of knowledge. Knowledge, though, has to do with understanding, rather than with memory. We can usefully think of knowledge as information placed in context. Wider and deeper knowledge are really greater knowledge of context.

In local history research, what we seek is knowledge; we seek it via the acquisition of information. We build our information from thousands of data of various kinds. To be effective in research, we have to get used to looking after data in safe and tidy ways, extracting information from them and recording that too. We acquire our knowledge more unconsciously, often realising that we have (or do not have) it only when we come to try to create a product – some kind of written or illustrated history.

In this chapter we are considering the collection, ordering and filing of data – data that you yourself gather. Here, and in the following chapters, we consider some aspects of the use of data to generate knowledge of people and events.

WRITING IT ALL DOWN: THE MATTER OF KEEPING RECORDS

Just as soon as you start asking people questions, as soon as you consult a document such as a register or a minute book, you start needing to make your own records. If you have found something interesting, you had better write it down. And if you have found nothing of interest, you had better write that down too. After all, you will not want to look in that place again for the same thing. If you do not write down which books you have searched and for what, and what you saw there; and if you do not record in writing things that somebody said, you will very soon find yourself probing your own memory: 'What exactly did old Mrs Roberts say?' 'Is that the same spelling as I saw in the municipal graveyard?' And so on.

When it comes to holding data, tiny items of text or number, the human memory soon gets overloaded and confused. Even if your memory is basically very good, it is best not to ask too much of it. Always, write it down! If you do not get into the habit, very soon you will have good cause for regret.

ON THE SPOT: USING A FIELD NOTEBOOK

Much of the local study I have done has been at a considerable distance from my present home. I drive a long way to reach the places and documents that I study. Several of my early journeys to search for data excited me very much, but ultimately they yielded a lot less than they should have done. I was ill prepared. My paper and pencils were insufficient, I did not write down what I had found in its entirety, and I did not record where I had looked for it. Because I was trying to do such a lot (far too much in fact) in the available time, I made up abbreviations. Unfortunately, when I got home I could not remember what they all meant. In some cases, I was not even sure what data had come from what document. I have frequently regretted the inadequacy of those early notes.

These days I carry a good quality A4 notebook of grid pattern paper, with a tough stiff cover. The one currently in use is bright blue. The previous one was uniform with it, except that the cover was brown. Its predecessor, also a book of the same design, had a green cover. I have thus an on-going series of field notebooks, colour-coded for approximate date. Inside them, each occasion upon which notes have been made is dated, and the location recorded. For example: *Devon County Record Office, Exeter 2.8.90; 'at St John's Church Burslem, 17.6.87'; Public Record Office, Chancery Lane, 22.7.86; Dr James Dunwoody, notes taken by telephone, 12.12.93.*

If a document is being scanned, the name of it is recorded, as also is its piece number, if it has one. (The piece number is that number the record office or library puts upon it, for their cataloguing purposes. Recording this not only identifies it unambiguously, but also will enable me to obtain that document on another occasion with a minimum of trouble.) My field notebooks are not models of tidiness, but they are the source I rely upon and return to – the first appearance of my own primary data. They are especially precious, since almost everything I later write, in part at least, depends on their contents.

However, vital though their function is, the field notes are even more than simply the original dated records of what I read or saw. Together, the series of notebooks is a diary of the whole journey of my research. In fact this is literally true, for I never travel without the current field notebook, even if I am not envisaging doing any kind of research, since I so often come across things I want to remember.

Tactics in note taking

When I am taking material down into field notes, in or out of doors, I always make the utmost effort to transcribe or describe things literally. Any abbreviations I may be forced to use are defined and standardised. The series of field notebooks contains my original notes ('primary record') of interviews, impressions received on location, excerpts from documents, transcripts of monumental inscriptions, sketch maps, drawings, important questions and thoughts as they arose, and much more, such as addresses and telephone numbers of local contacts. Particularly at interview and in searching documents, I commonly make 'mind maps' of what is emerging; writing some data items in spatial relation to others, so that a connected picture begins to form. In this way too, questions arise, that might be answerable there and then.

ON THE SPOT: USING A CAMERA

There are many occasions on location when taking a photograph may be much more effective or efficient than writing things down in a notebook. I have taken many records of views either for reference or for illustration of text. I have taken many more to serve as reminders to me of the current state of the landscape and buildings. Since some images may be used in talks, I take many colour transparencies. However, for documentary purposes I take black and white negatives using 35 mm format. This sometimes necessitates carrying two camera bodies. Sometimes I travel with a friend who carries a large format camera. Between us we have a wide range of lenses, including standard 50 mm lenses, a 28 mm wide angle and some telephoto zoom lenses.

In the event of travel to a distant location, we take care to have plenty of film of several types, spare meter batteries, a tripod, a hand-held meter and a means of writing notes about the photographs being taken.

In some circumstances, but always with permission, we record large documents using black and white film in a camera on a tripod. Using this approach, whole manuscript books can be copied fairly easily, whereas writing a transcript would have been quite impossible. We also often copy precious photographs on site, when borrowing them from the owner is not permitted. When they are available for borrowing, they can be copied on an illumination stand, permitting a top quality result.

WHAT IS DONE WITH IT ALL WHEN I GET HOME

Notes

Back in my study, I write up by hand or type on a word processor fair copies of the notes, as appropriate. Interview notes are set out on A4 lined paper, my asides are added in square brackets as also are some footnotes, where statements I recorded were found to be borne out by something in another source. I never, ever amend the field notes, which thus always remain as a record of what I wrote at the time. The final written up script is given an identifying code ('numerical identifier') and put into the appropriate A4 ring binder, e.g. for a set of interview notes, say INT017, the seventeenth interview in the INT ring binder, which has in it texts from many interviews.

Births, baptisms, burials and marriages are added to the PRTR (parish register transcript) binder, while impression notes made on location are written up, numbered and placed in a 'location file' called LOC. Literature notes, i.e. notes from books, go into a file called LITR; correspondence goes into a CORR file. Ring binders are, as far as possible, of distinctive colours: red files for interviews and correspondence, grey for literature, green for transcripts and blue for extracted numerical and nominal data. As these ring binders fill up, second ones are created such as red file 3, blue file 2, etc. Field notes are thus translated and transcribed into my secondary archival records.

The contents of the different types of paper files vary, in that some are mostly raw data, while others have low level information. All have their place in a paper file system. Of course, the original field notes are always retained and can be returned to for query.

The written-up archival records have within them, in square brackets, asides, annotations and questions, that I have added. These are early signs of connections and emerging patterns that I am discerning in the data. They, like the mind maps, are the beginnings of a higher level of information. I do find that in the course of time, I get many thoughts about this information, and lots of ideas about ways of processing data. Sometimes I apply extensive processing, producing tables or graphs. The results of data processing are written down in PROC files. More global thoughts that emerge as a result of studying processed data, I write as text, and place in TEXT files. The PROC files are definitely information files. The content of TEXT files represent the beginnings of my knowledge about the local history.

More about the insides of the files   The PROC files are the most complicated files. They each contain several subsets of selected, processed or plotted data. Sets which relate to particular places are distinguished by appropriate identifying place codes. For example, material on surnames in Sheffield are coded Shefnam001–023. Surname material relating to Wales as a whole is coded Welshnam001–015, while that specifically from Caerleon records are Caernam001–016.

Large files are thus sometimes subdivided. However big or complicated the file, or however extensive its content, all pieces – data, refined information or text – have their own letter and number identifier. This describes their 'home' file and subset. Under Shefnam, Welshnam, or any other label, numbers are allocated in order of acquisition.

Supplementary research materials

During research, one selects and accumulates many materials and objects beside written notes and data sets. Some of them, like pieces of newsprint, contemporary booklets, leaflets or photocopies, are chosen from the mass of text written by other authors. Other materials, such as photographs, maps, certificates or legal documents, are selected for reference to the problems being researched. As objects requiring filing, few of them come easily to a ring binder unless they can be put in transparent envelopes. For some of these sorts of objects, like whole newspaper pages, I use box files. In my file set, these boxes currently number 1 to 42. Their contents are segregated and labelled by origin: recent newsprint in one box, my own family's papers in five more, regional booklets and publicity materials in several others. Other materials are boxed by geographical region. Regional boxes include some concerned with Sheffield, another on the Potteries, and several on Somerset and Wiltshire.

All these types of items are kept, at least partly, for consultation; as reminders of actual words used currently, or in the past, by other writers. They are kept for supply of dates, images, and local colour. In a sense, though, they are nearer to being a library for browsing than they are to an extracted data set. Each item within each box is marked with an identifier, so that when it is consulted it can always be returned to its place. For my collection, I keep a typed list of boxes and of each box contents.

Maps

Probably to be added to a collection of research material is a selected set of maps. Mine contains both old and contemporary editions of folding maps, at various scales ranging in imperial or metric equivalent from ½ inch to the mile to 25 inch. I do make much use of ½ inch and 1 inch Third, Fourth, Fifth and Sixth Edition Ordnance Survey (OS) maps, occasionally studying maps of OS First and Second series. These were all obtained from dealers in second-hand maps. I also have some modern reprints of old 2½ inch mapping. Many of my maps are photocopies of 6 inch or 25 inch editions from libraries, photocopies of tithe maps and their schedules or of manuscript plans. The folding maps are stacked in plastic boxes. The large photocopied sheets are folded to A3 and placed in transparent pockets in an A3 ring binder. The maps run to some hundreds altogether, but are not sufficient in number to create a serious finding problem.

Photographs

I have mentioned that I take many photographs as part of my search and documentation process, and I have therefore many films, transparencies and prints. But before I discuss the handling of photographs, it is as well to be clear about the overall range of photographic material that one can accumulate.

Photographic material relating to a research project can be of four kinds:

(1) original old photographs including postcards; (2) modern (archival) copies of old photographs, both negatives and prints; (3) recently taken (modern) photographs, both negatives and prints; (4) transparencies. Both (3) and (4) may bear images of documents, objects, people or locations.

Each of these categories presents different storage and filing problems. Many things could be said about looking after and filing photographs; indeed it is recognised by bodies such as the major museums that image filing is a taxing problem. The most important points seem to be the following.

1. If you have the negatives of print material, make sure that they are stored in archive quality, transparent, PVC-free slip sheets, with labels that give date and place. The strips of film or individual negatives should be kept such that their sequence is clear. Purpose-made ring binders are available from photographic dealers. These should be stored in a cool, dark place of normal humidity.

2. If you have ancient prints, take archival negatives of them as soon as possible and store them as in (1). Keep the originals and negatives in separate and preferably fireproof places.

3. If you have mounted transparencies, give them numbers; write on the frames the date taken, the subject and the place.

4. Store unmounted transparencies in strips as in (1), with date and place labels, in a ring binder.

5. Create a catalogue of all prints, negatives and transparencies. This could employ a card index or a computer file. Check the state of all modern prints at regular intervals. The usual method of print preparation employs resin-coated paper developed in a machine and then machine-washed. Often, even though the fixer solution is frequently changed, prints will later slowly go brown. This is something much less likely to happen to prints made by the old bromide paper process, which is unfortunately much more expensive and much slower than resin paper technology.

CATALOGUING

I have amassed a library concerned with local studies running to more than 500 books. But 500 books, especially ones chosen by yourself, are not so many that they necessitate a complicated catalogue. I know what books I own, and what books I do not own. The only need I have is keeping them in some sort of logical order, so that I can find what I want.

A collection of over 300 maps, though, is not as simple a matter. I find it quite hard to remember what I have got and what I have not got. It is particularly difficult to know if I have anything covering a certain hamlet or house. A typed-up list would be quite useful in finding the maps, showing each map with the box in which it is kept. But such a listing would not tell me the coverage of each map. With such a list, I would possibly have to scan the whole to find a map showing some specific feature or for use in some particular purpose. Only a filing system using attached words to describe each map's coverage would help me out of that difficulty.

My ring binders and box files altogether offer a demanding problem. I need to be able to identify all the pieces of material I have, its file or box, with how it relates to a particular topic, be it a place, a person or an event. This is not a small matter.

Nevertheless, perhaps the worst of the filing problems I have is handling the collection of photographs. Above 2,000 transparencies, ancient prints, hundreds of old topographical postcards, many hundreds of modern negatives of details in lots of localities. And then there are $8'' \times 5''$ and $10'' \times 8''$ prints taken from those negatives. If I can find a way to overcome the photograph filing problem, then the others will certainly be beaten also.

In fact solving this sort of catalogue problem requires the making of two sets of arrangements. The first is the appending of descriptors, which tell the contents of the piece or set; not merely a title or a number, but a group of words (the 'keywords') which include all the important topics mentioned, or related to, or imaged therein. The second is to give each filed object an identified storage place, and to know the way that that place fits into the whole system.

The second of these requirements can be met, if I wish, fairly simply by the creation of a single ring binder containing a listing of all the other ring binders, box files and photograph files, made in such a way that I know which pieces come in which box or binder. The first requirement is far more complex. Describing photographs or newsprint with keywords, and sorting via them, is quite definitely a job for a small computer. Only with such a device can I sort for two or three requirements at the same time. *What images do I have showing both buses and the town bridge, before 1935?* At the start of my work, I had no filing problem – but that was fifteen years ago. The pile of material has grown and grown, and now it stares me in the face.

COMPUTERS FOR LOCAL HISTORY

I attended a lecture a few years ago entitled: 'Can we be saved from computers?' The speaker's conclusion, if I understood him correctly, seemed to be that we could not. However, he did not seem to believe that having these machines enter so many aspects of our lives was by any means a bad fate. Once I was deeply suspicious of modest electronic calculators, but I have got over that. Now I am more worried by the idea of hidden machines analysing what I buy in the supermarket. At the same time I am sometimes disturbed to find how hard it is to work, when I am separated from my own computer.

But how am I to address the subject of computers here? This book is about the study of local history, not about computers. It is not even a book about computers in local history, but these machines do get into the doing of this subject, just as they insinuate themselves elsewhere. Not only are we likely to need them for filing, writing, drawing and calculating, but also they have already helped to make the subject of local history what it presently is. This leaves me with the unavoidable task of writing about them. I shall write not just about the terrible filing problem mentioned above, but more generally (and I hope more interestingly) I shall write about things you can do using computers, which are unlikely to be done at all without them.

What do I mean by 'a computer'?

You cannot really buy a computer (*micro*computer really) without first learning a bit about them. Both learning about them and buying them are difficult, rather like trying to board a moving train. The models change with bewildering rapidity. The computer market advertises continuing rapid innovation. Prices are kept buoyant by always offering, in the next model, more performance than available in the last, yet for the same amount of money. Consequently, the available machines never get cheaper, but they do get better. The drawback is that a functional machine that you own can be seriously out of date in a few years. And as the latest programs are made for the newer types of machines, having an old machine limits your scope.

If you are going to plunge in and buy a computer, the best thing to do, over a period of weeks, is to buy various computer magazines (e.g. *ComputerShopper*), and read them. They are by far the best source for explanations of how the machines work, and of what various software packages (programs) can achieve. Comparative reviews of both program packages and computers are commonplace there. Magazines are the only place in which to find the information with which to weigh up the market. But evening classes too are good places to learn many beginner's things before you buy a machine of your own. Do note that any prices quoted in this chapter are for rough guidance only. You should use a magazine to obtain more up-to-date figures.

You will find in all these places that there is a large body of specialised and curious language associated with microcomputing. Furthermore, a text like this one is no substitute for a hands-on beginner's course. But if you are not familiar, Table 4.1 offers definitions of some of these terms.

Getting a microcomputer for local history

So what sort of machine do you need to help you with your local history? Bearing in mind that you may want to use it for several different purposes – to store and catalogue ordered information, to write text, perhaps to draw and print – you will not be looking for a toy. Your requirement is more for a serious office machine than for a home games outfit. The range of Apple Macintosh machines will do everything you want, and so will 'IBM clone' machines (PCs). The number of available makes and models of these is now very large. The 'bottom of the range' PC machines are now so priced as to make the purchase of a lesser machine than a PC entirely pointless.

In fact, the ones at the bottom of the range do not stay on the market long as they are about to become outmoded. Probably the best advice, whether you go for the Apple range or for a PC, is to buy not the cheapest machine, but rather the best that you can afford. What is 'the best'? First, this is the one with the fastest central processor (CPU), because it will stay up-to-date longest. Second, this is the one with the best visual display unit (VDU). If you are going to spend many hours staring at the VDU, it will pay you to buy a good quality one. The more stable and adjustable a VDU is, the less strain it is to look at it for long periods. The ones called non-interlaced SVGA (Super Video Graphics Adaptor) are best. If you can afford it, a 15 inch screen is better than a 12 inch.

The data and information you will handle will be stored on magnetic disks. These are either 'diskettes' (floppy disks) or hard disks, which have a much larger capacity. The PCs at the lower end of the price range offer hard disks as standard with a storage capacity of much more than 100 megabytes; this is huge capacity when translated into printed text. (One megabyte is the equivalent of a 300 to 400 page printed book.) However, many programs are themselves large, and they operate in a *Windows* working environment, which itself increases the storage capacity required. PCs with a hard disk storage capacity of 500 megabytes are now quite common.

Many computers are fitted with a CD-ROM drive. A CD (compact disc) has a larger capacity than a floppy disk. They will soon come to play an important role in local historical research; you may find yourself being offered data sets on CD-ROM to borrow or to purchase.

Table 4.1   Glossary of terms in microcomputing

Algorithm	A solution to a problem in defined steps
Argument	A variable used to make a specific search command
ASCII file	File in universally agreed code for information exchange
Assembler	A low level computer language
Backing up	Making a spare copy of a file
BASIC	A programming language
Baud rate	Speed of data transfer by telephony
Binary	Notation using only digits 0,1
Bit	Any one binary digit
Boot up	Procedure for starting computer
Bubblejet	Printer which uses vaporised ink
Byte	The set of eight bits equalling one character
C	A programming language
Case specific	Where DOM and Dom are not equivalent
CD-ROM	Compact disc storing data
Central processor	'Nerve centre' of the computer (CPU)
Character	One of a set of symbols – may be numbers, letters, commas, etc.
Chip	Small piece of semi-conductor
Clone	Computer of the same form as IBM-PC
Code	May mean instructions written by a programmer; may also mean hexadecimal
Coding	Applying numbers to sections of text
Compact disc	High capacity read-only storage medium
Co-processor	Extra processor added for maths
CPU	Central processor unit
Cursor	Flashing character showing where next character will be placed
Daisy wheel	Printer with font held on a wheel
Directory	List of files on a disk
Directory tree	A branched hierarchy for efficient file access on a hard disk
Disk	Flat, circular, magnetic storage device
Disk drive	Device for spinning a disk and reading from or recording to it
Dos, MS-Dos, PC-Dos	Types of operating systems. Dos literally means disk operating system. Current versions include Dos 6.2
Dot matrix	Image made up of dots
DX2	A form of 486 central processor chip – also DX, DX4 and Pentium overdrive
Electronic notebook	Computer even smaller than a laptop
Fanfold paper	Folded linked paper especially for matrix printers – continuous stationery
Field	A subdivision of a record
File	Anything on disk represented by a directory entry, e.g. text
Fixed disk	Same as hard disk or Winchester disk
Fixed length field	Has a maximum number of characters

Table 4.1 (cont.)

Floppy disk	Flexible small disk, alias diskette
Font	Selection of characters available for printing
Formatting	Preparing the surface of a magnetic disk to accept data
GEDCOM	Facility for genealogical data exchange
Hard copy	Printed products
Hard disk	Fast disk of large capacity and rigid construction
Hexadecimal	Numbers to base 16. Includes as symbols 0 to 9 and A to F. One hexadecimal number takes up four bits
Integrated software	Multiple applications programs packaged together
Keyboard	Pad of keys like a typewriter for addressing computer
Keyed file	A database file stored by sequence of one of its fields
Keyword	Word added to a record to aid specific retrieval
Lan	Local area network
Laptop	Portable, folding, battery driven computer
Machine code	Low level language in binary
Mainframe	A really large computer
Matrix printer	Impact printer using array of needles
Menu	A list of choices to be made via the keyboard
Merge	To fuse two or more files, usually retaining sorted order
MHz	Megahertz, unit describing processor speed. So DX2-90 is a chip that runs at 90MHz
Micro	A small table-top computer
Microprocessor	Electronic device that performs logic functions on receipt of signals
Minicomputer	A computer bigger than a micro but smaller than a mainframe
Modem	Computer to telephone coupler
Mono(chrome)	Single colour (VDU)
Mouse	Device whose movement on a flat surface yields equivalent cursor movement
Network	Several computers linked together
NLQ	Near letter quality
Operating system	Programs that supervise the running of other programs
Package	A set of programs written for general usage
Paper white	Mono VDU that displays black characters on a white background
Parallel port	One in which bits making up characters are transmitted all at the same time on multiple wires
Pascal	A programming language
Path	Sequence of labels specifying and leading to the subdirectory containing a particular file
PC	IBM, IBM clone or equivalent computer
Processor	Any device carrying out operations; often equals central processor
Program	A set of instructions for solving a problem
Prompt	Message inviting you to do something
Proportional spacing	Print in which each character has its own appropriate space

Table 4.1 (cont.)

Public domain software	Software bought for the price of a disk; needs no licence
Qwerty	Key sequence like common English typewriter
RAM	Random access memory
Record	A group of associated pieces of data
Relational	One file can access related information in another file
ROM	Read-only memory
ROM drive	Drive for compact discs
RS-232-C	Standard for passing serial data to printer or modem
Sector	The smallest addressable part of a magnetic disk
Serial port	One through which bits are transported sequentially on a single wire
Shareware	Software sold after use on approval
Sheetfeeder	Printer attachment for feeding in single sheets
Software	Programs
Sort	Put records into sequence
Source	Where information was obtained
Spreadsheet	Software for analysing information in tabular form
String	A sequence of characters or digits
Suffix	Set of characters after a file name indicating the type of the file
SVGA	Type of VDU (Super Video Graphics Adaptor)
Tape-streamer	Machine for backing up to tape
Tear-down paper	Fanfold stationery that can have the edges torn away to leave a rectangular sheet
Text retrieval system	Databases of text with no or few fields, relying on string searches
Track	Channel on a disk
Variable length field	One that adjusts itself to the size of the contents
VDU	Visual display unit
Window	A discrete portion of the VDU screen in which one application runs
WINDOWS	A well-known operating system providing an almost universal working environment
WORD	A variety of word processing package
WORD PERFECT	A variety of word processing package
Word processor	Computer used to handle text
WORDSTAR	A variety of word processing package
Write protection	Disks modified to prevent receipt of data
WYSIWYG	What you see (on the screen) is what you get (on the printer)
8086, 80286, 80836, 80486 or 586 alias Pentium	Species of central processor chips (see also DX2)

Candidates for inclusion in this glossary were very numerous; this selection concentrates on those that will be encountered in the kind of work discussed in this chapter.

Portable computers and electronic notebooks

I have been talking about table-top computers, but folding computers small
enough to take on the bus or train rapidly get more common. Many types
allow you to carry around a large armament of information as well as a
sizeable slab of computing power. You can enter the county record office
with most of your own records on board. All the varieties of program I
mention later in this chapter will work on portables; finance apart, it is not
difficult to visualise oneself typing from an original source directly into an
electronic data file, bypassing paper notebooks. However, as many people
have found, it is difficult to completely replace a field notebook with a laptop computer or an electronic diary, and for a variety of reasons. Some
record repositories will not permit the use of such machines. For those
people that can take up the laptop approach, and are permitted to start
typing directly into an electronic database, there is still the problem of getting printed copies and extra copies for security purposes ('backup').
Someone after all might steal the machine, or it might fail. Where before
there have been ring binders of hand-written notes, there will now have to
be ring binders of printout from the computer files. In one way or another,
paper still has an assured future in historical research. But should you buy
a laptop? Well, I would love to have one, but it is probably an extra for
those with funds to spare.

Moral and practical support in computer use

Learning to use a PC is much easier than it used to be. First, the machines
are more reliable, and second, they are delivered in a much more user-
friendly state. It is likely that if you buy a new machine, you will find that
the operating system and working environment, and maybe several programs, are already installed. The accompanying machine and software
manuals are much improved over those in the 1980s. Even so, the literature
does often fail the user. You will still need somewhere else to turn, such as
a computer-experienced friend. You will also need to get hold of some
books. Generally, published books about computers and software are
superior to supplied manuals. It took me ages to learn that the computer
section of the local bookshop had good things to offer me.

Choosing a printer

Printers are not an extra: you will certainly need one. The number of different types and models of printers seems almost endless. There is probably
something in the rather jaundiced remark that 'the number of new types al-

ways on offer is a sure indication that no one has really produced a design that definitively solves all, or even *most* of the problems'.

Dot matrix printers are the cheapest and noisiest. They are also the most troublesome printers from the paper-feeding viewpoint. Daisy wheel printers are good for mimicking a typewriter, but can be more expensive and slower than matrix printers. Laser printers are the most expensive, the most trouble-free and the sharpest for product. Developing fast are the ink and bubblejet printers. The best of these take A4 paper, are as sharp in print quality as mid-range laser printers, and are as cheap as matrix printers. A bubblejet is much quieter than a matrix printer. Here are some questions to ask yourself when you are trying to choose a printer.

1. What is the maximum price I can pay? (Cheapest matrix printers are about £120 including VAT. Laser printers are about £600–£2,000.)
2. What sort of quality of output am I satisfied with? (If you want to draw with it, you may need a high resolution laser printer.)
3. Will I want to send a fax taken from the copy? (If so matrix printers are unsuitable.)
4. Do I need a wide carriage machine, e.g. for A3 paper? (It is hard to get a big family tree on to A4, though many people offer ingenious programs to help you do this.) Many database formats give fields with line lengths exceeding the VDU width. A wide carriage printer can be very useful for printing records from such files.
5. Do I have any programs such as word processing software that pre-clude any makes of printers?
6. Is the noise that the printer makes an issue for me? (If so, you may need to avoid the matrix printers.)

So how may the computer be useful?

It goes almost without saying that the computer you buy might be used to type up neat copy of all of your archive notes, correspondence, reports and articles. Indeed modern word processing programs are very versatile and can be used to do other text-based tasks such as preparing indices of texts, sorting name or other lists, searching text for particular words or numbers, preparing numbered lists and so on. It is very likely that some sort of word processing package will be supplied with the machine. But at least two other types of programs will be exploitable: spreadsheets and databases.

Although as I have expressed it, these all sound like entirely distinct functions, in fact software packages are evolving constantly; all big packages will do a huge variety of things. The capability now overlaps from package to package: spreadsheets can be used as databases. These in turn accept free text (see p. 97). Because of that, it is perhaps more useful here to largely overlook the nature of particular named packages, and to concentrate on some functions you may need to perform in your research.

Structuring and storing information

Most talk and text contains many extractable data, and much information. However, though talk may have a sensible sequence, it is not highly ordered information. In fact, highly ordered data and information are often to a degree very repetitive in form. They are not intended for protracted reading or listening. At any one time, you are intended to hear or read only selected parts. Yet their constant sequence is that which makes the data there into information, and it is what facilitates the finding of the fragments of what you want from among the whole that you scan.

DATABASES

A body of data relating to a particular subject, that has been ordered and put into a standardised form to allow searching, is called a database. The name is significant: it contains accessible data and information, rather than immediately available knowledge. It could be concerned with almost any topic, for instance, with town buildings. Information concerning each building would be stored separately, for example on a record card, and each would then constitute one 'record'. Each record in the database would be divided up into data fragments called fields and the type of datum in each of them be standard for that particular database. For example, in the case of buildings, there might perhaps be eight fields per record:

1. numerical identifier
2. street name
3. location or number
4. date of construction
5. materials used
6. current occupier
7. current owner
8. notes.

Field 8 should contain references to all other aspects of interest not covered in fields 1 to 7, or perhaps could contain a list of deliberately added 'keywords' to aid in later record retrieval. Such keywords about buildings might be: Georgian, empty, restored, shop, ashlar, listed, church, warehouse, etc.

While you might make such a database on index cards, it is hard to escape from the thought that a stack of a few hundred cards would be very tedious to sift through, especially if it was to be done often, or if two criteria had to be matched. A computer employing electronic records would be much more effective at the sifting task. The extra ease of sifting would certainly facilitate the realisation of knowledge from the stored information.

Figure 4.1 illustrates another example of a simple database. This time the subject is people – the members of a chapel as listed in one of a series of membership books, this one of 1827. The structure is straightforward. Note the name is all in one field, surname first. The book date and membership number are in another field. There are notes at the bottom of the record concerning transfer to another chapel and exclusion from membership. The structure has been kept deliberately simple to facilitate data input. There are spare fields at the bottom of the record, in case new fields have to be added. Using a database of this sort, I can search for individual examples of records showing certain features, maybe search one only or all of the fields, or segregate records of certain types, a process sometimes called partitioning.

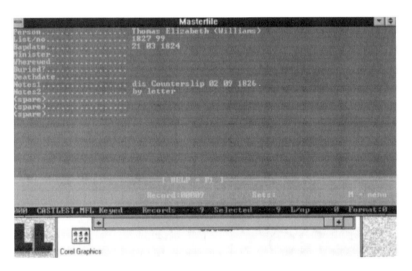

Figure 4.1   A computer screen showing one record from a simple, flat database devoted to entries in a set of chapel membership lists. The lists are defined by year and entries on it by number, in this case 1827 99. The record selected shows that names are entered surname first (maiden name in brackets). There is a date field for adult baptismal date, a Yes/No field referring to burial in the chapel yard, a keyword field to aid searching. Note that this member received a letter of dismission when she moved on to a Bristol chapel.

A data filing system in operation

The different electronic files inside computers are there for various purposes. They may contain text we have decided to store, numerical data of some sort or possibly programs of code used to effect various operations within the machine. All the files have names. The names often have suffixes ('file extensions') which describe the file type. Thus operational program files are often found bearing the suffix .COM (for command) or .EXE (for execute) or possible .BAT for batch operation. Data files may carry the suffix .DAT and text files .TXT, while extra copies of them may be called .BAK (for backup, i.e. a spare copy). The files we have been talking about creating are what are sometimes called document files and may carry the suffix .DOC. They are sometimes referred to simply as 'DOC files'; they describe the contents of paper files. In non-dedicated, general purpose database programs, the files also have special extensions, e.g. .DBF indicating that the contents are structured data.

The first of the two tasks I identified when I was discussing cataloguing, i.e. filing my own paper records can be computerised as follows.

Consider my categories of ring binder file called LITR, INT, PRTR, LOC, CORR, INFOR, THOR, TEXT and so on. These paper files can now be listed in a computer taking the names: LITR.DOC, INT.DOC, PRTR.DOC, LOC.DOC, CORR.DOC, INFOR.DOC, THOR.DOC, TEXT.DOC, etc. Each of these becomes one record in a database that catalogues all the paper files, and which I chose to call DOCLIST – the file that documents the documents. Each record in this database has only two fields, one of which is the identifier, e.g. INT.DOC, and the other a three-line description of the contents of the relevant paper file, i.e. INT. This description includes keywords. In this particular case there are several names of people, topics and places, all things discussed at interview. Also present in this field are the ring binder numbers, Red File 1 and Red File 2.

The forty-two box files I mentioned before are also, naturally, listed as an entry: BOX.DOC. Each record in DOCLIST represents a category of paper record and there must necessarily be another database for each of these. Thus the database INT.DOC contains 119 records each representing one interview script described in two fields. Thus:

Field 1   INT009
Field 2   Jones, Bessie, 1985, Middlezoy, WW2, Levels, Gullidge,
           Lockyer, Canada, orchard, cider, shoe factory, 1910,
           Bridgewater, Red File 1

Field 2 thus contains a description (it was conducted at Middlezoy, Sedgemoor, in 1985), keywords and the name of the ring binder in which the paper file INT007 is to be found.

The database called BOXES contains (of course) forty-two records of this general form with Field 2 of each describing by keywords many of the contents of a particular box file. The map collection is in a database called MAP.DOC, containing 320 records.

Dedicated database software

The databases which I have created to catalogue my own collection of historical material and with which I have illustrated this account so far were made using software that I purchased from the Church of Jesus Christ and Latterday Saints. It is called *Research Data Filer* (RDF) and it is remarkably inexpensive for such a well-written package. It allows for the creation of two types of database, one composed of vital event data about individuals (.DAT files) and one that records documents (.DOC files). Both create records in which the field structure is already determined, that for .DOC files being made up of two fields only. Field one is the document number 'docnum' (e.g. INT007) and field two has room for three lines of text describing the document, including as I have mentioned before title and keywords, plus the paper file in which the material is to be found. The advantage for me in using this ready structured ('dedicated') software is something more than the avoidance of the labour of designing my own field structure. It guides me past a particular pitfall, that of making the record structure more complex than I need. It is very tempting when using non-dedicated software to create records containing large numbers of fields. This subsequently slows down data entry; while it appears to make later searching more specific, in fact it makes difficulties, since there is more chance of having empty fields. The RDF software not only is outstandingly documented and conveniently structured, but also produces beautifully organised printout, with numbered pages, eleven records per A4 page, and with document numbers (docnums) in bold type.

What other database software could I use?

The RDF and *Personal Ancestral File* (PAF) packages sold by the Church of Jesus Christ and Latterday Saints have all the strengths just mentioned. They also have a drawback. Since the user does none of the programming, the user consequently cannot easily tailor the databases to fit the peculiarities of the data. The software is not designed for flexibility, rather for ease of use in a particular purpose – genealogy.

The software market offers literally dozens of different 'all purpose' software packages for database work on PCs. Occasionally in magazines you will come across critical reviews of some of them. The packages vary greatly in their complexity, versatility, ease of use and price. They are all adaptable to innumerable uses. Bearing in mind that the dedicated software that I have been describing cost £30, the more costly general purpose packages seem expensive at £250–400. However, there are among them some excellently flexible ones which find important work in running offices.

The lower end of the price range of general purpose database software includes *Cardbox Plus,* a well-known package that presents information with a record card-like layout, and *Masterfile PC,* quite easy to use and reasonably priced at about £60–70 (see Figure 4.1). *Rapidfile* is another package that I have seen working well with historical data. All of these would have done my paper cataloguing job very comfortably and would also be ideal for making the sort of database mentioned earlier, involving 'eight field' records of buildings. Furthermore, there are also some cheap shareware database packages, such as *PC File Plus* and *PC File DB* which also provide structured record storage.

Data sets have a habit of growing. Even those which one thought would run only to a few hundred records can suddenly threaten to acquire thousands. If data sets are going to be very large, it is necessary to think seriously about the software that is to be employed. I offer some thoughts about such a situation on pp. 91–4. But first it is necessary to fill in the picture more, by asking how the stored data set you are making is to be searched.

Searching the files

Most database packages share certain search procedures. First, you call the file that you wish to open, then when you have opened it, you type out a small search statement of some kind. In the case of RDF, the command to open a file is GET followed by the name of the file, e.g. GET BOX.DOC. Having opened BOX.DOC it can be searched by either of two commands, FOCUS which will identify all the entries carrying a certain word or keyword (and therefore define a subset of the file) or LOCATE which will prepare and permit you to leaf through, a list of all the records containing some selected word, phrase or number in one or both fields. There is also a SORT facility which places any selected group of records in order, alphabetical or numerical, based on any chosen field. It is further possible to ask for a second level of FOCUS on some aspect of a group of records already isolated by use of the FOCUS command. The parallel operations in non-dedicated software such as *Masterfile PC* could naturally be rather more flexible than in RDF, though in principle the same. The search command generally takes the form:

Field name   comparison symbol   argument

The comparison symbol can be =, <, >, <>, or any of several others, while 'the argument' is the general computing term for the word, phrase, number or 'string' being used as the item searched for. So one is specifying the field to be searched (in the case of DOC files usually field 2), the argument and the way one wants the field contents referred to in the argument. Thus you may ask the computer to find records that match the argument either numerically or in words (=), or to find numeric records which have values less than (<), greater than (>) or not equal to (<>) the argument. Incidentally, the word 'string' in this context means any specified successive series of characters. In *Masterfile PC* and similar non-dedicated packages, there are many more search command possibilities, including the isolation of records with certain attached dates or ranges of dates, the creation of major subsets of records, and others. The dedicated RDF package beneath its exterior uses search commands of the same general sort as a non-dedicated program. It is, however, so user friendly that one is largely oblivious to comparison symbols.

Larger numbers of records

The databases which I or you might generate for cataloguing purposes are rarely likely to be especially large. My 320 maps make quite a body of records, but my other catalogue database files seldom exceed 100 records. However, if I was to turn to some of my information ring binders, those to be found in the INFOR.DOC catalogue, I would find inside some very large bodies of records on paper. Electoral rolls, census extracts, monumental inscriptions, baptismal lists and membership lists are all examples of large bodies of records. Some of these run to several thousand records, and all of them could reasonably be regarded as having not fewer than six fields per record. The listings of vital events such as baptisms and marriages could be entered into an electronic database as DAT files using the RDF software package. Electoral roll data and dated membership list can also be squeezed into this format. Monumental inscriptions and census extracts both of which may well contain data about several related individuals can be stored using RDF, particularly by making use of that package's ability to store appended notes about individual people.

Although RDF would do the job, you may well feel that data like those on electoral rolls, come more easily to a flexible non-dedicated database. *Masterfile PC* or *Rapidfile* will achieve this on a budget, but you might also find good use for a package of the larger kind such as *Microsoft Access, Borland Paradox* or *Ashton-Tate dBASEIV.* These larger packages can be

Table 4.2 Example of a database made from an electoral roll

Field 1	Identification number of person
Field 2	Surname
Field 3	Given names
Field 4	Street
Field 5	House number
Field 6	House name
Field 7	Ward or district
Field 8	Voting registration number

An example of a simple flat database made up of data extracted from an electoral roll. The table can be usefully compared with Figures 5.10 and 5.11.

used to store, categorise, sort and retrieve all the vital records for a parish for a long period, baptisms, marriages and burials, or the products of a nationwide one name study. Software packages of this sort primarily sold for office and business use will, on a suitable computer, easily handle databases of tens of thousands of records, provided the CPU of the computer is fast enough.

Table 4.2 shows one way in which electoral roll entries may be broken into fields for storage as an electronic database using a package such as *Paradox* or *dBaseIV*.

Here each person is given a numerical identifier. Why is this so important? The short answer is, because there may be several people of the same name. There may also be several spelling versions of the name of the same person, all of which have to be somehow collected together. In the case of buildings and of many types of objects, there is a different problem – the individuals have no unique names. Creating numerical identifiers for individual records helps to deal with the often awkward matter of keeping separate those individuals that are distinct, and also connecting several supposed records of the same object or person; what is usually referred to as detecting 'record linkage'. In practice, once numbers are applied, they provide a rapid, unambiguous way of identifying one record out of thousands.

When the primary sources of data on people or land use are ancient documents, they will probably contain names in obsolete spelling forms. In order to control this, the field structure in the database being created has to have one field for the name as spelt in the primary source and another for the modern version. This allows the user to use the software to partition the data on the basis of the modern names, carrying along in the process, the old variant spellings.

Types of fields

The fields making up each record in a database are of three common kinds or 'attributes': some contain text, some numbers and some dates. (Actually, there are others, but they can be ignored here.) The computer requires that each field be given one of the three attributes. In the event of one asking the computer to 'sort' the records (i.e. rank order them), one has next to specify by which field this is to be done. The sorting can proceed then by number (e.g. numerical identifier), by date or by alphabetical order of text as desired. Note that it is sometimes convenient to store dates as numerical fields, especially when only the year or year and month are known.

It is also possible to have fields in which the entry contains only + or −, or perhaps Y or N or 'true' or 'false'. Thus one could use in, say, data from a rural parish Y or N to define is or is not a husbandman, or in data from Elizabethan Norwich is or is not a wool spinner. In this form, records can be entered very rapidly.

If there are more than two possibilities (and hence Y or N will not do), two or three letter codes in capital letters can be used. Then searching can be done using case specific commands. Thus: employment=SPI, or =HUS, or =OTH (for other).

The coding of data in this way (adding categorising markers to the original material) is essential, if the most is to be got out of a large data set. Naturally you can lay useful markers only if you have some idea of the questions you will want to ask of the database when it is compiled.

Dates: you may be troubled

A historian's dates are not the same as a business person's dates. In commerce, few sales records go back to 1770, while shopkeepers rarely wish to record a purchase as taking place 'about 1932'. Most general database software is compiled for business use. You may have to persuade it to accept dates before 1900, or to compute ages from lists spanning two centuries. Generally, these packages have several date forms. You will need what are called 'eight figure' dates.

MAINTAINING SEVERAL DATABASES IN PARALLEL

Once you have established one database, you may need to create a second and a third, which store related data. For instance, having put up the electoral roll for 1918 or for 1930, you may want to put up some other year's roll in parallel, which would allow you to obtain information about the frequency with which new people arrived, or the extent to which families changed their address. You could also think of databases of school admissions, church baptisms, war casualty lists and other name compilations for the same place. These various sets of data naturally have certain records with coincident surnames, identical individuals or similar addresses. If these several databases are created using the same software (*Masterfile PC, Paradox, dBASEIV,* etc.) it is possible to build in connections between them. During their construction the computer is informed that these databases are 'relational' to each other via certain fields. Having been instructed that two databases are relational, during searches of one base, the computer will point out places where the search word or string of characters ('string') appears also in the other base. Thus a surname sought in the electoral roll listing may also be noted as occurring in the school admission book. It is possible of course to use a non-relational (so-called flat or flatbed) database to store records from multiple sources. If this is to be done, they must in some software, all be fitted into the same field structure, something which is not always easy. One great advantage of a relational database system is that the individual bases need not have the same overall field structure. They must though have at least one coincident field. Certain newer flatbed databases (see p. 97) will tolerate records in a variety of field structures.

Contemplating something even bigger

A colleague of mine has recently been supervising the construction of the database of apprenticeship records for the Cutler's Company of Sheffield; this database currently has 30,000 records. While this is a lot more than most family historians might get together, it is still by some standards modest. Many document, map, plan or photograph collections run to hundreds of thousands. On the subject of personal records, if you add up all the possible traces there may be for the present and past people of a modest sized town, say one of 5,000 current residents, the total of records you might find would easily pass into hundreds of thousands. If you contemplate a database on that scale, take professional advice. (No, not a psychiatrist, an information scientist!)

DATABASES OF A RATHER DIFFERENT KIND

The databases discussed so far are all of a particular 'traditional' field structure, but databases do vary greatly in form, partly because the material in them varies so much in its source. There are two extremes. The first is a database in which all the data are taken from a single type of primary source, and hence the records are likely to have a modest number of fields and a rather uniform degree of field filling. The second is where the records have very many fields, and the data entered in them come by collating numerous disparate sources. The completeness of filling of individual records may then vary widely.

The latter type of database, though structured, is much harder to design successfully than the former. Furthermore, it may be necessary in the latter type to cite the sources for the data entered. This poses extra problems: it may be necessary to resort to additional 'infosource' fields or text footnotes. The presence of many unfilled fields may also prejudice attempts to partition or calculate from the stored data.

Many people have learned by hard experience that despite much investment of effort, complicated flatbed designs can be very limiting, when it comes to data analysis. I once attended an expensive database course, but even on that, although they said a lot about software, nobody told me about sourcing my data! Yet it is of the utmost importance. No one else can depend on your accumulated data unless you cite your sources. On that course too, no one explained the limitations of databases which have variably filled records.

Undoubtedly, the use of relational data sets gets around many of the problems inherent in multisource flat databases. There will be no need to source many of the data, since they are in already labelled data sets. Even so, in cases where numerous diverse sources of information have been employed, sourcing can still be a problem, but relational structures are to be preferred to ones employing lots and lots of fields with contents of diverse origin.

OTHER MODES OF DATABASE

Text databases

As well as the structured type of database, there are several other types that might be of interest to you for storing data of a historical kind, particularly qualitative data. The first of these is what is sometimes called a 'text database manager'.

Imagine you have carried out a substantial series of interviews with the residents of a town. You have recorded them on tape and perhaps prepared a typescript from each of the tapes. To make best use of all this material it must be stored in some way that makes it searchable, even though the data it contains are neither quantitative nor structured like a telephone directory or an electoral roll. Each text is essentially a single record composed of a single field, albeit often a large one. Indeed the texts may be very large or very small and thus the records may vary a great deal in length.

One way of dealing with this matter is to give each text a numerical identifier, in a second field add a set of keywords that describe its salient content, in a third the name of the speaker, in the fourth a date, and so on. In other words do a cataloguing operation. The ability to search the set of texts, however, would then be limited to a search among them. Our only way of searching *within* all of them would be via the set of keywords. Even if we have chosen them skilfully, the search will be on a sketchy basis to say the least. But what if we type the whole of each text into the computer? Can we not then search the whole of each of all of the texts? We certainly can. We could for instance employ the 'word find' subroutines of a word processing package. These are very effective these days. Even more powerful is a program called *Wordmatch,* which will quickly give a listing of all the words in a document.

The second way of dealing with this matter is to type each text into the machine as a record in a single large (variable length) field working under suitable text managing software. The resulting data resource may then be searched using 'strings'. Any string of characters may be used. Public domain software such as *Ask-it* (available at about £5 a copy) will do this job admirably. Some packages will pick out all instances where one specified word or phrase occurs closely adjacent to another specified one. This is called proximity searching.

The third way is to go through each typescript, segment it (i.e. separate it into pieces) and then numerically code each segment for sentences, phrases or reference of any particular type or character. Once that coding material has been entered into the computer system the resulting resource can be searched for all 'concordances'– instances of any chosen numerical code. This has something in common with keywording, but is much more detailed, and related characteristics or references can be given related (though non-identical) numerical codes. This allows very refined sorting of all the instances of chosen types of remarks, styles of speech, topic, dialect words, and so on. Several programs are sold specifically for this type of research. The more expensive packages will extract the environment of each occurrence and dump it into a new text store. This is the preferred approach when dialect, word use and things of that nature are the primary objects of study. A modest job can be achieved on a budget by adding codes to the text and then searching it serially with word processing software.

Note that the numerical coding approach has in it much input from the researcher themselves, who is assessing every line of each and every sample of text. This naturally is a very great deal of work, but might be very fruitful.

Easy to use freetext databases

Since the late 1980s there have been major extensions of the flexibility of common office software packages. In particular, some modern database packages now allow one both to add new fields to the records of an existing database, and to mix records of different field structure in one database. *Blackwell's Idealist* is a flat database package that allows record types to be mixed and which allows large blocks of text of varying lengths to be stored with the minimum of trouble. It is particularly useful for searching for records among a large set that contain particular words or numbers, and in situations where the records will be modified or updated during searching. However, if extensive record sorting and partitioning is contemplated, its use should be put aside in favour of *dBASEIV, Paradox or Microsoft Access,* or some other relational system.

Trees

Some data storage problems are about matters of place, that is, the place of one fragment of information within a mass of fragments. If it is useful to know that Mr and Mrs Robson live at house number 47, it is even more useful to note that it is 47 Bladon Street. It is significant also that it is Bladon Street, Newcastle upon Tyne, and not in some other city. Some data have a natural place in a hierarchy. One photograph is an enlargement of one portion of one frame that comes from a particular reel of film, one of six taken in a set. The six reels were taken by one of three photographers co-operatively recording churches threatened with demolition. This they replicated on six different days each in a separate city, all in 1989. The enlargement can be traced to its parent negative, which in turn nests into a parent film, which nests into a set of six films, which contribute to the products of one day, which nests with the products of five other days to make the complete available archive.

Many individual data originate as nested sets of this general sort. You might have many things in your files whose origin should be recorded according to a hierarchical tree. Sometimes it is particularly valuable to be able to trace an individual datum to its ultimate origins.

Several pieces of software are on the market for storing data in trees. *Treebase* is one, an inexpensive public domain package that I have used for geographical data, keeping a record of what names appear on what edition of what type of map. *Treebase* will store trees of up to twenty-two branch levels, with up to twenty-two twigs on each. Few problems need more than five or six levels. In fact, it is quite hard to generate a problem with more levels than that. My DOX.DOC system (described on pp. 88-9) has a tree structure like this example: DOX.DOC / PRTR.DOC / GREEN FILE 2 / CAPEL SEION MIs / JENKINS FAMILY / JOHN (JUNIOR). Each / represents a level of branching. Using *Treebase*, I can clearly see where each data subset fits.

MORE REMARKS ABOUT STRUCTURED DATABASE DESIGN

Although I have said all this about freetext databases and treebases, the place a beginner is likely to start is with a field-structured database. Both making and using structured databases are important skills.

Of the three main uses to which microcomputers are put – word processing, spreadsheets and databases –it is often said that databases are by far the most difficult to master. In the first two types of use, a set of commands is learned which drive the computer through a task, which it performs very well to standard settings (though you can alter them if you wish). In database work you have to do much more designing, both for making the record structure and for displaying it and printing it.

In addition, you have to decide on codes for marking the records in various ways, with a view to subsequent sorting or calculating. For instance, you may not want merely to record all the resident males in the district, but rather to code each for their locality or for some personal attribute. To be as flexible as possible during data file searching, partitioning and printing, and to be economical during data input, you have to design the record structure and the codes used very thoughtfully. Large books have been written about such database design and operation. There is room here only to offer a few brief do's and don'ts.

When creating a database

Do ask yourself what the database will be used for. Is it for collating incoming data from numerous sources? Or is it for speedy reference to certain already complete data?

Do consider if you need a highly compartmented field structure, or if you need just one or two large fields on which to do string searches.

In any case do make sure you have plenty of spare fields so that your database can be later changed or developed.

Don't forget to give each record a numerical identifier.

Don't be inconsistent with spellings and abbreviations.

Do make use of yes/no fields where possible.

Do make up a series of upper-case key terms to aid searching. (Case specific searching then allows one to use short strings.)

Do try to give yourself as many options as you can for searching and partitioning of records.

Do make sure that you have a field for the modern version of any personal or place name culled from ancient documents.

Don't omit to prepare a 'thesaurus' for the database, that reminds you and other users and compilers of the terms being employed for standard abbreviations, key terms, and so on.

Do try to be clear before you enter data, what form the printout will be taking. Will you be able to print single records and part records?

DETACHING THE DISCUSSION FROM COMPUTERS

It is very easy, once one gets on to the matter of computers and software, to forget that they are only an aid. The researcher has to make all the choices, not only of subject and source, but also of method of data processing and evaluation. It is your choice too, of how to process information and hence the sort of knowledge you gain. These circumstances are not altered by the possession of a computer. The facility only offers you more choices; it does not make them for you. Many directions, steps and stages grow inevitably out of the material you study, with or without assistance.

RECORDS OF PEOPLE

Much of what I address in this book is to do with identifying people and then gaining information about them. Often in this work, collating all the different references to the same person is central.

During the lifespan of an individual person (or a building for that matter), they may be referred to numerous times in written records, and appear on further occasions in oral testimony. It is generally true to say that on the occasion of the creation of each of these original records, the recorder had no ambiguity whatsoever in their mind, concerning the identity of the person they were recording. However, those of us who come many years after, having no personal experience of the people mentioned, often find ourselves questioning whether any two records we discover mentioning them, do refer to the same individual. Even if we find our parish has nine references to a Henry Baker, smith, can we be sure that there were not two or three smiths called Henry Baker alive during that period? Was the Jeffard Earbury, pointmaker, I read of really a different man from Gifford Yerbury, whitawer, of the same town? Our computer cannot make any of these sorts of decisions for us. We need to decide which records are linked and which are not.

Deciding if linkage is real

Provided we make an adequate field structure, we shall be able to record accurately and in full each record. Our computer will remind us of every instance where the name occurs, in all our lists, so that we can evaluate them all as a set, rather than making a decision based upon a single occurrence. Figure 4.2 illustrates the use of two windows carrying name lists to facilitate linkage decisions.

Next, we can help ourselves considerably by the way that we record early names in our own records. One field of each record may usefully contain the literal transcription of the name, while another field records what appears to be its contemporary form. For instance, *Skargyll* would be recorded as well as the better known *Scargill,* and we would insert alongside the older *Amere,* its common nineteenth- and twentieth-century analogue, *Emery* (see also Chapter 7). I recommend this even though the latest versions of most office quality word processor and database packages now have *Soundex* or soundex-like facilities, which are able to find Scargill for Skargyll or Jones for Johnes.

You should not suppose, however, that linking one record of a person to another record of the same person is difficult only in ancient records. In Chapter 5 I describe research on the records of men and women serving in the First World War. Due to the low quality of some of those records, and because of the commonness locally at that time, of certain family and given names, the problems of linkage there are quite acute.

A variant of the linkage problem occurs in census work where individuals and their families may be required to be identified on consecutive decennial censuses. Not only may they prove to be differently spelt, but also family composition mutates. In addition, the way that districts and addresses are specified depends upon the date and the quality of the enumerator. A mapping aspect of research may be introduced.

Finally, in trying to handle all linkage issues, making objective guidelines with respect to the acceptance of spelling variants, and especially with regard to the closeness of fit of dates and the defining family units, is best practice. Avoid decision-making 'on the hoof'. Guidelines will help to avoid creating extra inconsistencies and introducing them into databases. Rigorous consistency of all our own decisions should be our aim.

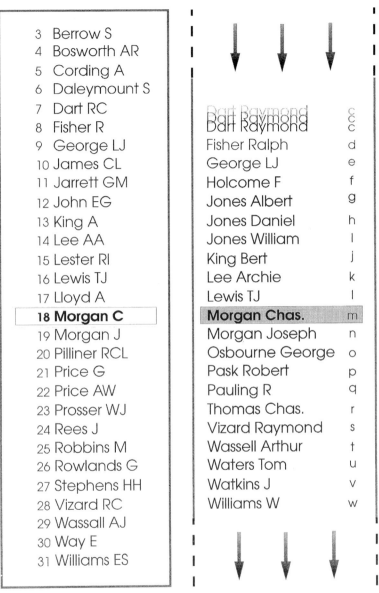

3 Berrow S		
4 Bosworth AR		
5 Cording A		
6 Daleymount S		
7 Dart RC	Dart Raymond	c c
8 Fisher R	Fisher Ralph	d
9 George LJ	George LJ	e
10 James CL	Holcome F	f
11 Jarrett GM	Jones Albert	g
12 John EG	Jones Daniel	h
13 King A	Jones William	i
14 Lee AA	King Bert	j
15 Lester RI	Lee Archie	k
16 Lewis TJ	Lewis TJ	l
17 Lloyd A		
18 Morgan C	**Morgan Chas.**	m
19 Morgan J	Morgan Joseph	n
20 Pilliner RCL	Osbourne George	o
21 Price G	Pask Robert	p
22 Price AW	Pauling R	q
23 Prosser WJ	Thomas Chas.	r
24 Rees J	Vizard Raymond	s
25 Robbins M	Wassell Arthur	t
26 Rowlands G	Waters Tom	u
27 Stephens HH	Watkins J	v
28 Vizard RC	Williams W	w
29 Wassall AJ		
30 Way E		
31 Williams ES		

Figure 4.2 Diagram illustrating the passing of one nominal list past another, in order to search for cases of linkage. This may be achieved via a split computer screen, via two screen windows or by literal, physical movement. Note that detecting linkage may involve making decisions on the validity of various spellings and of informal names. Arthur Wassell is the same man as AJ Wassall, but is A King the same man as Bert King?

FAMILY TREES AND CHARTS OF DESCENDANTS

Much of the effort expended by family historians is directed towards deciding who is the parent of whom. Much local population study involves tracing family trees. Genealogy is a very particular sort of record linkage. In family reconstruction, it is necessary not only to link all the records of the same person, but also to find the specific bridges between the sets of records associated with various different persons. Sometimes, the pitfalls lie in making false connections rather than in missing true ones. Computer software can be of assistance in cataloguing and listing, thereby making much more evident the coincident names and the coincident dates and places, and reminding us not to overlook various individuals we have found. It is helpful to plot on paper the links and relationships we think we have revealed. The researcher still has to decide which possible links to believe and which not. The computer, obedient machine that it is, will plot and print false conclusions just as neatly as it will true ones. In the handling of family trees and charts of descendants, the value of the genealogy software lies largely in the neatness and convenience of the printed product and in the short time it takes to produce copy. For more on this subject, see *Computer Genealogy* edited by R.A. Pence (1991) and the valuable shorter account *Computers for Family History* by David Hawgood (1994). Personally, for value, I have seen little to improve upon the *Personal Ancestral File* (PAF) package made available by the Church of Jesus Christ and Latterday Saints for about £30. Using a machine with a colour VDU and a mouse, the results are very impressive. The more expensive *Roots III* is also excellent.

THE PROBLEM OF TRACING FORWARDS FROM AN INDIVIDUAL

For a number of very good reasons, most familial reconstruction studies are attempted backwards. First, they often start with a living person (frequently the researcher). Second, the causes of events, including human conception, birth, marriage and death, lie in their past rather than in the future.

If you have already defined a population or family group living at some date in the past, however, you may have good reason to want to trace forward to present-day families. If you try this, an important aspect of personal records quickly makes itself plain: many types of records are constructed specifically to permit retrospective tracing. The General Register Office records have no indices for the *children* of particular people. Rather, they have indices of the parents of new children. Similarly, we are not required to deposit with the new owner our onward going address when we move house, or to supply an address when we leave the city for a job elsewhere. On the other hand, when we are filling in the decennial census return, we are asked where we were born. If our vital records so determinedly look back, how then am I to look for the descendants of my great-great-grandfather's brother Joseph Gray, always supposing that he has some?

The difficulties of forward tracing studies in England and Wales are compounded by the hundred-year rule on census material and by the offering of register office indices rather than of the full register office certificates. The latter not only have to be bought, but also bought blind. The excellently readable *Scottish Roots* by Alwyn James (1981) makes clear the advantages enjoyed by those making their research in Scotland, both with regard to census returns and to civil registration. They also have access to monuments and parish records which frequently cite the women's maiden names.

Suppose that in England you want to trace the descendants of men or couples listed on the 1861 census or in church records of that time, how would you start? The obvious step is to go to the returns of later censuses. There is possibly information you want on the 1871, 1881 or 1891 census book. If the family name is rare, a sound approach is to collect all references to it over a wide area: most if not all are likely to be relatives. The process of using later censuses is hugely facilitated if the county census has been compiled as an electronic database, as whole counties can be searched at speed.

Coming down to even later times, and when surnames are commoner, it may be fruitful to write a form letter to all or some of the people carrying the names in the regional telephone books. Although many will not reply, and indeed may not even be related, those that do will often know their connections back two generations. There may already be a national one-name study underway. This should be checked with the listing at the Federation of Family History Societies.

The success rate in tracing to the last fifty years can be increased by studying an intermediate residents list such as the 1930 electoral roll. This will show which names survived the first fifty years from the 1881 census. Data may also be obtainable through the members of family history societies. It is worth reflecting on the great assistance which would be rendered to work of this sort if access to selected contents of local registries was to become general.

GEOGRAPHICAL RECORD KEEPING

It is possible that some aspect of your research will prove to be about distribution. Questions may be spatial; you defined your locality for study geographically. It is not a large step from that to a geographical study within it: name patterns by street, causes of death by district, and so on. If this is your need, look for professional advice. You can utilise computer packages called Geographical Information Systems (GISs), which will store and plot map-based data.

GOOD HOUSEKEEPING: TAKING CARE OF ALL YOUR HARD WORK

Do you keep second copies of important documents? Although this is not always necessary, it is best to make photocopies or second prints of anything you have spent work on. Important originals should be photocopied or photographed too. Anything new in manuscript should be copied. And what about material in the computer? It is quite hard at first to let oneself trust a computer, especially when one has laboured so long and hard to obtain all the data that it is consuming. Perhaps it will refuse to reveal them later? Or could it just forget them?

Unlike humans, computers do not tire, forget their place in the list, get cross, or change their mind. I sometimes leave mine in my office switched on, with its cursor sitting perhaps half way through the word I was typing when I was called away. It stays there faithfully, marking the place until I get back, maybe several hours later, to take up the use of the keyboard exactly where I left off. On balance, the machine is much more reliable and predictable than I am.

There are two ways of losing data and text from a computer. First, the machine breaks down: there is some major malfunction or 'crash'. The second way is by a human mistake; what one might call 'pilot error'. Crashes happen to all machines, sooner or later. The most serious major malfunction commonly experienced is the sudden demise of the hard disk. Last night it was fine, this morning you have switched on the machine, and it cannot access the hard disk. On a machine with a 100 Mb disk this could be akin to losing a library of fifty to a hundred printed books, only worse, because it is not text you have bought, but material you compiled yourself.

When it comes to mistakes, everybody, however experienced, makes lots of them. Such an error is usually small and may lose nothing, but it could conceivably, at worst, wipe clean or contaminate an entire hard disk or large file that represents years of hard work. My habit of going away and leaving the machine with a file open is a dangerous one. If there is a power failure, I will probably lose the whole of that file. It is only worth the risk with small correspondence files.

A common way of losing files is to copy over them in error, some other file or an earlier version of the same file. If this is done, the automatic back-up facility of a word processor can then unfortunately overwrite the backup file too.

It is essential to make extra copies of all files on floppy disks for storage outside the machine. If you have files containing important information, it is *gross folly* not to make at least two extra copies on disk (backup copies). One copy is to be kept locked in a drawer near the computer, the other safe in another place, preferably a different building. Even if your house burns down, that is no excuse for losing your local and family history data! M.R. Smith (1989) has written a book called *Commonsense Computer Security,* which is a useful guide on how not to lose your data.

It is good practice also to keep *up-to-date* 'hard copy', i.e. printout of all data files. These can act as 'last resort' copies of the data, but will also prove useful as reference documents. My cataloguing databases are printed out and bound together as a booklet, which is handy for browsing.

Special backing-up equipment, kept permanently connected to the computer, would allow you to copy your whole hard disk contents at intervals in a period of minutes. A tape-streaming facility of that sort currently costs about £150, though they are getting cheaper all the time. For price information you should consult a recent magazine. Anyone involved in a major research programme, or in the writing of books, should consider buying such a device. It gets around the inertia problem, that 11.30 p.m. lassitude, 'I can't be bothered to copy it just now. I'll back it all up tomorrow, or on Sunday, or . . .'.

REFERENCES AND FURTHER READING

Harvey, G. (1993) *DOS for Dummies Quick Reference*. San Mateo, USA: IDG Books [The title jars a bit, but one of a supportive series of books].

Hawgood, D. (1994) *Computers for Family History: An Introduction*, 5th edn. London, Acton (self-published) [Very handy little book, especially for family historians].

James, A. (1981) *Scottish Roots*. Loanhead: MacDonald [About the Scottish vital records].

Maudsley, E. and Munck, T. (1993) *Computing for Historians*. Manchester: Manchester University Press [Useful beginners' text on databases and spreadsheets in historical work].

Moseley, M.L. (1991) *Windows 3.1 Instant Reference*. California: Sybex Inc [One of a handy series of books for when the manual fails you].

Oliver, P.R.M. and Kantaris, N. (1994) *DOS – One step at a time*. London: Bernard Babani [Really is a low cost, beginners' book].

Pence, R.A. (1991) (ed.) *Computer Genealogy: A Guide to Research through High Technology*. Salt Lake City: Ancestry Inc. [Gives useful detail of genealogy packages].

Penfold, R.A. (1991) *Understanding PC Software*. London: Bernard Babani [Starter's text with introduction to the various categories of software].

Smith, M.R. (1989) *Commonsense Computer Security: Your Practical Guide to Preventing Accidental and Deliberate Electronic Data Loss*. New York: McGraw-Hill [Speaks for itself].

Yarborough, N.K. (1992) *Friendly Macintosh*. London: Random House [Beginning, with AppleMac].

CHAPTER FIVE

One Society at One Particular Time: Caerleon in the First World War

MAKING A SYNTHESIS

It will be evident from the way I have treated the subject of interviews and oral evidence in Chapter 2 that I have a particular interest in the ways that people of the past came together to make the community of a particular place. Indeed, although many of the questions asked of older people do relate to family, I also mention neighbours and persons of the same street or immediate locality. My interest is in building pictures of who knew whom; whose lives were linked to whose, by genes, by proximity, and by the bonds of employment.

Oral evidence appropriately collected and directed, and additional, relevant, documentary verification, can be used to reconstruct the form of local societies in the period seventy to a hundred years ago. The study can take in an identification of the high profile local gentry, the landlords, the members of the local council and its officers, churchmen and deacons, trades people and shopkeepers. It can also define, to some extent, who worked for whom, and those the local people regarded as authorities, the makers of opinion, advisers and mentors. Direct memory will probably reveal much about local employers; about the membership of churches and chapels, about schools, clubs, sport, politics, in-migration and departure. There will be good opportunities for studies of one further generation of residents as they are reflected in the memories of today's old people. Their recollections will be an entry into the lives hinted at in directories or electoral rolls, or reported upon in newspapers and minute books.

The gathering of data for a social reconstruction naturally gives ample scope for interviewing skill, for record keeping, documentary verification, database construction and data processing, and the writing of reports and illustrated accounts. Every method discussed in Chapters 2, 3 and 4 might play a part. However, there will be a need to define the period to be studied as well as the boundaries of the place in question. In fact, as far as time is concerned, we can distinguish two aspects: a society as it proceeded through some roughly defined period, and that society in relation to certain specific events. The latter gives us both definite dates and bases for inter-personal connection. It is thus the easier to grasp.

ONE TOWN'S WAR

I have chosen as an example a study of Caerleon and district during the period of the First World War, which commenced over eighty years ago, but is still within the memory of many old people, who were children at the time. Even in the mid-1990s there are a few genuine veterans left. During the course of my study (commenced 1982), there were still significant numbers of veterans available for interview.

As a research focus, the war of 1914–19 is significant because it made a deep mark on British society. It is thus not difficult to get old people to remember it and comment on it. In fact, quite the contrary; it is almost impossible to talk to old people without the subject of that war entering the conversation.

THE BRITISH EXPERIENCE OF WAR

Before starting to describe the study itself, it is useful to consider briefly the general matter of war in modern British history. In the last 200 years, in England and Wales, war has been part of the experience of most natives. It has happened rather often: the Peninsula Campaign, the Crimea, the Indian Mutiny, the Zulu Wars, the New Zealand Land Wars, the Nile Campaign, the Matabele uprising, the wars in South Africa. Frequent as it has been until the twentieth century, war was something that certain men and occasionally women went away to take part in: the 'face of battle' was never seen on home soil. This has tended to give the British a very particular view of war: in wartime some people go away and come back, some go away and come back much less fit, some go away, and do not come back at all. Something very unpleasant happens somewhere over the sea. Those who come home have harrowing stories to tell, though they do not always tell them.

But the two world wars were new sorts of experiences in several ways. They were the first wars in which almost any adult male under 50 years old might be pressed to service. They were the first wars in which every family had someone serving, and in which actual civilian effort (as opposed to simply suffering) was very relevant. Even then, air raids apart, war still largely happened somewhere else. British world war experience is still very different from that of the Belgian, Dutch and French peoples, to whom war has generally meant invasion, occupation and confiscation of property. Curiously, the British vision of remote war is reinforced by a transatlantic view. For modern Americans too, war happens 'over there'. And distance lends curiosity at least. When visiting in North America, I have more than once been asked by young Americans what I remembered of the Second World War; in particular, had I seen or heard any bombs fall?

HOW I STARTED STUDYING WARTIME CAERLEON, AND WHY

As far as the First World War is concerned, the first condition for successful oral research is satisfied: oral sources do exist. Furthermore, many, many relevant documents are available. However, although I was aware of these crucial advantages, I did not start my study of wartime Caerleon on the basis of any argument about sources. I got involved in First World War studies through asking, or trying to ask some factual questions about the war experience of my father and of his brother Gilbert. I knew that my father had volunteered at an early age (16 or 17 years old I thought), while I knew from family remarks that Gilbert (Figure 5.1) had been 'gassed on the Somme'. My initial questions were really about family history, and they were asked of elderly residents, rather than of documents. My queries were about a war of which, I came to realise, I was very ill informed.

Despite starting with such a narrow family view, the answers I was getting soon caused me to wonder just what that war had been like for my family's neighbours and friends, and for other people in the town. Just who was involved? How many? What did they all do? What was the scale of the local loss and injury? How did local people view the events? Is it possible to discover and report on a collective war experience?

As the questions dawned upon me, I saw that there were many data to be collected. After I had begun collecting them, I realised that I needed to learn not only about who served in the forces, but also how to make a reconstruction of the social nature of town and district at the time of the war. I saw that more extensive interviewing would be valuable. It should ask of a panel of people who lived through the war, questions about relatives, neighbours, political figures and gentry, and use as prompts, names taken from the local electoral rolls and memorials.

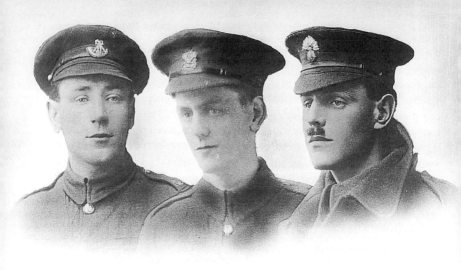

Figure 5.1 Three privates: Ivor Arthur Williams, Trevor Gravenor Williams and William Gilbert Williams. The picture is a composite one made from separate negatives. The two on the left appear to date from 1917, the third from 1916.

LOCAL WAR HISTORIES WRITTEN BY THOSE WHO WERE THERE

Before I committed myself to a large-scale project, I thought it wise to check whether anyone had already written a history of the town's or the county's part in the First World War. After all, some of the local happenings must surely have been remarkable. Did anybody write any of it down?

For some towns and cities, somebody did indeed write much of it down. W.H. Scott (1923) for instance, wrote *Leeds in the Great War 1914–1916*, which he described as a 'book of remembrance'. It contains in fascinating detail much about Leeds volunteers, the call up, local factories, hospitals, local health and a host of other matters. It also contains a list of the 9,640 Leeds persons who were killed or who died in that war. Some of them were local born men who had enlisted in the armies of the Empire, especially Canada and Australia.

The town of Swindon too, has an excellent book, *Swindon's Effort in the Great War,* compiled by W.D. Bavin (1922). This offers (among much else) details of the local concern for the plight of Belgian refugee children, some of whom were evacuated to Swindon, or to other English towns and cities. Birmingham, Bristol, Leicester, Middlesbrough, Portsmouth and Preston are all among the places which have good between-the-wars publications about town activity 1914–19.

I noted that books of this kind, written close to the time, include much information that would now be impossible to obtain. Inevitably too, they have a different perspective from anything a writer might compile today. The lapse of time prompts questions they did not ask.

I was not surprised to find that the only regional publication at all relevant to Caerleon in the First World War was a Book of Remembrance for the nearby town of Newport; it comprised a list of the fallen, more than 1,500 local men and women, with their service numbers, ranks and units or ships. Among the names there I recognised a few Caerleon men. The *Newport Book* was in spirit like many memorials and rolls nationwide. It concentrated on details of local people who fell in the war, paying little attention to the service of the majority.

Furthermore, a town's life during wartime is as much about the responses and actions of those who live, work and worry at home, as it is about those away on service. We cannot make a town history from a list of fallen. To compile an account, we might want to know not only who fell, but also who else served in the forces, who did war work in the mercantile marine or in the dockyards, and who was an active figure on the 'home front'. We might ask how life at home was changed by the war; how those at home behaved in relation to their friends and relatives away on service; what was felt at home at the worst of times, or at moments of great change.

RECENT RESEARCH AND WRITING

Apart from 1920s writing, there is a quantity of second- and third-generation literature about the First World War. Among much still written about that time are some regional books. They include Gerald Gliddon's (1988) book on East Anglia, *Norfolk and Suffolk in the Great War,* and Alan Peacock's (1993) *York in the Great War 1914–1918.* Before you start a study on a town or county, it is wise to check if anyone has recently published anything about the area. Many books about the First World War are reviewed in *Stand To,* the magazine of the Western Front Association. Enquiries in local bookshops will undoubtedly turn up the increasing number of small books about life at home during the *Second* World War (and especially reminiscences concerning the Blitz). It is not unusual for local verbal enquiries about the First World War to be answered with information about the Second World War.

GETTING SERVICE DETAILS OF SOLDIERS, AIRMEN AND SAILORS

While a town's experience of war does add up to much more than just the experiences of the young men and women who went on active service, the latter are at the heart of it, involved in primary events. Many local initiatives were reactions closely connected to their being away. To know of life at home it is then appropriate to ask how one might establish the numbers of those who served, in what units they served, when and where, and with what rank. To obtain numbers, one has to establish identities. So what sources are available for ascertaining the service details of local men? And can we construct an exhaustive listing of local serving men and women? The answer to the last question is a qualified '*Yes*', but the possibilities for research on surviving persons are much different from those for studying war dead. A complete listing of serving persons means obtaining and combining two quite separate nominal lists.

ORAL EVIDENCE: BEGINNER'S LUCK

My specific enquiries about my father and his brother might have produced very little, but I was in luck. Enquiries among local people and through the Western Front Association led me rather quickly to personal contact with a man in a nearby town, who was interested in the local Territorial Force regiment, the 1st Monmouths. On hearing of my interest, his first question to me via the telephone was straightforward: 'Given a choice, what would you most like to find in the way of sources?' Having a vague notion that my father had been in the Monmouths, I replied that what I would like most was to meet a veteran who could confirm this. His reply was that he knew of only one veteran of 1914–18 of the 1st Monmouths who was still alive, but he would telephone and ask him if he had any recollection of my father. When he called back the next day, he left me astonished.

'He remembers your father at Oswestry and also in France. You had better hurry up though! He is more than 91.' As soon as possible, I drove from Sheffield to Newport. Tom's memories of my father were from 1915 and 1916. Our new friendship lasted until he died aged nearly 95. As well as his army recollection, Tom had boyhood memories of my father's brother Trevor, who was his particular school friend, and of things and people far too numerous to relate. My father, Jack (actually Ivor Arthur) Williams, he said, had been in the 2nd/1st Monmouths, and afterwards in the 1st/1st.

MORE LUCK: THE REWARDS OF PERSISTENCE

My second piece of luck concerned a document that I did not know existed. In the course of reminiscing, a family friend mentioned to me that some months before, he had seen a hand-lettered 'Town Roll of Honour' for the First World War behind a piano in the Caerleon church school room, though he had been disappointed to see that his late father, a former RAF veteran, was not on it. We made a trip to the vicar for a key to the school room. The Roll was not there, however, only an empty picture frame. Visits to three other addresses followed before most of the Roll was cautiously lifted from the top of a wardrobe and placed into my hands. Some of it was handed over as powdery fragments in an envelope. It took some patient work to piece the Roll together. Tom lived just long enough to help me solve the crossword of the part-defaced names. I have since spent further time dating the Roll and studying the significance of name groupings upon it. Finally, the Caerleon Roll, which was compiled in April 1915, is made whole again, and hangs in Caerleon Community Centre, in a room just off the old Drill Hall (Figure 5.2).

One cannot state too strongly the value of oral enquiry in this field. Many details, including knowledge of the existence of documents, are lodged only in the minds of older people. Some details are exclusively known to veterans. Even now, First World War veterans can occasionally be found. But if you cannot find one, ask for descendants of veterans. Work of this kind needs as much help as it can get from the families of the men who served. This can be obtained only by talking to them and having their confidence. Between them, they have countless unrecorded items of information. Without my questions the Roll of Honour might have stayed on top of the wardrobe. There are no substitutes for tea and talk.

GETTING THE RESEARCH ON TO A TIDY FOOTING

It would be quite possible to take much more space at this point describing further where I have been lucky and where unlucky, and all the byways I took in the early stages of a long study. From here on, however, my account sets out the straight path by which this sort of study can most efficiently and effectively be done. The key steps in it are as follows: defining the place of study, building a list of those who served, and discovering a societal structure at home.

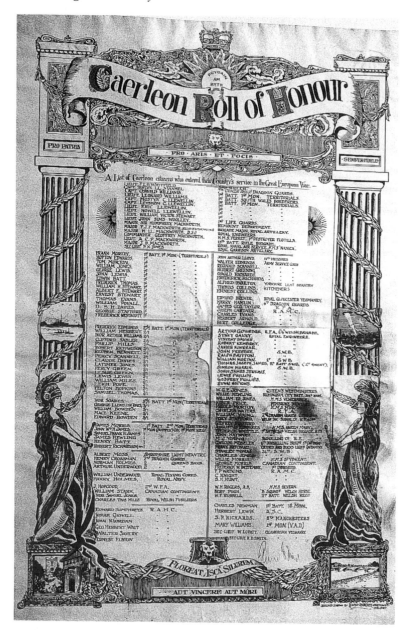

Figure 5.2 Caerleon Town Roll of Honour. It is largely a list of serving men compiled early in 1915, but that list was briefly added to much later in the war. Now restored by the author, the Roll hangs in Caerleon Community Centre.

Defining the place of study

Although we think we know what we mean when we name our home town or our birth place, our understanding may not entail any precise geographical definitions. Our town may not entirely map either with the way some other people define the place of the same name. However, when it comes to working definitions, personal pictures are of little use. The place of study has to be defined in some unambiguous and rational way. Furthermore, the definition has to be one that fits the dates being studied. Modern Cardiff and modern Sheffield do not have the same boundaries as the Victorian towns with the same names. If the place is not tightly defined, it will not be possible to decide who belongs to it, and hence which people belong in the study. Clear definitions are important especially because of the amount of family and business movement taking place in the period 1880 to 1920.

After several trials of different sorts of definitions, for reasons which will become clear later, I concluded that for studies of the First World War, the most watertight means of defining places in England, Wales and Scotland would be the constituency compositions and boundaries used for the 1919 general election. It is especially fortunate that a Boundary Commission under the chairmanship of Sir James Lowther MP sat during 1917 and produced a three-volume report published by HMSO. This contains 109 schedules with maps defining the constituencies in each county and the districts making them up. In towns, the maps are often 3 inches to the mile; in the countryside four miles or occasionally eight miles to the inch. In the countryside the constituencies used blocks of civil parishes, rural districts and urban districts. Fortunately, only rarely were such local units split. On the electoral roll produced for the 1919 election, the voters are defined in their districts, with house addresses attached. One can therefore define a place outside the big town, by means of these voting district boundaries.

Inside the larger towns and cities, definition of areas has to be via ward boundaries. The contents of wards in terms of streets will be obvious on the voters' list. However, tracing boundaries on the ground requires the use of ward maps. Many local libraries and record offices do have Ordnance Survey or other maps overpainted in colour to show ward boundaries at various dates. Note that caution is called for in tracing both ward boundaries and the limits of towns and cities. Due to the requirements of the *Representation of the People Acts,* boundaries have been adjusted very frequently. One may not assume that the town or ward boundaries in 1903 or 1935 necessarily applied in 1919 or 1914.

Be circumspect too, when you believe that you have discovered the town boundaries. The boundary of a town as a county borough does not have to be congruent with the boundary for the same town in its role as a parliamentary borough. Note also that the units employed as registration subdistricts are not entirely equivalent to administrative units. Consultation of the summary volumes of the 1911 decennial census reveals the care that has to be taken to ensure that the correct type of boundary is being used in the study. In those volumes, population data are given for each of registration subdistricts, administrative units and ecclesiastical units.

Building a list of those who served

It is not possible to gain a realistic picture of local life between 1914 and 1919 unless the magnitude of the service commitment of local people is made clear. One often comes across references to, and even whole books, about the names on a war memorial. In a way, the long effort of eighty years' remembrance has concentrated attention on the many war deaths, making transparent the efforts of the many who fought, carried stretchers, nursed or laboured and then returned. The fallen were always (fortunately) a minority.

In many ways, the involvement of people on the 'home front' was coupled to the group of people away. So the numbers and identities of people away have to be known, in order to gain insight into the preoccupation and involvement on the home front. A consolidated list of serving persons should ideally be compiled. This will contain soldiers, Royal Flying Corps (RFC) and RAF men, Royal Navy, Royal Naval Reserve (RNR) and Royal Navy Volunteer Reserve (RNVR) men, Merchant Seamen, civilian war workers, and women in the Field Ambulance Nursing Yeomanry, Voluntary Aid Detachment (VAD), Queen Alexandra Nursing Corps and the Women's Army Auxiliary Corps (WAAC). As far as is reasonable, the list should include each person's unit, ship or workplace, because these determined what war events the person was involved in. It should be noted, though, that there is no necessity for minute detailing of the war service of all involved individuals. The final local list will include both fallen and survivors, and among servicemen will distinguish regulars, volunteers, territorials and call-up men.

Amassing such a list for Caerleon and district has proved manageable only by treating the fallen and the survivors separately for investigative purposes, by compiling two separate lists and then combining them. This approach was necessary because the fallen not only pose different research questions from the survivors, but also involved different information sources.

Discovering a societal structure at home

A consolidated list naturally tells much about the character of the service of local people: in which theatres of war men served and died, who volunteered, who was a territorial soldier, the number and identity of officers and much other detail. Some of this directly connects to matters of social status and wealth. It leads naturally on to consideration of the local territorial battalions, the popularity of regular soldiering as a livelihood, and the recruitment to regular battalions of the local regiment of the line.

It was possible to connect serving sons with their fathers' lives locally, and to identify men who knew each other through school days, church, chapel, a sports club or a workplace. The list of serving men and women was a foundation on which to build and to which can be added the social fabric of the place in those times. Much relevant information for these purposes I found resided in newspapers, council minute books, school records and parish magazines. The possibilities were almost endless. In this chapter much space is given to the means of accumulating the list and the associated insights into local military matters. The building of a picture of the home front is restricted to a few chosen aspects: the part played by gentry and professional people, and the local scale of war deaths and how that matter was handled.

STRATEGY INVOLVED IN COMPILING A CONSOLIDATED LIST OF LOCAL SERVING PERSONS

Figure 5.3 is a flow diagram summarising the way that information has been amassed. Starting with the 'Final List' on the left of the chart, you can trace two main streams of incoming information: that to do with survivors, and that to do with fatal casualties. In my work, I have found it useful to keep these two streams separate. While they both generated plenty of paper-based records, I directed my effort towards creating two separate electronic databases. Originally these were compiled in *Masterfile PC* software (see Chapter 4). Later I transferred these to *dBASEIV,* a much more powerful package. If I was commencing the work now, I might well use the more flexible *Access* or *Paradox* software. During the course of the work, it has been very convenient to carry lists of names to various record repositories and on location in cemeteries. To do this I created text files using a word processor package, surname first (Figure 5.4). This enabled me to annotate names in the field, and then to re-sort them in the computer, as required.

A major recurring problem was record linkage. The two major lists,

FLOW CHART OF SERVICE LIST COMPILATION

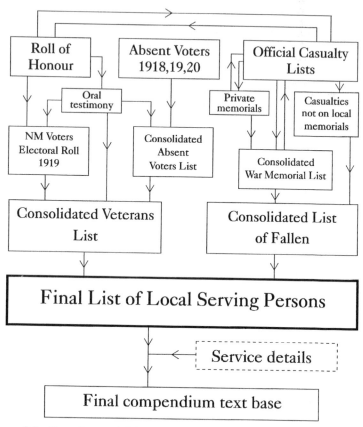

Figure 5.3   Flow chart explaining the compilation of a comprehensive list of local serving men and women for Caerleon and district, for the period 1914–20.

survivors and fallen, could not be fused until I was certain exactly how many William Joneses and John Morgans there were, on either list, and hence in total. The local name selection was not a wide one, and distinguishing true links from false was not always simply done. When the final 'Final List' was made, it was intended to create a freetext database using *Idealist* software (see Chapters 4 and 10). This would carry a textural account of each serving person, and would be readable like a book, but searchable and sortable electronically. My Final List had 704 names on it: there were 4 women and 700 men. So, exactly what tactics did I use to

```
18 19 Ball William Henry
18 19 Banner Henry Jacob           later butcher
   ● Banner Thomas Victor
18 19 Banner (William) John
18 19 Barnes Archibald
   18 Barrett Charles
  18 9 Bartholomew Albert Wilfred
18 19 Batt Edward George F          Henry Batt (Roll 15)
18 19 Baulch Harold
   18 Beavan Francis James
   18 Bennett Ruben
   ● Berrow William Sam    died 17/2/19 Ponthir
18 19 Berrow William Zephania   of Greyhound Inn
18 19 Bissell Thomas
18 19 Bodman Frank
18 19 Bolton Arthur
18 19 Bolton Harold T
18 19 Bowden William
   ● Bowen Charles                18 Bowen Frank
18 19 Bowen Edward Wintlow
18 19 Bowerman William F          the postman?
18 19 Bowles John Stanley
   18 Bradley Ernest
   18 Bray William Henry
   18 Brian Christopher          PoW
   18 Britton Samuel Ralph      Cricket Club photo 1912
18 19 Bromham Leo
   18 Bromham Philip Henry       School Admission Book
   18 Brown Cyrus
   18 Buck Harry
18 19 Burrows Francis Arthur
18 19 Burrows Percy
18 19 Busby George
   18 Carter Charles          Civilian war worker
18 19 Carter John
   18 Champion Edmund W        18 Chadwick TB
   ● Charles Albert Victor
18 19 Charles George (Henry)
```

Figure 5.4   A word processed list of service people, in the course of being annotated.

arrive at it? Can I be sure that the total in it is somewhere near the truth? It is time to talk again about the boundaries of the place.

DEFINING THE BOUNDARIES

I defined my geographical unit of study as follows: the Urban District of Caerleon, as it then was, which was the town in the ancient parish of Llangattock juxta Caerleon. To this was added rural Llangattock, and the portion of Christchurch parish known as Ultra Pontem, and the parishes of

Llanhennock and Tredunnock, which were parts of Magor Rural District. To this combined area I added the hinterland of the town – the parishes of Llanfrechfa, Llanthewy Vach, Llandegveth, Kemeys Inferior and Llanwern. People from all these places came to the town regularly – to meet socially, to fairs or shops, to the Magistrates Court or to school. And indeed, as it turned out for some, to appear on a war memorial. The physical boundaries I used were those implied by the 1919 electoral roll for the Monmouth Division (Figure 5.5).

BOUNDARIES IN TIME

Both my interview material and my study of the Roll of Honour showed me that long-time residents knew very well indeed whom they considered to be 'sons and daughters of the town'. Yet there were war casualties, who in official records were born, enlisted or resided at 'Caerleon Mon', but who appeared on no local roll or memorial, and were mentioned by no one in conversation. Evidently, the town population has to be defined not just in space. When and for how long should someone have lived there, to be counted as part of the study?

Several local people regarded one man I studied as 'local', even though he was a resident for only about five years before the war. Another man was born there but lived many years in the next parish. He was apparently forgotten. A third man had a war grave in the churchyard and a next-of-kin address in the town, but was recalled by no one to whom I spoke, and is omitted from the local memorials. How a son or daughter of the district qualified socially to be regarded as local is obscure, and presumably depended in part on involvement. I decided that the soundest definition would not be local birth, but local residence at the outbreak of war. There was no document to supply a list of residents in 1914, therefore I decided to opt for the next best thing – residents as specified on an electoral roll. I chose 1919. As far as the fallen were concerned, this would translate to a presumption of a 1919 roll entry, had they survived. Fortunately, war grave data almost always supplied at least a partial address or a locality.

RESEARCHING THE FALLEN

It is a curious fact that researching the fallen is very much easier than researching the survivors. Indeed the richness of the record for the fallen could lead one to develop and write a study based entirely upon them, and more than one researcher has done just that: see for instance *No More*

Figure 5.5 Portion of the Boundary Commission map for the County of Monmouthshire, 1917.

Strangers by David Gray (1992). a collection of biographies of the First World War fallen of the town of Peterborough. However, I am putting a study of the war dead first in my account, only because they present the easier identification problems. Results of research on them can act as a platform for the equally important but harder search for service detail of survivors.

War memorials

The most natural-seeming place to begin a search for a complete list of fallen would be a local war memorial. Personal memorials apart (and there are quite a lot of those), almost all towns and cities have public memorials, though some keep the names of their fallen out of sight in a book of remembrance, the public memorial being a plain structure. Some parishes also have their own memorial. Nevertheless, you can depend neither on the existence of a memorial, nor on the accuracy of any entries that may appear on one.

Until the First World War had taken place, memorials to fallen soldiers were mostly regimental affairs. Many of the older regiments have a memorial to the casualties of the Boer War. Some have them to members lost in the Crimea or in India. The York and Lancaster Regiment, for example, has a fine bronze in Weston Park, Sheffield, listing Boer War dead, the Devon Regiment has a like memorial in Exeter cathedral and the Lincolnshire Regiment has memorials in Lincoln Minster.

The dead of the County of York (various towns and regiments) in South Africa, 1899–1902, are remembered on a public memorial in York, and paralleling that, a list of the men of Monmouthshire lost in the same campaigns was placed in St Mary's Church at Monmouth. These memorials were the forerunners of the thousands of post-1919 war memorials.

Inspired by many nations placing major monuments in capital cities and on the battlefields, many people across Britain – citizens, landowners, clergy and councillors – planned their own local tributes. Thus it is that we have innumerable forms of memorials executed in many materials. The data on them were chosen by local people, thus the record found there can vary much in coverage and in accuracy. Some structures have no names at all; some have a meticulous, detailed list, with ranks, regiments and death dates. Many have names but no dates, ranks but no regiments. As documents (see Chapter 3), they vary greatly in meaning; they cannot always be understood well enough to identify the men unambiguously. Often too, their credibility can be questioned. Soldiers' ranks are frequently distorted, and regiments named sometimes do not match official records. But local memorials do, despite their faults (or maybe because of them), tell much, not least about their compilers.

The war memorials of Caerleon and district

In a study of local war deaths, I noted and studied six war memorials in the district I was studying. There are two in the town: a public one that formerly stood in the town square, but now stands in the local park, which was constructed substantially at the instigation of the members of the Baptist chapel, and a tablet within St Cadoc's Church. Both of these give names, ranks and units of the fallen.

Christchurch parish has a fine memorial, a grey granite structure placed on a high point overlooking both Severn and Usk. This memorial (Figure 5.6) was the only one locally to include dates of death.

Capel Seion, the Baptist cause at Ponthir, has a list of fallen (presumably members), though without any service details; inside All Saints Church, Llanfrechfa, there is a fine incised brass plate with the names and ranks of fallen of that parish, but again no units or dates. Finally, at the north end of Llanfrechfa parish is a further memorial in the yard of Pontrhydyryn chapel. Again, no ranks or dates, but again, presumably, representing chapel members.

In addition to these six, I studied four other major memorials: the Newport Book of Remembrance (1,532 names with service details); the Orb Iron Works memorial, Newport (121 names with the department they worked in: Figure 5.7), the plaques erected by the Guest, Keene & Nettlefold Company at Cwmbran, with names only of fallen from that company's iron works and coal mine, and finally, a photograph of the now lost parish memorial of St John's Church, Maindee, which gave 384 names sorted by rank and regiment. Maindee district was formerly in Christchurch parish.

All these four extra memorials were sited within a relatively short distance of the area studied. Scanning them was essential, since it had become clear that placement of names on local memorials was a haphazard matter. A man could appear on several memorials, or occasionally on none, while a casualty that seemed to be a local man might be written only on a public list outside the area. There are several reasons for this kind of result: some memorials represent institutions, some parishes, others attempt to be the centre of a district. When it comes to content, one may have been compiled from records kept during the war, another made retrospectively. One may be a fine artwork carrying unchecked data, while another may be carefully crosschecked for detail.

The two war memorials actually in the town had twenty-four names in common. The public memorial had 30 names though which were not in St Cadoc's, while the latter countered this by having three that were not on the public memorial. However, of the public memorial list, twenty-one were shared with other memorials in the area, including some who were on the Llanfrechfa, Capel Seion, Maindee and Newport lists. Only nine of the names on the Caerleon town public memorial were unique to it. A similar story could be told about Llanfrechfa church and the two chapels nearby. Finally, Christchurch memorial had twenty-three unique names and shared

seventeen more with Newport Book. Thirteen were shared with St John's and eight coincided with those at Caerleon town. All of this complicated story could well be illustrated graphically with Venn diagrams, but I will refrain, even though such approaches do give insights into the sorts and sites of social boundaries that were acknowledged in the district about 1920.

The foregoing makes it very clear that a basic (though not final) consolidated list of fallen may be made by combining all memorial lists, then identifying and eliminating all instances where several entries seem to refer to the same man. In practice, though, this was not as easy a matter as might have appeared, because of the high frequency of certain surnames in the area. This meant that if one assumed that all references to Arthur James and to A. James meant the same man, there was a good chance of making a fallacious deletion. All entries referring to the same man had to be linked beyond reasonable doubt, yet all references to different men had to be kept separate, in spite of any name sharing that occurred.

The difficulties with collating memorials were compounded by the presence among the war survivors of further men with the same or similar names. The overall magnitude of these connection problems can be seen by the figures: in a total final list of roughly seven hundred names, there were twenty-six instances of two or more men sharing both surname and first given name. Of those twenty-six coincidences, five had either three, four or five men involved.

In practice, I carefully passed one memorial list past another (and later did the same for survivors lists), a process that can be much facilitated by using either a split screen facility on the computer, or working two lists in separate windows (see Figure 4.2). In either case, the lists would be sorted alphabetically before any attempt was made to find linkages. Sorting can be achieved either with a text handling package such as *Word* or *WordPerfect,* or via a modern spreadsheet such as *Excel.* Once the draft name list has been tentatively made, other records can be used to discriminate between similarly named men. For the fallen, date of death is one of the best discriminants. Other 'first resort' discriminants are the arm of the service (army, navy, etc.) and home address. Further means of separating men are discussed on pp. 130 and 134.

Official war death records

Men and women who were killed in the First World War are well documented; in fact they are much better documented than those who survived

Figure 5.6   The public war memorial, Christchurch, Gwent. [Photo M. Turton]

Figure 5.7 The bronze war memorial plaque at the British Steel Corporation Orb Works, Newport, Gwent, which gives the works department where each fallen man was employed.

the war. This is partly due to an accident and partly due to the 'rules of the game'. By a terrible irony, the personal records of British soldiers serving in the First World War were largely destroyed by enemy action in 1940. However, the war grave and casualty lists, being kept in another place, were not lost.

The First World War casualty lists were published in 1921 and the war grave and memorial records of service personnel killed can be searched on request. (Cemetery registers can also be purchased.) In contrast, the personal service records of a soldier are available only to himself or to his next of kin, i.e. the closest surviving relative, a rule that greatly restricts access to even the few papers that have survived. In a curious sense, the soldier passed from the private to the public domain when he was killed.

Among the sources that were available for resolving the identity problems were the published casualty lists, the records of war graves, the General Register Office (GRO) Indices of Service Deaths, 1914–21, the GRO list of Naval Deaths and the public list of Mercantile Marine deaths. These all proved valuable for the study of the local war dead. In addition to these official lists is the *Roll of Honour Royal Flying Corps and Royal Air Force for the Great War 1914–18* compiled by H.J. Williamson (1992). There are several other useful published lists, including *British Red Cross and Order of St John Enquiry List 1917* (Anon. 1917, republished 1989) and the list of officers taken as prisoners of war in various theatres.

Casualty lists

Lists of dead, missing and wounded which, during action, were publicly released at frequent intervals, were often extracted to local newspapers. For most research purposes, the consolidated lists of soldiers who died, first published by the War Office in 1921, are most convenient (Anon. 1921b). These have been reprinted (Hayward 1989), in approximately eighty parts, as a regiment by regiment, battalion by battalion listing of the First World War fallen, some 635,000 other ranks' names altogether. I have found it appropriate to buy ten volumes of this publication, plus the volume containing officers' names, even though the whole is available on microfilm in my local city library. The officers' volume has lately been much reworked, extended and re-presented in two volumes, *Cross of Sacrifice,* by S.D. Jarvis and D.B. Jarvis (1993–95); these now include army, naval, marine and RAF officers.

The 1921 casualty list entry for each man gives his full name, birth place, place of enlistment, place of residence if different from birth place, rank, regimental number, theatre of war in which he died, and date and manner of death. Entries sometimes also give the name of a former regiment. It is noticeable that the entries for the members of infantry and cavalry regiments give more unit detail than the equivalent for horse and field artillerymen or for members of the Machine Gun Corps. On the other hand, the Royal Engineers' list usually gives company detail.

Using the published casualty lists

Using my consolidated memorial list, I attempted to find an entry for each man in the huge national lists. In addition, I took certain segments of the national casualty lists and scanned them for men who were described there as having a local birth place, or who were stated to have lived in or enlisted in the area. Several interesting things emerged from these searches, including a few local casualties who were not on any local memorial.

First, a significant proportion of the men named on the local memorials could not at first be identified in the lists: either I had no information of a battalion, or no one of that name appeared among the casualties of the stated battalion. Sometimes in the latter case, the man was later found in another battalion of the same regiment, though often he was not. Often men were identified, but with a different rank. (The war memorials commonly gave highest acting rank attained, rather than substantive rank.) Some of the men were finally found in the lists of altogether different regiments or corps.

Where I still had doubt regarding the service of a local casualty, or had an awkward problem of identity, I sought more information in the GRO register of Military Deaths 1914–21 or Naval Deaths for the same period. Armed with fresh information, I returned to the casualty lists.

The General Register Office

Each person killed in the war has a death certificate, which may be purchased from St Catherine's House. I sought out many of the local casualties in the St Catherine's Military Death index and ordered certificates for a proportion of them. When these arrived, they variously said things such as 'died of wounds'; 'reported missing 20–22.12.1914'; 'poison gas 2.5.1915'; or 'died of wounds 49 c.c.s. 12.1.1918'. They usually confirmed other ranks' regimental numbers, battalion identities, rank and given names. Sometimes on an officer's certificate, the reverse was annotated with a remark about birth date or place.

I found that the most useful items at St Catherine's were not the certificates themselves, but the indices, both to the Military Deaths and to Naval Deaths, which cut across all unit boundaries (in the case of Naval Deaths, ship boundaries). This meant that they helped me to find soldiers who were concealed in some unsuspected volume of the casualty list. In many instances, aided by the death year given, the GRO indices enabled me to clarify the identity of a man.

The GRO lists do make clear just how many men there could be nationally, with the same or a very similar name. If you are unfortunate enough to be supplied with only a family name and one initial, or a name plus 'artillery' or 'RFA' (Royal Field Artillery), or finally, a name and simply 'Gnr', then unless the surname is a rare one, the chance of finding the right man in the GRO index is slim. In the cases of artillerymen, the consolidated casualty lists for the RFA and Royal Garrison Artillery (RGA) are the best starting places, and one should return to them. Studying both GRO indices and the casualty lists makes one acutely aware of how much less rigorous the military recording of names was, than that practised by civil register offices.

War grave records

Meticulous records are kept of the graves or official memorials of war casualties. The custodians of grave and memorial records and of the graves themselves are the Commonwealth War Graves Commission (CWGC), Maidenhead, Berkshire. They maintain card indices of those who died in war since 1914, and for a small fee will search their records for a named person. Their success substantially depends upon the completeness of the information with which they are provided in the request. Commonly their index gives not only the grave (memorial) site and date of death, but also rank, regimental number and recorded next of kin. The latter detail will often confirm that you have identified a local man.

Of the first eighty-two individuals I asked them to seek in their indices, some seventy-six finally yielded definitive identifications. It will be evident that a war memorial such as the one at Christchurch, which includes regiments and dates of death, is especially helpful for setting up war grave searches, while the finely crafted brass plate at Llanfrechfa, which has names and ranks only, is much less so. Of the six entries of which the Commission found no trace, one proved to be a suicide and another was an accident not classified as a war death. The remaining four were unidentified due to having a common name and no regimental information. Incidentally, four local men who lay in war graves, but who died in 1919, were not listed at the GRO as war deaths.

For the tracing of entries on 'name only' memorials, it is worth noting that in all districts of England, Wales and Scotland, many more local men will have served in the local regiments than in regiments associated with far away places; the casualty lists for the batteries and battalions of the locally connected artillery and infantry regiments are the places to look first for the really problematical war dead.

Cemetery registers

The cemeteries and memorials maintained by the CWGC (see Figures 5.8 and 5.9), frequently near the locations of death, all have a register. These can be consulted on site, or copies may be purchased. The entries in them sometimes give detail extra to that returned by the commission in a grave trace. Of about sixty overseas grave visits that I made, the book entry gave added information in six or seven instances .

THOSE THAT CAME BACK: RESEARCHING VETERANS

During 1918, steps were taken to start the creation of the first comprehensive electoral roll for the adult males of the nation. (Just previous to the war, little more than 60 per cent of men had the vote.) Accordingly, data were collected house to house and from serving troops, and the first rolls were prepared. Serving men filled in slips explaining who they were, and their unit of service. The roll for 1918 represents men (and some women) alive and of age on 18 August 1918. Those men away from home on military or on defence work (the latter could be munitions, shipyard or foundry work), were listed separately on what was called the Absent Voters' List (AVL). On the main list, those away were also marked with a lower-case *a,* while the qualification to vote was described as NM, meaning naval and military. On the AVL, many men on active service, but distinctly under 21 years old age, were included. Figures 5.10 and 5.11 show the form of the AVL and NM voters' lists.

In 1919 a further electoral roll was completed based on notifications before 18 February of that year. This too carried many servicemen, since it covered the last months of 1918; in any case, some call-up men served in the Rhine Army or fought in Italy in 1919, while some others were retained as late as 1920 or 1921, in Egypt, India or Africa.

The NM voters on the main electoral roll of 1919 make up the bedrock reference source for compiling lists of veterans. Used for this purpose, the NM entries have three huge advantages. First, the roll precisely defines the area of study. Second, it places individuals in their family groups, at their home loci. Third, the NM voters include the AVL names from both 1918 and 1919.

Figure 5.8   Ponthir cricket team, 1909, with G.M. Jarrett highlighted, and his war grave at Artillery Wood, Belgium. Cpl Jarrett is also commemorated on Caerleon Town War Memorial.

Figure 5.9 The war grave of L. Cpl Jack Rees MM, at Llanfrechfa parish church, Gwent. He was a day labourer who sometimes earned his money by carrying beer to the men at the Ponthir rolling mill. [Photo M. Turton]

POLLING DISTRICT C.		PARISH OF CAERLEON.	DIVISION 2.
(1)	(2)	(3)	(4)
No.	Names in full. Surname first.	Residence or Property occupied and abode of non-resident occupier.	Nature of Qualification.

CROSS STREET

a782	Green, Percy Arnold	Post Office	NM
a783	Green, Leslie Lovall	Do.	NM
a784	Green, Donald Edwin	Do.	NM
785	Gear, John	12	R
786	Keene, Henry Edward Mace	Myrtle House	NM
a787	Edmunds, Walter Henry	18	NM
788	Edmunds, Arthur John	18	NM
a789	Soares, Ivor John	18	NM
790	Rawle, Joseph	21	R
791	Stafford, George	25	NM
792	Stafford, James William	25	NM

Figure 5.10 A redrawn segment of the NM portion of the electoral roll for Caerleon, Monmouth Constituency, 1919. [M. Turton]

Absent Voters' List.		Monmouth Division .	Polling District C.
1	2	3	4
No.	Names in Full. (Surname first).	Qualifying Premises.	Description of Service. Ship, Regiment, Number, Rank, Rating, &c., or recorded adress.
1189	Green, Percy Arnold	Post Office	2nd Lieut., 2nd Mons.T.F.
1190	Green, Leslie Lovall	Do.	Lieut., 2nd Mons.
1191	Green, Donald Edwin	Do.	2nd Lieut., 4th R.W.F.
1192	Keene, Henry Edward Mace	Myrtle House	18236 Pte., A.P.C.
1193	Edmunds, Walter Henry	18 Cross Street	MT/04814 Pte., A.S.C.
1194	Edmunds, Arthur John	18 Do.	Sig. WZ/2920, R.N.V.R., H.M.S. "Amethyst"
1195	Soares, Ivor John	18 Do.	26678 Pte., 1st Mons.
1196	Stafford, George	25 Do.	276719 Spr., R.E.
1197	Stafford James William	25 Do.	59999 Pte., Welsh

Figure 5.11 A redrawn portion of the Absent Voters' List, Caerleon district, Monmouth Constituency, 1918. [M. Turton]

An important first step: checking NM voters against AVL entries

Working with these lists, there are few problems of ambiguous identity, because the rolls and AVLs both supply addresses, which can be used to back up identification by name. Useful secondary discriminants are service arm, and the presence or absence of a commission. Service detail from the AVLs provides further means of discriminating one man from another.

There are (of course) some fairly small numbers of men who, though surviving the war, remain undetectable in this way. They include men who joined early, but were invalided out before 18 August 1918, and some young men who were called up in 1918 when they became 18 years old. Some of the former group appear on the electoral roll (see Figure 5.10) for 1919 simply as voters qualified by residence. The group of men born in 1900 mostly did not get on to the 1919 roll, and have to be detected by interview with families, photographs, newspaper reports or medals. At Caerleon, I could guess the names of some of them from the dates of birth of local boys, as entered in the boys' school admission book.

At Caerleon, the men who joined the army in 1914 and early 1915 were fortunately recorded on the Town Roll of Honour. That document, rescued from the top of a wardrobe, is proved by Urban District Council minutes to have been compiled by Cllr William Williams in March and April 1915, and was stated to the council to be complete, at a meeting reported in the press on 8 May. It is a compilation of all the regular soldiers, recalled men, territorials and volunteers of the district, as their families submitted them, over a few weeks during March and April of that year. There are several men there whose regiments are stated, but who, by the time the 1918 AVL was made, were again ordinary town residents, which is how they are recorded on the 1919 electoral roll. They were presumably by this time unfit for service. The Caerleon Roll of Honour is a truly historic and rare sort of document – the town looking at, and reporting on itself, at a precipice in world affairs. It gives many insights into the way the populace were thinking and acting in those days.

Tidying things up: two lists combined

It should be noted that the schema outlined above, wherein two lists are compiled and combined, is disturbed only by a very small number of men who appear both on memorials and on the AVLs or main electoral roll. Once the two lists were complete, fallen and survivors, they could be fused with little problem to make a 'final list' of local serving men and women. Even with few personal details appended, this tells a tale about the First World War in that locality. The total people away at the war from Caerleon and district was 704 (700 men and 4 women). While I would not wish to assert that 704 is precisely the total, I believe it to be close to it. If any persons are missed from the list, they are probably either men who were volunteers in later 1915 or call-up men of 1916 and 1917, invalided out before August 1918, but are not locally resident, or they are women, who would not have been placed on the electoral rolls simply because they were women.

The number taken alone is insightful – frighteningly large for a small place. Imagine the impact of 704 people being away from home, out of a population of about 6,000. Imagine 22 per cent of them being killed. On top of that figure, imagine many more sustaining injury or gassing.

Putting flesh on servicemen's bones

Many details of the service of individuals were available to be collected, examined and appended to the names on the final list. From the AVLs and the grave records, and from the Roll of Honour, it is not hard to know who was a commissioned officer, who an NCO; who was in the navy, who in a submarine. The Roll of Honour told who were pre-war territorials, and indicated too who were recalled regular men. Newspaper reports, interviews and relics such as medals, photographs and discharge papers, all contributed to pictures of the records of service.

The collectible data could be set too with great advantage against two different backgrounds: the regional aspect of the army in South Wales at that time, and the social fabric of the town of Caerleon and its district.

Locally connected regiments of south-east Wales

Following the Cardwell army reorganisation of 1881, the old regiments of the line were grouped in pairs and given names and local recruiting patches. Though there was resentment at the loss of their venerable numbers, the new regiments did become closely connected with particular regions. The 10th Regiment, for instance, became the Lincolnshire Regiment, while the new identity of the 53rd was the 1st Battalion the King's Shropshire Light Infantry. After 1881, men joining as regulars very often joined the new locally connected regiments.

In 1908, local connection was fostered further by the way the new Territorial Force was created. This too was within counties and had training and sectional organisation, based on the local drill halls formerly used by the 'old volunteers'. Finally, in 1914, the regional regiments of the regular army were used by Lord Kitchener as a foundation, when he created his so-called New Armies. These added many new battalions to the regional regiments created in 1881.

It will follow from this potted history that in 1914–16 local men were particularly likely to volunteer for service in the regiment they knew and saw, and which had barracks not too far from home. Researching a district or town thus requires a knowledge of the local battalions. If one has a record of a town casualty, but no associated regimental details, the casualty lists of the local battalions are prime places to seek the man.

The local regiment of the line in south-east Wales in 1914 was the South Wales Borderers (SWB). Previous to 1881, the 1st Battalion of this regiment, a very proud one, was known as 'the 24th'. I was fascinated to discover that that title was still in casual use in 1914, several families referring to the 1st SWB by that name in conversation. Furthermore, veterans I spoke to used that name as late as 1988. To estimate from the casualty lists, about 40 per cent of men in the regular 1st Battalion SWB were Welsh born, and more than half of those were Monmouthshire men, some 25 per cent of the battalion. They had barracks at Brecon.

The 2nd SWB, which was also a regular battalion, was quite different in the sense that it recruited more widely: Wales, Ireland and the north of England were all in its catchment. The proportion of Monmouthshire men in it seems to have been about 10 per cent.

The 1914–15 New Army volunteers who presented themselves at a local drill hall, or at Brecon barracks, were processed into a series of New Army battalions, the major ones of which were as in Table 5.1. Later, when more than ten battalions were away at the war, call-up men went to the reserve battalions, and when trained, were sent out in drafts to top up the other units.

The local significance of all these battalions becomes clear when I say that 14 per cent of all the local serving men spent some time with one or more battalions of the SWB. Of course, this is not as simple to interpret as it might be, as many men over the duration of the war served in two or three different battalions or corps. As Table 5.1 shows, many of these were entirely independent units that could take you to France, Mesopotamia, Macedonia or Gallipolli. However, knowledge of the places and occasions that each battalion knew in the war does give great insight into the war experience of many local men. E.A. James' book *British Regiments, 1914–18* (1978) gives the war service of each battalion summarised in a few lines.

The Territorial Force (TF)

In the county there was, at that time, a rather unusual military body, a wholly territorial regiment: the Monmouthshire Regt. It was really an his-

Table 5.1   Battalions of the South Wales Borderers, 1914–19

1st Regular	served France and Flanders
2nd Regular	served China, Gallipoli, France and Flanders
3rd Reserve	located Brecon, Pembroke Dock, Liverpool
4th formed 8/14	served Gallipoli, Mesopotamia
5th formed 9/14	served France and Flanders
6th formed 12/14	served France and Flanders
7th formed 9/14	served Salonika, Macedonia
8th formed 9/14	served Salonika, Macedonia
9th Reserve formed 10/14	located Kinmel Park
10th formed 10/14	served France and Flanders ('1st Gwent')
11th formed 12/14	served France and Flanders ('2nd Gwent')
12th formed 3/15 (bantams)	served France and Flanders ('3rd Gwent')

The 11th and 12th battalions were disbanded in February 1918.
In addition to these named, there was the 1st/1st (Brecknockshire), a territorial battalion which served in Aden and India, and approximately eight other home service battalions.

torical offshoot of the 24th; as such its cap badge was a dragon picked from the centre of the old regimental badge. Three TF battalions existed before the war, 1st, 2nd and 3rd, which in 1914 became known as the 1st/1st, 1st/2nd and 1st/3rd, to accommodate the newly forming reserve battalions known as the 2nd/1st, etc. Things even developed as far as the 3rd/3rd and the 4th. These battalions were very regional indeed, the 1st/1st being Newport-based and manned by residents of the south of the county. The other two battalions were based at Pontypool and Abergavenny respectively.

Many Caerleon men joined the 1st Monmouths before the war and trained in Caerleon Drill Hall and on the town cricket pitch. The town speciality was machine gunnery. Alhough there was no hard rule about where you should join, in practice the TF catchments of these units were rather sharply delineated. Almost all men of Caerleon town who joined the TF went to the 1st Battalion. Only about five out of seventy joined the Pontypool battalion. Yet up the road at Ponthir, no more than two miles away, almost all men chose Pontypool, even though it was no nearer. Perhaps it reflected the places they ordinarily went to work. Whatever the basis, it possibly proved a life or death choice. The 1st/2nd (which has a published history) was one of the first territorial battalions to arrive in France (7 November 1914) and it saw much distinguished service. The 1st/1st arrived in France in February 1915. All three battalions were heavily involved in spring 1915, during the Second Battle of Ypres. Rather more than one-fifth of the local serving men of the district spent at least part of their war service with the Monmouths, a place where they surely had the company of many friends, or at least of other boys from home.

Other local volunteer units included the Welsh Brigade, Royal Field Artillery (based in Newport and at Panteg, Pontypool), the RGA Glamorgan battery (TF) and the Royal Monmouthshire Royal Engineers (RMRE). However, Caerleon men joined all these in only small numbers. The Town Roll of Honour clearly sets out the list of pre-war TF men, and in a separate list (Figure 5.12) the local members of the 2nd/1st raised in autumn 1914. This was mostly men well under 20 years of age, boys really, for some were only 16 or even 15 years old. If you compare their names to the names of the boys in the Caerleon boys' cricket team of 1913 (Figure 5.13), or in the Baptist Sunday School class of the same year, it is not hard to imagine how they all came to join up together.

If one separates out the war history of the battalions of the SWB and the Monmouths, one can gain a picture of the war experience of a significant body of local men. Using the AVLs, the newspapers and interviews, the way that the boys of the 2nd/1st and 3rd/1st Monmouths passed on their way to fighting units at Somme and Passchendaele, to commissions, and in some cases to the military cemeteries of Belgium, can be traced.

The availability of the brief war history of every infantry, cavalry and yeomanry battalion in Brigadier E.A. James' book, and the many individual published regimental and divisional histories, makes the tracing of most

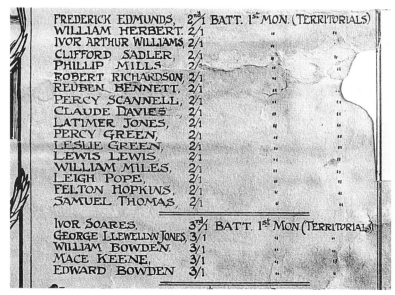

Figure 5.12 Detail from the Caerleon Roll of Honour compiled by Cllr William Williams showing the volunteers to the 2nd/1st and 3rd/1st Mons, September 1914 to March 1915.

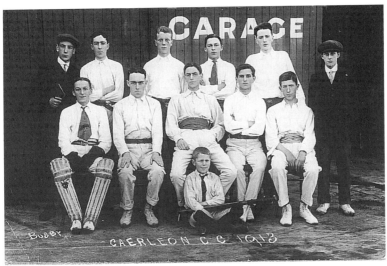

Figure 5.13   The boys' cricket team, Caerleon Cricket Club, 1913. Back row: Ivor A. Williams, Ernest Pope, Clifford Sadler, Leslie Green, Reginald Scannell, Walter Young. Front row: Percy Green, Leigh Pope, Trevor Williams, Ivor Soares, Alan Cross. Below: Henry Pope. The names in many cases coincide with those in Figure 5.12.

men's war careers possible, in outline, provided their battalion is known. The investment of concentrated effort can be rewarded with much detail. For this purpose, the series of small books by Norman Holding (1982, 1984, 1986) is a great asset. Other invaluable works are A.S. White's (1993) *Bibliography of Regimental Histories of the British Army* and A.F. Becke's (1935–45) series of volumes, *Order of Battle of Divisions,* but there are numerous other printed resources useful for tracing the movements of battalions and batteries. For researchers who do not want to purchase, there are fine collections in the British Library and at the Imperial War Museum. There are also several specialist military booksellers, whose lists should be scanned if histories of particular units are sought. It is important to realise that battalion and battery movement was determined largely by divisional movement. The published histories of divisions are therefore significant. Copies of the war diaries of battalions, brigades and higher formations such as divisions are kept at the PRO Kew.

Regarding the estimation of the dates at which particular men joined their units, any available clue may have to be harnessed, including studying the regimental number of the man in relation to the pattern and range of numbers carried by the battalion or corps concerned, the medal rolls at Kew and surviving correspondence.

War news

Until about August 1915, the local newspapers of the county carried remarkably full details of the military involvement of local units, including lists of casualties: dead, missing and wounded, by battalion. There were numerous letters and excerpts published including some from hospitals, men out of the line and even prisoners of war held in Germany or the Netherlands. A few explained the last live sightings of comrades. Some letters were from surviving officers describing occasions of disaster involving many men of the county. For example, the catastrophe that befell the 1st/1st Monmouths on 8 May 1915 is referred to many times in the local papers, often by actual participants. Many of their letters and extracts make very sombre reading. Often local men were picked out for report, especially if they were wounded.

Service with other regiments and corps

Scanning my records of servicemen, concentrating on the regiments they served in, I find that about half were with the local connection, but the others were spread very widely. There were three major ways this came about. First, service in the regular army was a long-standing local way of earning a living. While local men often did join the 1st SWB, they also joined other regiments. The 2nd Dragoon Guards ('Queen's Bays') was much favoured in the area, but some men joined the Rifle Brigade, the Shropshires, the Cardiff-based Welch Regiment, the Royal Welsh Fusiliers or the Royal Field Artillery. Of the modest number of local men who went out to France before 22 November 1914, and who thus could claim to wear the 1914 star, more than half were either in the Queen's Bays or the 1st SWB. The recalled men did include some who were in a variety of other regiments, including York & Lancs, the Dorsets and the Royal Gloucester Hussars.

A second way that recruitment was broadcast was through the Derby Scheme call up, a process which commenced early in 1916. At this stage men were being called in a manner that deliberately mixed men from different counties. This sent Llanfrechfa men to the Highland Light Infantry, Caerleon men to the Royal Fusiliers (see Figures 5.1 and 5.14) and a Christchurch man to the Norfolk Regiment.

Finally, a third factor operated to place men in army units which had either no local connection, or no regional roots at all. Men could be transferred: by the abolition of battalions, by request, through special training, after commissioning (see Figures 5.14 and 5.15), or after they had recovered from wounds. On these occasions, their second unit of service could

Figure 5.14 Lt Donald Edwin Green, Royal Welsh Fusiliers, in Egypt, 1919. He commenced his service in 1916, as a private in the Royal Fusiliers, was commissioned to the RWF, and served in France before going to Egypt and remaining there until 1920.

be quite remote from their first. Thus one man went from the Monmouths to the Machine Gun Corps, another to the Labour Corps. A third was commissioned into the Welch Regiment, a fourth into the Indian Army Corps.

It must be understood that while the men serving in the infantry and cavalry claim much attention, armies depend on other groups to provide and maintain transport, to repair or build roads and canals, organise and deliver food and ordnance, and do the paper work. As the war went on, the number of men committed to these support tasks increased both absolutely and as a proportion of the army. Inevitably many call-up men were drafted to the Army Service Corps, the Royal Engineers, the Army Ordnance Corps, the Labour Corps and so on; all hard-working organisations, whose members found life by no means free from danger. Tracing the experience of individual men in these corps can be very difficult. If this is contemplated, the reader is recommended to read the booklets by Norman Holding which particularly address problems of these kinds. Other relevant sources are the medal rolls held at the PRO Kew, documents such as discharge or transfer

Figure 5.15   One of a series of photographs taken by Lt D.E. Green in Egypt, 1918–20. It shows members of the 4th RWF waiting to relieve the 46th Punjabis, who are in mid-ground of the picture. They were to guard the Turkish prisoners seen at the rear.

papers handed down in families, photographs and oral evidence. In some cases, obituaries published many years after the war will have important service details in them. Sometimes the original subscription lists of the local branch of the British Legion survive with details. At Caerleon, up to the time the Town Roll was made, about 73 per cent of men were in or liable to be drafted to units called upon directly for combat, whereas by the time the AVL of 1918 was compiled that figure had fallen to 64 per cent, an indication of how the character of the army was changing.

Regimental numbers

It seems remarkable that when the First World War started, the British army did not have a standardised numbering system for its servicemen. Each regiment did its own numbering exercise, as it saw fit. Consequently, when the army was hurriedly expanded in 1914–15, new soldiers were given numbers in whatever way the particular corps or regiment happened to use. This meant that no soldier, in the first part of the war at least, could be depended upon to have had an unique numerical identifier.

Older-style regimental or battalion numbers ranged from single digits for 'old sweats' up to four or five digits for the incomers of 1914–15. As we are not generally able to view original nominal rolls, we can work out the range of numbers in use by a particular unit at a particular date, only by reference to the relevant casualty lists or the medal rolls.

It is often possible to analyse the casualty lists so that the approximate range of numbers in use when the unit went abroad is established. The 1st SWB, for instance, landed in France on 13 August 1914. Their first occasion of serious loss came at the Aisne on 26 September. The men who died then (and must have gone out in August) mostly had personal numbers in the range 7,000–9,000. It has been possible to establish from interviews with veterans, that some former SWB members re-called to the colours in early 1914 had personal numbers near 8,000. Replacement drafts of men carried higher numbers. Consequently, a man carrying the number 13,500, while he was in France and Belgium perhaps at the end of 1914, was possibly not there in August. Men arriving even later had numbers over 20,000 and some even over 40,000. The matter is not simple, however, because certain blocks of numbers were given to the regiment's New Army battalions. The 4th SWB, for instance, had men with numbers mostly in the range 23,000–30,000.

When men changed battalion they generally changed number as well. Only later in the war did six digit numbers become widespread (the 1st/1st Monmouths were renumbered in 1916 with six digit numbers, which commenced mostly with 225, 226 or 227). In some battalions even a few months from the end of the war, many men retained old numbers of five digits, which presumably had been given to them in 1914 or 1915.

SERVING AT SEA

The Royal Navy

I noted in the Caerleon area that RN, RNR and RNVR men amounted to about 9 per cent of the total serving persons. Though not a large percentage, this is a higher figure perhaps than the national average; it probably reflects the proximity of the district to a large port. Apart from mariners, several men were sent to work in naval dockyards as riggers. One of these worked on the 1918 reconstruction of *HMS Furious*, then the navy's most advanced aircraft carrier.

The RN sailors of the district served on many different ships. Indeed, according to the 1918 and 1919 AVLs, almost every Caerleon sailor was on a different ship from every other. The latter included several such as *HMS Minotaur*, *HMS Barham* and *HMS Queen Mary*, which were at the Battle of Jutland, and some like the balloonship *HMS Manica*, which was at the Dardanelles. The only ships with more than one local man aboard were HM

Ships *Vivid*, *Revenge*, *Valiant*, *Carnarvon* and *Wildfire*. Several of the ships mentioned were large warships of the then most modern pattern.

For the roles of naval ships in the war, several good reference works exist. The official HMSO publication *British Vessels Lost at Sea 1914–18* (published in 1919 and republished in 1977) includes details of very many ships, because it includes any that were simply fired upon. It contains references to most troop and transport ships. Even larger is Charles Hocking's *Dictionary of Disasters at Sea in the Age of Steam* (1969, republished 1990). This offers much information about ships sunk in battle, including by submarine attack. It catalogues ships present in many of the major battles including Coronel and Jutland. For anyone requiring technical detail and specification of naval ships in the First World War, *Jane's Fighting Ships of World War I* (Moore 1990) makes accessible much material, using both text and images from the 1919 and 1914 editions of *Jane's All the World's Ships*. The regularly updated *Ships of the Royal* Navy by F.E. McMurtrie (1938) is also very useful.

The Mercantile Marine

Christchurch and Caerleon war memorials both have inscribed upon them the names of men who died serving in the Merchant Navy. The great coal, engineering and shipbreaking docks at Newport were one major source of local employment and wealth; it was not uncommon for youths to join ships as deck boys, and later to go on to become Ordinary or Able-Bodied Seamen (ABs), while the parish of Christchurch was a place that traditionally was home to Master Mariners. Tracing individual men's careers in detail would be heavy work, and require reference to registers of shipping and to crew lists. The men away in the mercantile service 1914–18 have for our purposes to be counted as war-serving men. If killed by enemy action they were officially war dead. Like other war deaths, their graves and memorials are kept and recorded by the CWGC.

The national total of war deaths on merchant ships in the First World War was about 17,000. Tracing their deaths is most easily achieved by first approaching the CWGC. However, those with no known grave can be found on the national memorial outside Trinity House at Tower Hill, London, and in the attached eight-volume cemetery register. The memorial gives an alphabetical list of ships with about 12,000 names of crew members lost at sea. Reference of a ship name to the book by Charles Hocking will then give the likely date of death.

ANOTHER SORT OF BACKCLOTH: THE PEOPLE AT HOME

Wartime induced many changes in life at home. These included new work practices and hours, new roles and opportunities for women, the creation of special administrative bodies and a general preoccupation with, and consciousness of, war news. Interview materials contain much that is revealing about work experience. At Caerleon, for instance, not only were men sent on war work in foundries in northern and midland towns, but also Caerleon Forge was in an active phase; men who came to the town to work in the forge just prior to the war stayed on and became absorbed into the community. Round-the-clock shift work was introduced, and older men who had been in forges and mills when they were younger were asked to return. A well-established Caerleon baker, for instance, went to the Caerleon Works as a plate shearer, a trade he had left at Abercarn some years before. Local newspapers carry much detail about workplaces.

The parents, sisters and wives of older men were acutely aware of whom had gone to the war and who was in a reserved occupation. Resentment towards reserved men by the families of serving men, and by men themselves, was often considerable, and still smouldered even sixty years later. Veterans I spoke to scarcely ever failed to point out some of the 'reserved' men, just as they could also name men, who for reasons of infirmity or accidental injury, did not serve at home, or share in their adventure abroad.

POPULATIONS AND PROPORTIONS

It is difficult to be absolutely sure that one has identified *all* the serving persons, but my failure over the last few years of searching to add to my list suggests that rather few escaped my attention. If 700 really is close to the serving total for the district, what proportion of the total available men were away? Put another way, how many men of eligible age remained at home?

A useful estimate can be made using the 1911 decennial census. The returns for 1911 for administrative areas and registration subdistricts can both be used to compute the total population of the district. The returns even supply the numbers of inmates in the Newport Asylum and the Orphans' Home, both at Caerleon. If these are removed from the total, in 1911 the district contained 6,164 people.

Two other items of data are pertinent: the population of the County of Monmouth on that census, which was 395,719, and the number of county men aged 20–40 years at that date. The latter, which is published in the deliberations of the Executive Committee of the Welsh Army Corps 1921, was estimated to be 69,657.

These figures assume that the situation was static, when it was not; men entered and left the age range as the war went on. They ignore also men either side of the age limits who may have served. Nevertheless, despite these weaknesses, if extrapolated, these estimates do give a valuable indication of the likely total number of eligible men in the district. This comes out at 1,086 (slightly more, if adjustment for population increase 1911–14 is included). Thus, since the number away at the war was 700, the balance of men remaining at home was roughly 300–400. These would have had to include men retained to work forges and rolling mills, and to work on farms. The number would also include those precluded from service by ill-health or disablement.

Much more could be written about all these matters. However, I want to move on and pick on two other particular sets of questions. They concern, first, the casualty rate of the district, and second, public voices and community action. I set the clusters of questions out below:

1. • What proportion of local serving men was killed?
   • Is that proportion typical of the country as a whole?
   • Is it typical of the county or of the principality?
2. • What actions and events could be regarded as community responses to the war?
   • Who took the lead in them?
   • Who gave voice to the thoughts and wishes of the local people at that time?

LOCAL LOSSES

The total local deaths from all war-related causes numbered 152. This is about 22 per cent of the local serving persons. At first, when I calculated this figure, I thought it very high and searched for errors in the counting. I wondered if somehow I had counted war deaths which were not really local. I searched for a figure to compare it with – a national estimate perhaps – but this proved harder to find than I expected. First, it was surprisingly difficult to establish a reasonable national total for war deaths. Second, it was even harder to establish how many British people served.

Very tentatively, using data from the *Statistics of the Military Effort of the British Empire during the Great War 1914–20* (Anon. 1922), I came to the conclusion that a national index for war deaths was about 13–14 per cent of those who served. If this figure is close to the truth, the Caerleon district percentage is nearly double the national average. At present, I have no means of knowing if other parts of the County of Monmouth or the principality of Wales yield similar percentage military death figures. It is very possible that, rather than this being a random matter (bad luck so to speak), the selection of battalions and squadrons served in by local men offers an explanation. However, to determine if this is so, other parts of Wales as well as parts of England and Scotland have to be studied, both for war deaths and for numbers serving.

One piece of evidence that indicated that the makeup of the local serving men was not average was the proportion of officers among local men. This was 9–10 per cent. However, what might be a national average figure proved hard to ascertain. Perhaps 4–6 per cent might be near the true national mean. According to electoral rolls, the adjacent district of east Newport had an officer proportion of only about 3 per cent. But Caerleon town was near woods, fields, farms and country houses; it was hunting country, a community with more of the social class that traditionally produced officers. At present, I am still not sure how important this point is. I have much work to do, both to verify and to explain my data. Undoubtedly more understanding would accrue from a study of more districts.

VOICES AND ACTIONS OF THE TOWN

My first tentative conclusions about the life of the town and district during the period 1914–19 emerged from interviews. Identifying openly influential people is not difficult: in conversation with old people, certain names crop up again and again. Those who had the respect (or even servility) of local people were mentioned repeatedly, and descriptions of their behaviour, style of dress, mode of transport and manner of speaking were available. Follow-up questions often exposed some of the sources of their wealth, and detail of the land and houses that they owned.

The people who were teenagers or young adults at the time make very clear the respect and fear with which they viewed those for whom they opened gates and doffed hats. They accepted without question, the inevitability of these families providing the officers in both the Territorial Force and the regular army, just as they also had provided much of the management at the local iron and brick works and the benefactions available to local boys.

Interesting and encouraging as this sort of testimony is, it cannot be claimed to be the result of thorough study. To create a more credible picture, evidence has to be obtained by more systematic and rigorous means, using printed sources. One way of doing this is to analyse the directory entries for the district in the war period and for some years prior to it. *Johns' Directory of Newport and District* (Anon. published annually) provides one good source of information on local gentry families, magistrates and holders of office. These data can be supplemented by reference to handbooks of local government, since they list the local government officers too. The minute books of the Urban District Council (UDC) and local newspaper reports define the active councillors, even quoting their words on particular occasions.

Newspapers refer to committees such as the Food Committee whose members scanned tradespeople and advised local residents on food availability and procurement, including the growing of vegetables. They also encouraged pig keeping. On the committee were some of the councillors, some councillors' wives, certain shopkeepers, a local grocer and the postmaster, who was also the rate collector and rent man for the town allotment gardens.

Some of the same councillors, with various local magistrates, served on the Derby Scheme Tribunal, which commenced duties in February 1916, and immediately dealt with fifteen cases of men who had given reasons for wishing not to be called up. The *Daily Post* records that the reasons offered by most of them were upheld. The figures for local serving men (mentioned above) suggest that the total of men of military age who were either reserved or unfit was probably under 400. These would have carried the weight in the forge and tin plate works and on farms. At the north end of the district some men were employed at the Guest, Keene & Nettlefold forge and coal mine; at the south end, some may have been Newport dock workers or employees at Lysachts Orb Iron Works.

The appearance of the same prominent local persons in a variety of public roles was very striking. Between twenty and twenty-five people provided the nucleus of responsibility in the area. They were at the forefront in the courts, on the council, on committees, organising parties for wounded men, running letter writing and clothing circles, comforting the bereaved, and raising funds. Many of those same people had important roles as employers, churchmen, landlords or professionals. Their names appear in the newspaper accounts of many local wartime events.

In March 1915 the *Newport Daily News* reported that Caerleon UDC had agreed to a suggestion of Councillor William Williams (my grandfather, Figure 3.1) that a Roll of Honour of local volunteers be compiled. I found this report only several years after I had researched the Roll, and about a year after I had finished restoring it. The arrangement of the inscribed names in particular groups, and the presence in those of all the sons of this core societal group – even when some of them had long left the town – vindicated my judgement when I defined this as the influential group.

Many questions could be asked about the place through the medium of this core group. However, for reasons of space, I have chosen to report here just two. The first is the names of the people who were the functional

Table 5.2   Societal core of Caerleon and district: local action 1914–18

Gentry and aristocracy

- Cleeves, Llanfrechfa Grange (*serving Brigadier*)
- Llewellin, Caerleon House (*formerly CO Old Volunteers*)
  Mackworth, Oaklands, Llanhennock (*Remount Dept*)

- Pilliner, Llanyravon — Fund raising
  Stewart, Brodawel ——————————————— House for events
  Whitfield, Vicarage ——————————————— House for events
  Williams, The Mount ——————————————— House for events
- Waters Williams, Llysbrechfa

Urban District Council (UDC)

J Banner ——————— Mrs Banner ——————— *Provision of*
D Bevan-Jones, pastor ——————————————— *comforts, letter*
F E Rickard ——————————————————————— *circles, support*
                                        of bereaved,
                                        parties for
- W Williams ○ ——————— Mrs A Williams ——————— *wounded men*
  W J Davies
  E Davies
  T Parry
  H G Brewer
  G W Stark

Officers and tradesmen

E A Green, postmaster ———————————————
W H Marsh, grocer ———————————————————

● = Member of the Local Derby Tribunal
○ = Compiled Roll of Honour on behalf of UDC 1915
These prominent social figures gave a public voice to the war and organised local action. The actions quoted are picked from among those verbally reported or mentioned in the press. No doubt all the individuals listed were active in other ways too.

societal core of Caerleon and district. The other is their family involvement in the war – the number of sons they had serving, and the fates of those sons (see Tables 5.2 and 5.3).

It is worth reflecting on the role that the local societal core had to play in dark times: to continue in the public eye, perhaps serve on the Derby Scheme Board, even when you had sons already dead or gravely wounded; to comfort the sons of others, as yours were silent and out of touch; to deliver black-edged telegrams, as Mr E.A. Green did, at houses you knew well. Only after the war was finished and the hundreds of men returned, did social divisions open in the community of the town. The Baptist chapel promoted one (the town) war memorial, the church congregation the other

Table 5.3   Societal core of Caerleon and district: sons away at the war

	Sons serving	Fate
Gentry[a]		
Cleeves, Llanfrechfa Grange	1	
Llewellin, Caerleon House	5	2 wounded and POW[b] 1915
Mackworth, Oaklands	5	1 killed 1915, 1 suicide 1917
Pilliner, Llanyravon	1	1 killed 1914
Stewart, Brodawel	1	1 killed 1915
Whitfield, Vicarage	1	
Williams, The Mount	2	2 killed 1915
Waters Williams, Llysbrechfa	1	1 killed 1915
Urban District Council		
J Banner	3	most of time in ASC[c] or LC[d]
D Bevan-Jones	1	1 lost leg
F E Rickard		
W Williams	3	1 badly gassed 1917
H G Brewer	1	1 killed 1918
T Parry	son-in-law	killed 1917
G W Stark	1	emigrant in PPCLI[e]
Officers and tradesmen		
E A Green, Postmaster	4	1 wounded 1917 of 3 commissioned 1 LAC[f], RAF

a Most but not all sons of gentry were commissioned
b Prisoner of war
c Army Service Corps
d Labour Corps
e Princess Patricia's Canadian Light Infantry
f Leading aircraftsman

(parish) memorial. Even so, the citing of names on both was generously done. Some returning soldiers took determined radical stances, founding ex-servicemen's societies and spreading political parties, seeking seats on the UDC. It was the start of a more confrontational age, and a new group of social leaders began to emerge.

REFERENCES AND FURTHER READING

Anon. (various dates) *Johns' Directory of Newport and District.* Newport: R.H. Johns.

Anon. (1917) *British Red Cross and Order of St John Enquiry List 1917.* Reprinted Newport: Ray Westlake Military Books (1989).

Anon. (1919a) *Officers Died in the Great War.* London: HMSO. Reproduced London: Samson Books (1979) [Invaluable source].

Anon. (1919b) *List of British Officers taken Prisoner in Various Theatres of War August 1914 to November 1918*. Reprinted London: London Stamp Exchange (1988).

Anon. (1921a) *Welsh Army Corps 1914–1919: Report of the Executive Committee*. Cardiff: Western Mail.

Anon. (1921b) *Soldiers Died in the Great War 1914–19*, in 80 parts. Separate parts republished Polstead: J.B. Hayward & Son and the Imperial War Museum (1989) [Essential research source for studies of the First World War].

Anon. (1922) *Statistics of the Military Effort of the British Empire during the Great War, 1914–20*. Republished London: London Stamp Exchange (1988) [Huge war data resource].

Anon. (1981) *The Naval Who's Who 1917*. Polstead: J.B. Hayward & Son [Gives names of casualties at Battle of Jutland].

Banks, A. (1989) *A Military Atlas of the First World War*. London and Melbourne: Leo Cooper [First World War in specially drawn maps].

Bavin, W.D. (1921) *Swindon's Effort in the Great War*. Swindon: John Drew Ltd.

Becke, A.F. (1935–45) *Order of Battle of Divisons, 4 volumes*. London: HMSO, four volumes, Republished Sherwood, Nottingham: Sherwood Press (1989) [Essential reference works for First World War research].

Coombes, R.E.B. (1983) *Before Endeavours Fade*. London: Battle of Britain Prints International, 4th edn [An illustrated travel guide to the battlefields and cemeteries of the Western Front].

Coppard, G. (1980) *With a Machine Gun to Cambrai*. London: Imperial War Museum. Republished London: Papermac (1986) [A fine and rare thing – an 'other ranks' memoir].

Englefield, V.E. (1921) *The History of the Twentieth (Light) Division*. London: Nisbet [Typical example of a divisional history].

Enser, A.G.S. (1979) *A Subject Bibliography of the First World War*. London: André Deutsch [Lots of books, listed by topic].

Gliddon, G. (ed.) (1988) *Norfolk and Suffolk in the Great War*. Norwich: Gliddon Books [An example of a recent regional study].

Gough, Sir H. (1931) *The Fifth Army*. London: Hodder & Stoughton [A general's view of *his* war].

Gray, D. (1992) *No More Strangers*. Peterborough (self-published) [Biographies of men on Peterborough War Memorial].

Hocking, C. (1990) *Dictionary of Disasters at Sea in the Age of Steam*. London: London Stamp Exchange [Monumental work].

Holding, N.H. (1982) *World War I Army Ancestry*, Plymouth: Federation of Family History Societies.

Holding, N.H. (1984) *The Location of British Army Records. A National Directory of World War I Sources*. Plymouth: Federation of Family History Societies.

Holding, N.H. (1986) *More Sources for World War I Army Ancestry*. Plymouth: Federation of Family History Societies.

Hurst, S.C. (1929) *The Silent Cities*. London: Methuen. Republished, London: Naval & Military Press (1993) [Original guide to Western Front Cemeteries, with early photographs].

James, E.A. (1978) *British Regiments, 1914–18*. Joint edn, London: Samson Books [The single most useful research reference book that gives war history of battalions].

Jarvis, S.D. and Jarvis, D.B. (1993–95) *Cross of Sacrifice*. Brimpton: Robert's Medals Publishing [3 volume listing of officer casualties].

Macdonald, Lyn (1978) *They called in Passchendaele*. London: Michael Joseph [An account of an infamous battle. Constructed from interviews with veterans].

Macdonald, Lyn (1989) *1914*. Harmondsworth: Penguin [The testimony of those who served in 1914].

McMurtrie, F.E. (1938) *Ships of the Royal Navy*. London: Samson Low, Marston & Co [Various other editions also].

Middlebrook, M. (1971) *The First Day of the Somme. 1 July 1916*. London: Allen Lane [Meticulous account with many veterans' quotes].

Moore, J. (1990) *Janes Fighting Ships of World War I*. New York: Military Press [Recent compilation from First World War editions – *the* reference on Naval Ships].

North, J. (1936) *Gallipoli The Fading Vision*. London: Faber & Faber [A fine commentary on an epic].

Peacock, Alan J. (1993) *York in the Great War 1914–1918*. York: York Settlement Trust [Local politics during the First World War].

Putkowski, J. and Sykes, J. (1989) *Shot at Dawn*. London: Leo Cooper [A book intended to shock – and which does].

Scott, W.H. (1923) *Leeds in the Great War 1914–1918: A Book of Remembrance*. Leeds: Leeds Libraries and Arts Committee.

Ward, C.H.D. (1919) *History of the Welsh Guards*. Republished, London: Stamp Exchange (1988) [A wonderfully gracious example of a regimental history].

White, A.S. (1993) *Bibliography of Regimental Histories of the British Army*. London: Naval and Military Press [Invaluable work of literature reference].

Williamson, H.J. (1992) *The Roll of Honour Royal Flying Corps and Royal Air Force for the Great War 1914–18*. Dallington: Naval and Military Press.

CHAPTER SIX

The Matter of Population

In the 1950s and 1960s, walking town pavements was something one did in the company of thousands. On a Saturday morning, town centre pavements could be so full as to force one to walk in the road or to take avoiding action in shop doorways. As a child in Wales, I remember Newport streets crowded with shoppers, people passing the time of day, Welsh women with babies in shawls, men selling newspapers. Later, as a student, I spent some years living in London where shopping areas were no less used. When I came to Sheffield thirty years ago that too still had a vibrant street life.

Things now are so changed in all these places, and in most other towns, that occasionally I catch myself wondering if what I think are memories are only things that I imagined. But no. All older people remember town streets crowded with pedestrians. The presence of so many people on the street at the same time left little doubt in the minds of all of us that we were town people. In fact, most of the nation were town people. This was the culmination of a gathering process that had been proceeding since early modern times. To us who lived in the mid-twentieth century, the results of many decades of town growth were all around.

The gradual congregation of people of small settlements into towns is well documented. Perhaps some particular towns can owe their growth substantially to such immigration. But local growth by immigration must be distinguished from the phenomenon of overall national population increase, even though these two things may not be completely separable. After all, might not population increase provoke movement? And may not the mixing of peoples or crowding of life in town in some way stimulate greater procreation?

However, before even trying to comprehend these sorts of issues, I would like to air some other more basic question. As the national population has grown very greatly over the last few centuries, is there any such thing as 'natural population growth'? I ask this because I have sometimes seen the term used in local historical accounts. If there is such a thing, then it is important to learn how this contributes to the growth of individual towns.

FACTORS IN TOWN GROWTH

When a town is said in a gazetteer or travellers' handbook to have had in 1921 a population of, say, 101,402, this is a figure based on the census taken that year. It is essentially a figure obtained by counting people on, or with respect to, a certain day in 1921. One week later, ten or fifteen of those people had died, and a roughly similar number of new ones had been born. A week after the census date then, the population was still no doubt very close to the census figure, even although the actual individuals present had been subject to an exchange process – or at least about 1 in 10,000 of them had. A year later, the proportion exchanged would have been nearer to 5 per 1,000. Evidently, although the total present (what we loosely call 'the population') may have changed very, very little, the situation has more components than just total number. Change continues to take place. Even if at the 1931 census the town had still had a quoted population of near 100,000, they would not by any means have all been the same people. The 100,000 is really not a total, but what is sometimes called a 'steady state' figure.

To understand the situation better, we can imagine that the population of a town (as shown in Figure 6.1) is influenced by four major factors: the birth rate, and the rate of arrival of immigrants, both of which raise population, and the death rate and the departure of emigrants, both of which lower it. In this model, the steady state town population is the figure inside the box, through which people are 'flowing'.

Although we have figures for annual deaths and annual births, only when we know something of the extent of immigration and emigration, and their net effect, can we say anything very useful about local population growth or contraction. To unravel the matter, we need to talk next about the national population, because this is the framework within which the happenings in one place occur.

The British national population has grown in size several fold since the year 1800 and even more so since 1700. While there has been a small amount of immigration from abroad, the great bulk of the growth has been due to excess of total births over total deaths. Indeed, the excess of births is even greater than at first appears, since nationally emigration has been quite heavy. Evidently, living conditions have been such that on the whole,

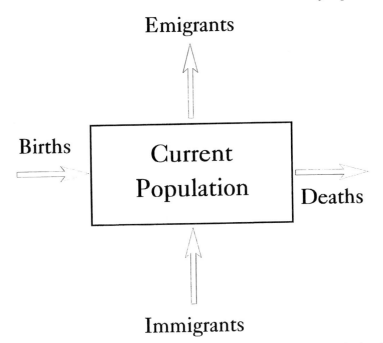

Figure 6.1   A four factor model for understanding population size. In the box is the population count at any given date. Each arrow represents a factor that would have its own rate value which might change at different dates.

enough children have been enabled to survive, to outnumber the persons dying. This situation has sometimes been described as 'natural population growth'.

Even that sort of growth is complex. If the children born in a short period of two to five years are considered, although they may be more numerous than the deaths of the same period, those babies take many years to reach maturity. Also they can die in adulthood without marrying, or they may marry, but prove infertile. Only if the births outnumber deaths for a period of rather longer than five years, can we say that an upward trend of population size is established. An examination of the poorest nations of the world confirms that generally human reproductive potential remains high at all levels of food supply, other than the very poorest. Child production by individual couples among a population on a subsistence diet is likely to be thus primarily modifiable by changing the age at marriage, or by the practice of contraception, as suggested by Wrigley and Schofield (1981) using evidence based on analysis of English parish registers.

However, the annual death rate is potentially subject to numerous variations, due to the influence of many factors such as infectious epidemic, environmental pollution, famine or detrimental behaviour. Potential human lifespan is evidently very long and has been, at least until the past hundred years, mostly under fulfilled.

It is not hard to accept that several factors influence birth rate, and rather more factors influence death rate. Birth and death rates can combine variously to yield an assortment of net rates of population increase or decline. The British national population has been showing net increase for more than 300 years, indicating that, over all, death rate has been less than birth rate. From this, and at least at first, ignoring national emigration and immigration, we can compute average growth rates for different periods. If we translate these into the situation for a particular place it is possible to get a very rough overall estimate of the population growth that there would have been without the effects of local immigration. (It is rough, because local conditions may not have matched the national average ones.) For all that, it is handy to have; it is this sort of estimate that some authors have, more usefully than above, referred to as the 'natural population growth'. It is in this way that I employ the term. When studying an individual place, the relevant local estimate is a useful pointer to the local significance of immigration.

THE GROWTH CURVES OF INDIVIDUAL PLACES

Recently, while teaching a class of human biology students, I had cause to show them a graph of the population of Sheffield over the last few centuries (Figure 6.2). Its shape is quite startling, as for much of the period in question, it steepens rapidly. Towards the end it seems to try to rise almost vertically.

It was on this occasion that I found good use for the estimate of 'natural population growth', which I obtained from the national population figures 1801–1931. By 1924, Sheffield had about five to six times as many people as the national average growth would have predicted. Immigration has played a huge part in the city's growth. Moreover, it has done so by a kind of 'compound interest' effect. The incomers have been coming for many, many years, not only adding directly to local totals, but also naturally showing their own multiplying ability after arrival. They thus contributed further to the acceleration of town growth by the birth of new little Sheffielders. Naturally, since it exceeds the natural population prediction by so much, Sheffield's rapid upward sweep of population is not reproduced in all the towns of England and Wales. Many different shaped population curves can be seen.

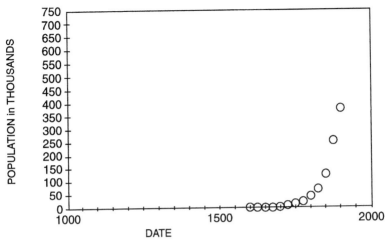

Figure 6.2 Population of Sheffield at various dates. Redrawn from the Abercrombie Civic Survey of the city published in 1924.

RARE AND EARLY LOCAL CENSUSES

Since population size change is the product of four forces, birth, death, immigration and emigration, and each of those is itself complex, estimation of population cannot be done only from sources such as baptismal or birth registers. The numbers of births or baptisms per year alone do not give a clear picture of population. Birth numbers and deaths per annum are only *rates* which could be associated with the appropriate arrow in Figure 6.1. The only uncomplicated way of knowing local population is to count it. Occasionally, in the seventeenth or eighteenth centuries, for one reason or another, the residents of a town, village or parish were counted or listed. Sheffield town population for instance was counted in 1615/16 when it was pronounced to have 2,207 inhabitants, and again in 1736 when the total given for the township was 10,121. These figures are among those used in the original version of Figure 6.2, which was published in the city's Civic Survey by Abercrombie (published in 1924).

When listings of this kind were made, they usually gave the householder's name and perhaps the number of people in each house. Exceedingly rarely, full name and age details are given. Censuses of this sort can naturally be used to derive a population estimate. Frome in Somerset has a listing compiled in 1785. This gives the head of the house, the number of residents of each sex and the number of cows. This yields a (human) population estimate of rather over 8,100.

157

If the annual baptismal rate around the time of the census is computed, this census figure can be used to calibrate the baptismal number at other dates, and thus to give rough population estimates for those other dates: 5,700 for the year 1700, and 4,400 for the year 1650. Other West Country places with eighteenth-century censuses include Trent (now part of Dorset) and Camerton, near Bath. Further, local inhabitants' lists that are useful in this way include that for Kendal in Westmorland (1695), the famous listing for Clayworth in Nottinghamshire made in 1676, and also the Marriage Tax lists for the 1690s for London and Bristol (the second of which is mentioned again in Chapter 8). Such listings are rare; local historians will not normally find one for their locality.

RETROSPECTIVE POPULATION ESTIMATION

The earliest national censuses – for 1801, 1811 and 1821 – give opportunities for retrospective population calculations. This can be done as follows: first compute the average annual number of baptisms for the parish, for the blocks of nine years that centre on the three dates. Second, express these per head of total population for each of the relevant dates. This average, generally fairly consistent for the three dates, may be averaged and used to calculate a population at an eighteenth-century date, by dividing it into the annual baptismal rate. The latter must be obtained by averaging a block of years.

When this procedure was carried out using data from the parish of Frome St John, Somerset, for a block of years clustered around 1785, the population estimate was rather close to that given by the local census mentioned above. Naturally, as the years studied get more distant from 1801, the population estimates become more suspect, since more changes of marriage practice may have been adopted, and more unidentified alterations in living conditions may have occurred.

Other methods of estimating are available too. Some of these are a bit rough and ready, but still useful. They are equivalent to what scientists sometimes call a quick and dirty experiment. The first of these concerns the Hearth Tax assessments.

The list of those assessed for this tax is taken to be a list of heads of households. Each house is assumed to have an average household size of 4.25 persons. Using this multiplier, taken from P. Laslett and R. Wall (1972) *The Household and Family in Past Time*, gives a first estimate of population. In most instances, this has to be adjusted for those persons exempt from payment or omitted from the list – the most uncertain part of the calculation. It is usual to multiply the first estimate by 1.5 to allow for tax-exempt poor.

A second rough method is based on the Compton Religious Census for 1676. (The returns have been reprinted in A. Whiteman (1986) *The Compton Census of 1676.*) Here, household heads (or sometimes whole families) who were Church of England worshippers were counted, as were dissenters and recusants. The latter two categories seem often to be recorded as individuals. Again it is necessary to multiply household heads by 4.25, then add the number of dissenting and recusant individuals. Finally, diocesan visitation returns can sometimes be employed for calculations, if they include numbers of church families and numbers of dissenters and Catholics.

I tried out all three methods, plus census-based retrospective calculation in the parish of Llangattock juxta Caerleon. The results of these various calculations, with the relevant dates are plotted in Figure 6.3.

It would be unwise to place too much reliance on any of the individual estimates. However, before 1800, all the estimates made do lie to a surprisingly smooth curve, indicating a measure of agreement. The population

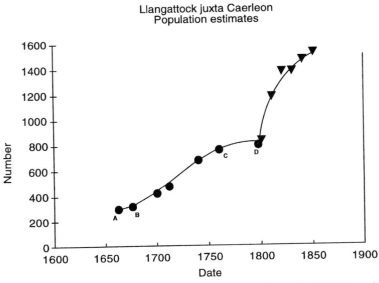

Figure 6.3 Population of Caerleon at various dates. Triangles indicate decennial census data. The earliest estimates are *A* from the Hearth Tax of 1663 and *B* from the Compton Religious Census of 1676. Estimates *C* and *D* represent the diocesan return of 1769 and the Vicar's count of 1798, reported to Archdeacon Coxe. The remaining points are obtained by back projection using census figures for 1801, 1811 and 1821 and the parish baptismal and burial records.

was apparently little more than 200 in the early seventeenth century and it rose very steadily to a sort of plateau at the end of the eighteenth. In or about 1800, there was initiated a violent population rise associated with the founding of Fothergill's tin plate works. This set the town off on an entirely new path of growth (see also Chapter 9). It is of considerable interest that the town and parish had such a modest population in the 1600s, since some two hundred years earlier, the town was an incorporated borough. That fact and the detail in surviving sixteenth-century shipping records cause one to wonder if any catastrophic set back in town population occurred at any stage.

LOCAL BAPTISMAL AND MORTALITY RATES

It is apparent from Figure 6.1 that the population of a town could stay constant even with increasing immigration, provided an increase in emigration also occurred. Putting this another way, a knowledge of the rates attached to any or all of the four factors does not confer knowledge of the population. However, longitudinal analysis of the two most available parameters, the baptismal and burial rates, can sometimes give useful indications both of changes in local living conditions and the occurrence of major population reshaping events, without putting a figure to the population itself.

In most well-established communities, there is a baptismal number/year that bounces along at a fairly constant rate. For places with populations already above about 400–500, the yearly total average is generally slowly increasing. At Caerleon, throughout all of the period for which records exist (from 1695), death rates, estimated as burials, were less than baptismal rates.

However, at Frome this was not so. A study of the period 1690 to 1760 showed that in Frome, burial numbers were most frequently 65–75 per cent of baptismal numbers. But for certain years this did not apply. In twenty-three of the seventy years of the period mentioned, deaths exceeded births, as indicated by these records. The worst spell was from 1726 to 1732, in which in all years but one, deaths well exceeded births. In 1737 there were nearly 300 burials against only 140 baptisms. Life at Frome was amazingly unhealthy at that time.

Comparing Caerleon death data for the same period with those of Frome indicates that, although the housing at Caerleon was poorer (houses were smaller and made of humbler materials), it was on balance a healthier place to live. Only in one or two years in the 1730s did deaths exceed baptisms, and even then, only by a modest amount. Caerleon's greater health may have been because the town was adjacent to a tidal river that daily carried away infectious effluent from the ground water.

At Frome St John, baptismal numbers rise steadily on a gently steepening curve, though the whole period of records from 1560 until the end of the seventeenth century, at which point there is a sudden steepening, which corresponds to the boom in house building in the Trinity district. Later, near 1830, there is a drop in town totals of baptisms associated with the assisted mass emigrations to British North America.

STUDYING IMMIGRATION

Poor though birth, baptismal and burial figures are as direct estimators of population, they are at least accessible vital records. If someone was to ask for the best sources of quantitative and qualitative data on immigrants into and emigrants from a particular parish, town or city one would be hard put to offer an answer that really satisfies. Movement is harder to measure than birth and death. What one offered as sources would depend upon the period that the questioner referred to. For the latter half of the nineteenth century, one would have to say as many other writers have, that the census enumerators' books are unrivalled as sources. For times previous to 1851, other means must be sought; these may include surname patterns and the homes of out-of-parish brides or grooms, as cited in the parish marriage register or banns book. Finally, if the period after 1891 is referred to, one might hesitate to commit oneself to an answer at all. The use of surnames as tracers of movement is feasible (see Chapters 7 and 8).

LOCAL NINETEENTH-CENTURY IMMIGRATION STUDIED FROM THE CENSUS ENUMERATORS' BOOKS

The nineteenth-century census books are so much written about, and so much used in teaching, that some justification is necessary before setting off to write yet more about them. My reasons for offering more are that I am promoting aspects which are less usual. They are to do with town to town movement, incomers from overseas and pattern analysis of incomers within the town or city. My examples are drawn from an ongoing study of the records of Sheffield, now a very large place; a busy town that was incorporated a borough from 1843 and created a city in 1893.

About the year 1700 there were in England thirty-two places with populations of 5,000 or more. Sheffield was not among them. By 1750 it ranked fourteenth in England with a population of about 12,000. At the census of 1801 it had exceeded 30,000 and reached rather higher in the rankings. Its growth and climb were rapid indeed, and they continued to accelerate. In the middle part of the nineteenth century, between 1841 and 1861, Sheffield found 70,000 more citizens. As Figure 6.2 shows, increments of that magnitude continued into the twentieth century.

For any local historian pursuing oral history, the 1891 and 1881 censuses are of special interest because they record details of many people mentioned in conversation. In small places where you have a body of interview material, the census enumerators' books for those years would be an obvious place to turn to for extending and verifying evidence. Despite this, the part of the census record discussed here is that reporting the rapid population growth of Sheffield in the period 1841–91, with particular reference to immigration. Studying just one of these censuses of the city from any point of view is a very considerable task. A preliminary study did, however, indicate that the sources of immigrants, though they perhaps differed in balance at different dates, nevertheless had some aspects in common over the span of several censuses. Deciding to start with one decennial census, I initially chose 1861 as this census was, from some points of view, taken at an especially interesting time in Sheffield's industrial history. The Bessemer process was perfected in 1857 and became much used in Sheffield during the 1860s, while the rise of the great armaments industry began soon after 1861. The town population at the time of that census was 185,172. Interestingly, the 1861 census was also the first to seek data on country of origin.

I was concerned at the outset, to clarify two aspects:

- the origins of the immigrants
- the geographical pattern of their settlement within the town.

Later, I became concerned with follow-up questions about the extent to which 1861 was similar to other dates in the later nineteenth century, and whether the mid-nineteenth-century incoming of certain groups that I detected on the 1861 census still showed in today's Sheffield. A search for contemporary families that exemplified the movement recorded on the 1861 (and later) censuses was instituted.

DATA COLLECTION

Data collection consisted of a line by line scan of the enumerators' books for the town, amassing cumulated counts of the numbers of individuals

- born in each English county, and the three Yorkshire Ridings, all recorded separately
- born in Wales
- born in Scotland, with cities and towns separately recorded with individual personal names of incomers
- born in Ireland, with individuals' names, towns and counties recorded
- born overseas, with names and places of origin.

The numbers were collected on to specially designed pro formas. The collection process was much facilitated by the availability of abbreviated and alphabetised census transcripts prepared by the Sheffield and District Family History Society (FHS) (see also p. 179). On these, data were collected county by county, entailing repeated readings of the lists. The three Yorkshire Ridings were not distinguished on the lists and the entries had to be individually evaluated. The procedure of repeated reading was tedious, but on balance much more effective than evaluating and allocating each succeeding line. However, the alphabetised lists did not always contain all the required clarity or personal detail; thus it was necessary to check a proportion of the entries on the microfilms of the books themselves. Towards the end of the study, some of the computer files used to create FHS transcripts became available for direct searching.

The borough being very large in 1861, I needed to make a strategic decision concerning the most productive way to proceed. I believed that I should, at the outset at least, work on a sample of the city, such that understandable results would emerge before a completion of the whole city. Here I had a problem, because my interest included the *pattern* of settlers on the ground. Since this was so, a genuine broadcast random sample, spread about all corners of the town, was not of use. Yet I certainly needed to take some kind of unbiased sample, in order to reduce the total workload. After some thought I decided I would try to complete a study of one sector, effectively a quadrant of the city. I needed to be conscious from the outset, however, that it may not be wholly representative of the borough as it was at that time.

The state of progress of FHS census transcription meant switching from where I had started and concentrating at first on the west of the borough. Later the zone covered developed into the west quadrant of the town. Figure 6.4 shows a map of a part of the borough with the quadrant referred to marked out in dark lines.

It has edges mostly traceable on the ground today (the exceptions are where roads have been lost to ring road, council flat, hospital or university development, or where it crossed open ground, since built upon). Internal

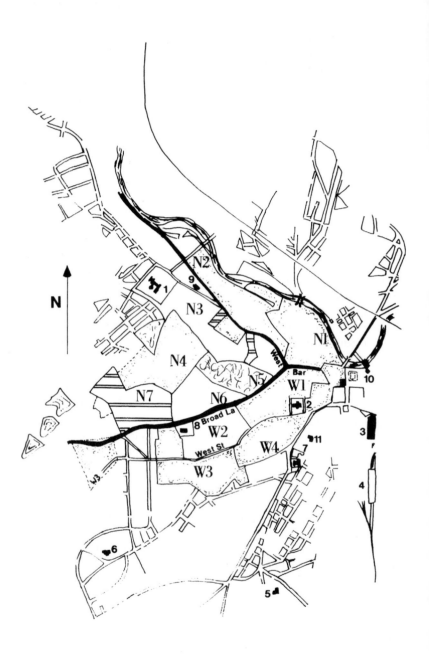

boundaries too were frequently traceable. It is almost exactly a quarter of Sheffield as it then was in terms of area, and rather more than a quarter in terms of population. The total population of the quadrant analysed was 50,746. The sample there taken had one particular great advantage, namely that it cut the city like a cake, thus appropriately weighting the areas that existed at different distances from the centre. If the sectoring was to be completed, the centre point would perhaps have been to the north of the mound of Sheffield castle, close to a point formerly known as the Irish Cross.

CONDITIONS ON THE GROUND

The area of the quadrant is bounded on the east by the River Don, as that water course runs in from the north-west to the town centre. The area is then defined by taking a sweep from the river anti-clockwise to take in some rising ground of the bottom of a spur of Walkley Bank, across the valley, up the steepening slope and over to the main thoroughfare called at different points, Brook Hill, Broad Lane, Tenter Street and West Bar Green, which mostly runs off the south part of the Crookes spur, into a shallow valley. From that line the sweep takes in the next slope and higher ground between that and the west to east town street called Division Street, going a little south of it.

Some large areas of housing included in the quadrant as it was in 1861 dated from the town's eighteenth-century building explosion and the first era of town overspill building in the period 1720 to 1740. On the map, these are the districts labelled W1 and W2.

Some of these early houses in courts near the Townhead (W1) were demolished in the late 1890s, necessitating the rehousing of 1,250 people. However, many courts of houses on 'the crofts' at W2 survived until the

---

Figure 6.4   A sketch map of mid-nineteenth-century Sheffield with the patches making up the quadrant studied drawn in. The River Don enters from the north-west and turns sharply in the middle of the city. Note that of the eleven patches studied, two have detached portions. The township of Sheffield also had a detached portion associated with W3. Numbered blocks are sites of: 1 Sheffield Infirmary, 2 St Peter's Church, 3 Pond's Forge, 4 Midland station, 5 St Mary's Church, 6 Broomhall, 7 present town hall with St Paul's Church, 8 St Georges's Church, 9 St Philip's Church, 10 Opera House, Blonk Street, 11 St Marie's Roman Catholic Church. Patches W1 and W2 had many poor eighteenth-century houses, N6 many from later in the eighteenth-century. W3 had many houses built in the period 1830–50. In N7, building was continuing in 1861.

zoning and clearance programme initiated under the Housing Acts of 1925 and 1930, and following the Civic Survey of 1924. By this time they were dilapidated and squalid, and conferred on their residents an ill reputation that was hard to shake off. A few older pictures of the Townhead houses cleared in 1898 do survive (Figures 6.5 and 6.6), and a camera can still capture a few uninhabited ones and small works also from the eighteenth century, in streets either side of Tenter Street and West Bar Green (Figure 6.7). The extent of the Sheffield slum clearance operation can be judged from the published figures: by 1935, under the three Acts, 16,247 people had been rehoused and 3,742 houses knocked down, almost all of them in the quadrant under consideration. Clearance and rebuilding schemes continued in the area of the quadrant at least until 1965.

The venerable housing that remained in the quadrant after the demolition of 1898 was reported on as part of the 1924 survey. At that time it was noted that the population density was as high as 262 per acre, when works ground area was included. It exceeded 400 per acre when works were taken out of the calculation. There is no reason to suppose that in 1861 population density in central Sheffield was any less than that just quoted. According to witnesses, some of the worst housing was merely of one room on each of the ground and first floors, or even of only a single room. These courts of eighteenth-century housing were long noted for their squalor and unsanitariness, which is described in Calvert Holland's (1843) report on *The Vital Statistics of Sheffield*.

On both the Don bank and in the most southerly part of the sector (W3), there was until the 1980s a large tract of houses, shops and small works built about 1830–40. These particular houses were thus quite modern at the time of the census in 1861. With mouldings around the six panel doors and over the Georgian-style sash windows, they had, even so, in some cases at least, only one downstairs room. They were mostly demolished about 1960–65, though a few houses and some shops (Figure 6.8) have been overlooked. The sector of the city studied included about half of the eighteenth-century built-up area which appears for instance on Fairbank and Cary's map of 1795. This included certain old streets of better dwellings. Principally, these were Georgian town houses dating from roughly 1770–90. They lie in what today is the business quarter of the city, housing the offices of lawyers, property firms and financial agents.

Figure 6.5 An eighteenth-century house in Hawley Croft (photographed in 1898 shortly before demolition), showing an example of some of the early housing that made up much of the quadrant. The form of the windows was typical of many houses of the period, as were the irregular bricks and stone roof tiles.

Figure 6.6 Also in Hawley Croft, a shop dating perhaps from 1830, now demolished. It was typical of much nineteenth-century property in the area, some of which still survives.

Figure 6.7 A recent (1992) picture of an old works building alive and well in Lambert Street, in the heart of the quadrant.

A redevelopment process applied to the main city centre streets chiefly in the period 1880 to 1900, involved widening and straightening certain roads, and furnishing them with much larger buildings mostly with ashlar frontages. During this period, much ramshackle eighteenth-century building stock was swept away, leaving just a few better buildings from that period. The restructuring process spread out along certain radial roads, including West Street, a shopping thoroughfare that passes through the

Figure 6.8   A recent (1992) photograph of shops from about 1835 that still stand at the end of West Street. This street corner was an enumerators' landmark during the 1861 census.

quadrant. Between 1899 and 1921 most of that street, which held many buildings from the first half of the nineteenth century, was rebuilt with far more substantial structures. In between these, and at the back of them, some houses and shops from prior to the 1861 census remain, plus a few work-shop premises possibly dating from before 1800.

DATA HANDLING AND PROCESSING

I worked on eleven separate film records: piece numbers RG9 3476–84. Each contained what I shall call a 'patch' of five or six enumerator's sub-districts. Altogether, the quadrant comprised thirty-five enumerator's sub-districts for Sheffield North, and twenty-one for Sheffield West. All were in the Township of Sheffield. Using a street map from a directory of the period, it was largely possible to plot these on to a modern street map (even though some streets are now entirely lost) and then, using that, to explore the territory on the ground. I kept extracted data from each patch separate. Thus I had eleven values for

- total population

- persons originating in each English county and riding
- total Irish persons
- total Welsh-born persons
- total Scots-born persons
- total persons born abroad
- certain other parameters.

From these eleven I was able to generate an 'average patch' for the quadrant. The birth place frequencies of people in the average patch are shown in Figure 6.9.

Because the data for each patch were separate, it was possible to apply tests for significance of difference between the data for the different patches, and to relate the composition of the patches to their position on the ground. In practice, the most significant aspect of position was distance from the centre.

Questions about patch composition in respect of geographical origin were approached in four steps. First, the Celtic incomers and overseas persons were abstracted and analysed separately. Second, various ratios were computed: Yorkshire-born versus various other English-born persons. Third, the frequencies of persons born in each of the major contributing English counties were plotted against each other, to search for correlations. Finally, the numbers of Celtic incomers were plotted against each other and against various sources of English persons.

LOOKING FOR CORRELATION VIA REGRESSION PLOTS

Regression analysis is a method of seeking correlations in data by plotting graphs of values for one parameter against those for another. Thus, if there are eleven patches, the eleven values for, say, Warwickshire-born people are plotted against the eleven for, say, Shropshire-born. The line that best fits the resulting scatter of points is computed and drawn. Personal computer software is commonly available to do this (one example is *Sigmaplot*), which is achieved by a method called computation of 'least squares'. There are tests to determine if the slope is 'real', i.e. genuinely >0. Not only is the slope of the line important, but so also is the remoteness of the points from the line – the so-called residual variance. The closer the points fall to the line the more likely it is that the slope is significant, i.e. 'real'.

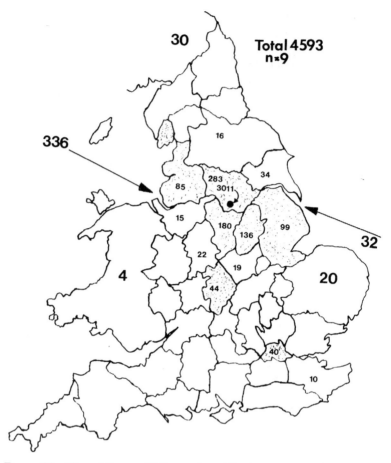

Figure 6.9 Map of the pre-1974 counties of England showing the sources of Sheffield incomers by county in the average patch of the west quadrant of the town. The total population of the average patch was 4,593. Counties in stipple were major contributors (average contributing numbers marked). Other counties with numbers given were less significant geographical donors. The number of patches analysed (*n*) was nine.

IRISH, SCOTS AND WELSH

The parameter showing the most outstanding variability in the whole set of results for the quadrant was the frequency of people born in Ireland. One of the patches had as many as 20 per cent Irish-born residents, and another 16 per cent, while at the other extreme, one patch had only 1.3 per cent. It was because of this variability that I felt it best to compute all quantities both with, and without, the Irish included. Many Irish-born couples had English-born children, who must nevertheless have lived in a home where the accent was Irish or maybe the language Gaelic. If all the children of these families are included in the calculation, a few districts in Sheffield had as many as 25 per cent Irish residents. There were eleven or twelve Irish born people for every Scot, but eighty-six Irish for every Welsh born man or woman. As discussed more fully in Chapter 8, the Welsh very seldom made their way to Sheffield in the nineteenth century.

Whereas the Scots were mostly town people from Edinburgh, Glasgow or another sizeable place, the Irish were apparently mostly from the distant parts of that island, especially the counties of Galway, Roscommon, Sligo and Mayo (Figure 6.10). I say apparently, because when it came to the Irish, the enumerators had a tendency to avoid detail, and just write 'Ireland'. My comments are thus based on those persons whose origins were more precisely stated. Some enumerators were much less rigorous than others, so the quality of the data varied somewhat from piece number to piece number. Fortunately, there were some hundreds of entries of Irish people available with the full data of origin given. In addition, the geographical name spectrum of Ireland can be used to confirm regional (in this case Connaught) origin in Ireland. The selection of names at Sheffield differs markedly from that in Gwent, for example, where the Irish people mostly arrived from Munster via Cork. A summary of R.E. Matheson's *Special Report on Irish Names* (published 1894) is given in Donal Begley's (1981) *Irish Genealogy: A Record Finder.*

Even today, the birth places of Sheffield's Irish incomers are not heavily urbanised. They were people from a remote rural economy. They not only formed local Irish zones in the town, but also tended to be segregated even among themselves. Most of the Galway people seem to have been in one area, the Roscommon people, more spread out. To judge from the birth places of their children, most western Irish had arrived from 1847 onwards, often in the 1850s. However, there were others who had come from Dublin or another town and these tended to have been in Sheffield longer, and to live in areas of better housing.

When Figure 6.10 is considered, the places and frequencies seem to funnel in towards Dublin, strongly suggesting that this was their main port of departure. (A minority did seem to have arrived via southern or northern ports, however.) Many of the Irish had Lancashire born children. The most usual route seems to have been (and here I speculate) perhaps a walk to Dublin, a boat to Liverpool, a temporary settlement in south Lancashire (usually Manchester), later a move east, perhaps on the Great Central Railway. So many of the Sheffield Irish children were Lancashire born, that

Figure 6.10 A map of the counties of Ireland showing the frequencies of Sheffield arrival. Figures represent numbers per thousand Irish incomers to Sheffield. Counties stippled are the principal donors of immigrants. Others with numbers given made a contribution above fifteen per thousand. It seems likely that those leaving from the province of Connaught walked to Dublin. A few persons appear to have left from Cork and from Belfast. Abbreviations: TIP'Y: Tipperary; WM: West Meath; LEIT'M: Leitrim; ROSC'N: Roscommon. The heavily bordered area is Dublin.

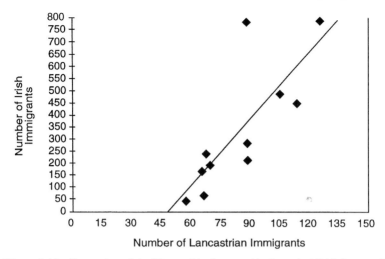

Figure 6.11 Regression plot of Lancashire born residents against Irish born residents for the eleven patches of the quadrant. Data were plotted and the line computed using *Sigmaplot*.

in studying the origins of the Sheffield people in English counties, it is necessary to estimate the number and employ it.

In Figure 6.11 you can see this being done by a regression plot (see above). Each batch of enumerators' subdistricts (piece number) had on average about fifty Lancashire born people who came independently of the Irish. Then for every eight Irish people there was one Lancashire born child. Allowing for the presence of Irish born parents, and for a few accompanying grandparents, the Irish incomers had very roughly one Lancashire born child for each four or five they brought from Ireland.

ENGLISH INCOMERS

It was noticeable that once the Irish were removed from the data sets, each group of subdistricts was rather like the others in population origin. Yorkshire disregarded, the leading source of English incomers in nine groups out of eleven was Derbyshire. Nottinghamshire was the other contender for first place (Lancashire being discounted). Lincolnshire was generally in third spot. The three counties together made up 10–13 per cent of the non-Irish population in the inner patches of the borough, but this incidence decreased as one moved outwards, especially to the north, where at the edge of the urban area, it was down to about 6–8 per cent. This might have been partly due to the greater distance of the north edge of the town from the counties to the south of the borough, though the distances involved are so small, that I am inclined to take the view that the English incomers, like the Irish, found the poorer, cheaper housing. Housing was newer, more spacious and presumably more expensive as one moved out towards the green fields and woods of the north. This view is supported by the data for natives of Shropshire, Staffordshire and Cheshire who were only at four-tenths of the density in the peripheral northern districts than they were in the central parts of the borough, and by similar results for the dispersion of Warwickshire and Leicestershire folk. When more data are available for other quadrants of the city, this matter can be explored further. It can be stated already, though, with regard to the west quadrant, and perhaps then for the whole borough, that regression plots indicate no pronounced correlations of arrivals from any one English county with any other. Undoubtedly, though, there were certain towns in each donating county, that were special sources of Sheffield people. For instance, in Staffordshire, Bloxwich, not a large place, was one from which a surprising number of people left for Sheffield.

It was very obvious, when all of the data were scanned, that many of the English and Scots migrants to Sheffield came from towns and cities rather than from the countryside. The Scots often came from Glasgow or Edinburgh, the midland English from Birmingham, Wolverhampton (or Bloxwich). The southern English came largely from London (especially Middlesex or Kent). When it came to Yorkshire, discounting the areas that were then rural, but which make up parts of present-day Sheffield, the migrant component of the 1861 population was very largely West Riding, with Leeds, Rotherham and Wakefield featuring among the places most often mentioned. To my surprise, of the 10 per cent of Yorkshire people who did come from more remote Yorkshire, only about one in twenty was from the North Riding and one in ten from the East Riding, mostly from Hull. This left more than eight out of ten to come from the West Riding, many from the towns just mentioned.

The fact that so many migrants to Sheffield came from other towns confirms a view of town growth and urbanisation discussed by Clark and Souden (1987) *Migration and Society in Early Modern England*. They point out there that migration to towns is not usually a matter of rural or village people getting up and going to a city. Rather, it is first a matter of them going to a place bigger than their current one. Then from there, they, or more likely their children, who perhaps held more relevant and saleable skills, and a willingness to learn, moved on to another, possibly bigger, town. From that place, further movement was likely to be to other towns or maybe to a city. Finally from a city, movement was often to another city.

By 1861 many places had already grown very large; city to city and big town to city movement was already commonplace. It is worth noting that if it took several generations for the descendants of an early-nineteenth-century rural family to become city people, during this time, national population was not static. Towns were increasing in size even as the country cousins arrived in them. But even in the nineteenth century, city to city movement was an ancient phenomenon. Whatever the era, once people have experience of life in a city, they are personally equipped to move from their present city to another. Even when most English people were still rural, in say 1500, there were, nevertheless, people moving from old cities, like Norwich, Salisbury or Coventry, to London.

THE GERMAN CONNECTION

In the west quadrant of Sheffield borough there were 101 people whose origin I have interpreted as German. Some of them gave their birth place as Germany, some as Prussia, a few as Württemberg and one as Hanover. Although some were single men, others were in families. From the stated birth places, it was apparent that there were a number of Anglo-German families in which English born men had German wives whom they had brought back to Sheffield. In some cases, evidence of a German connection in the grandparent's generation was noted. There were some men with English names, born in Germany as early as 1802. By 1861, the Sheffield connection with Germany was already of long standing. Indeed, some had come to Sheffield well before the huge emigration from Germany of the mid-nineteenth century: between 4 million and 5 million people left that country between 1841 and 1900.

The commonest trades among German men in Sheffield were pork butcher and watchmaker, though there were also cutlery dealers, spring knife manufacturers, tobacconists and some professional men, referred to as professors of language. Sheffield had, as revealed in the directories, as many as thirteen professors of languages in the mid-nineteenth century. To judge from their names, by no means all of them were likely to confine themselves to teaching German.

OTHER STRANGERS

In the part of Sheffield I examined, I found people from eighteen other countries besides those mentioned. They included well over fifty people born in the USA and some born in Canada. This confirms something not always realised: people in the nineteenth century moved to North America and back even at mid-century, with some facility. In some Sheffield families, it was abundantly clear that the parents, born near Sheffield, had been out to the USA. There they had travelled through various states, before finally returning to England.

The next commonest overseas nationality was Polish. In the nineteenth century that country was subject to domination by both Prussia and Russia. Some Poles fled this circumstance. One patch of Sheffield streets had nineteen Poles living near each other, and another eleven not far away. There were also in west and north Sheffield, a few Swiss, some Italians, Spaniards, Belgians, Greeks, French, West Indians, Moroccans and Arabs.

SOME GENERAL CONCLUSIONS

As I started this piece of work, I thought that studying only data from one decennial census might give rather specialised information, from which it would not be possible to generalise. However, while there are (naturally) features of the data in 1861 that belong particularly to that date, the study also reveals that much that was going on in 1861 had been in operation some time (two generations at least). An examination of later censuses and of directories confirms also that much continued afterwards. In the 1861 census, a great deal is being revealed about general and persistent aspects of town growth in the nineteenth century. The major English sources of migrants to the borough recorded in 1861 went on being major sources for many years afterwards. German immigrants too continued to come in the 1870s and 1880s; in fact the process endured so that Germans were still setting in train new pork butcheries as late as 1900. Yet some had come to England long before 1861. However, regarding German arrivals in Sheffield, I have no firm starting date.

The Irish had been arriving in the town since well before the famine of 1846–48, though the majority of those whom I recorded in 1861 were post-famine migrants. Regarding the arrival of English people from within a 50 mile radius, a directional selectivity seemed to be present. This was very like a directionality reported in the movement into Sheffield revealed by analysis of cutlery apprentices, recorded in the records of the Cutlers' Company starting in 1624. Such biases in the direction of apprentice movement presumably relate not only to the urge to self-betterment, but also to factors such as relative accessibility of the town. This in turn relates to landscape and means of transport. By 1861, much movement was related to places of equivalent business and perhaps the passage of goods and skills.

FOLLOWING UP ON THE 1861 CENSUS STUDY IN DOCUMENTS

Although I still look forward to being able to add more material to the present quadrant, and perhaps later to being able to compare the four quadrants of the borough, it was very tempting (and indeed proved very informative) to follow up the data already held, even though they do relate to only a quarter of the borough. I attempted follow up in several ways.

First, I took named individuals from my census extracts and searched for them in a series of directories extending in date from well before, to well after, 1861. The volumes that I made most use of were White's directories of Sheffield for 1833, 1841, 1858, 1862, 1871 and 1902, and Kelly's for 1934. Within them I looked for residents and for businesses. In addition to these, I had available, courtesy of an extramural group at the University of Sheffield, an index of the Sheffield census for 1841, and via the efforts of the Sheffield and District Family History Society, indices for the censuses of the borough in 1851 and 1871. There was also available the *Sheffield Who's Who*, published by the *Sheffield Telegraph* in 1905. This offered short biographies of about 500 prominent Edwardian citizens.

In some instances, individuals and especially individual tradespeople from the census were found in directories; for example, some like Louis Barnascone, the Swiss cutler, were followable for many years at various addresses in the town. Very few Swiss people came to Sheffield. He had come there many years before the 1861 census, and I was later able to find him on the 1841 census. In subsequent years his cutlery merchant's business was shown as having good premises in Waingate. Although I have traced no living descendants, Barnascone cutlery can still be found in use with its distinctive mark – 'Lewis Barnascone' and a large grasshopper. (I have some in my kitchen drawer.) His knives had remained on the market until well after stainless steel became the material of choice for table knives, subsequent to 1919.

Many tradespeople changed addresses every few years; even if they were in the quadrant in 1861, many proved to have been elsewhere in the town before or after that date. Quite a large number of persons appear in no directory and on no later census. This was particularly so of people from Germany or other countries. The 1861 census suggested that though some Germans established themselves as butchers, jewellers or watchmakers, many others were single young men, living in the poorer housing areas, who may have been in Sheffield for learning trades or establishing sales. Many of them may have returned home soon afterwards, while possibly others came and went between censuses, leaving behind no written record of their time in Sheffield.

A finding of some general importance that emerged when the census for 1841 and that for 1871 were examined for the same families and trades-people was that the general character of immigration was at least quali-tatively similar to that of 1861. Many sources of incomers were repeated; I suspected, but have not yet proved, that if I analysed the same quadrant for 1881 and 1891, I might obtain results still sharing some of the same charac-teristics. The German connection, for instance, continued after 1900. A consultation of the 1905 *Who's Who* reveals several people of German de-scent prominent in the life of Edwardian Sheffield. These included the then Lord Mayor, Alderman Sir Joseph Jonas, and many other men who had received their education in Germany. When I began a census follow up in the 1871 and 1881 books, the reservoirs of Sheffield population in Nottinghamshire, Lincolnshire, Warwickshire and Derbyshire were soon confirmed as continuing for these later decades of the century.

FOLLOWING UP ON THE 1861 CENSUS IN THE FIELD

To start this process I aimed to seek out people by verbal enquiry, who are current descendants of one or another category of nineteenth-century in-comer. I especially sought Sheffielders (or former Sheffielders) as follows: persons of German or Irish descent, descendants of mid-nineteenth-century arrivals from Lincolnshire, Nottinghamshire, Warwickshire and Stafford-shire. I asked also for anyone who was a grandchild or great-grandchild of immigrants from any Yorkshire town more than 30 miles away.

This verbal scanning could be done in several ways. These included ask-ing interested local groups such as Family History Society members, or at-tenders of evening classes at the Extramural Department of the university, or by contacting the elders of some city churches. It was also possible to make progress by telephoning people with certain names out of the current telephone directory, though that activity has to be pursued with circum-spection.

WHAT I OBTAINED FROM AMONG PRESENT DAY CITIZENS

A thing that struck me immediately as I attempted to locate current de-scendants of mid-nineteenth-century immigrants was how much change there has been in the city over the previous 100 years. I met not only many persons who had themselves arrived in the city, but also large numbers whose parents or grandparents had entered Sheffield in the Edwardian period or in late Victorian times.

There were also present Sheffielders with surnames which indicated that they may have been descended from families connected with the town and district since as early as the fourteenth century (see Chapter 7 on name-based tracing). Staniforth, Shirtcliffe, Creswick, Crookes and Burley were some of the regional surnames. To add to those there was a cluster of other names brought by very early arrivals from just west of the Pennines: Mottram, Hyde, Hollingworth, Duckinfield, Hadfield, Hattersley and Charlesworth. Finally, Sheffield also proved to have residents who claimed descent from eighteenth-century arrivals: for example, Thomas Gallimore, metal button maker, who married in Sheffield in 1737, had come from Wirksworth in Derbyshire, though originating in a Staffordshire family.

I recently met a person who was directly descended in the male line from a Joseph Cooper who was an excellent example of one of the categories of incomer that I had noted on the 1861 census. He arrived in Sheffield from Bloxwich near Cannock, Staffordshire, early in the 1860s. He had been apprenticed to a horse bit maker near Cannock, where he learned hand twisting of hot steel. In Sheffield, he was put to twisting augers and his family believed that the family works in Bath Street, Sheffield, in the 1920s, was the ultimate one twisting augers by hand. This is an excellent example of how a young man who had acquired saleable skills in one town could move to and prosper in another.

A second connection that I was able to make of the same sort was to a family called Duty or Douty, who are descendants of one who came from Warwickshire to work in metals. The males of the present day family (whom I have met) until their retirement worked also in metal at a Sheffield tube works. Their original immigrant ancestor arrived about 1850; latterly the family had collateral Irish relatives.

Unsurprisingly, when I turned in that direction, I found that Irish names were spread wide in twentieth-century Sheffield life. An analysis of the street directories for the 1930s indicated that the then new council house estates at the Manor and at Wybourn to the south of the city, contained up to about 5 per cent of residents with Irish names. Examples of names were Flannagan, Callaghan, Murphy, McQue, Molloy and Kerrigan, all of which appear on the 1861 census. To judge from interview information, many more people have some Irish ancestry. Of the hundreds of Irish names noted on the 1861 census, many (including most of those just cited) can still be found in the city telephone directories.

Although it is now not unusual to see Irish names on company letter-heads, they were slow to reach those positions. In the *Who's Who* of 1905, very few Irish names appear among the city's top 500 personages. However, by the first quarter of the twentieth century the Irish names were widely distributed through the districts of the city. Although one would now say that the nineteenth-century Irish arrivals are entirely assimilated into all aspects of city life, the process was a slow one. The city is not one of those generally referred to as having a large Irish presence – for more about this see the excellent *An Atlas of Irish History* by Ruth Dudley Edwards (1981) – for thousands of them, Sheffield did become home, albeit often a second destination one. They helped to leave a mark on the city in the form of a Roman Catholic cathedral, several churches, schools and certain public houses that today are known as 'Irish pubs', even though the courts of houses that were once home to their customers are fields of urban dust. In conversation, older Sheffield people may still mention the Sheffield Irish, and distinguish those of Dublin or other town origin, from those who in the 1850s came from the rural west. Like so many economic migrants before and since, these latter incomers were regarded with suspicion and sometimes hostility; it is significant that even now older citizens are as cautious about mentioning Irish ancestry as they are about saying that their family lived in a back-to-back house.

When attempting to follow up the nineteenth-century German Sheffielders, one of the first things I did was to contact the Sheffield German Lutheran Church, which has premises in West Street. However, this proved to be of relatively recent origin, its membership being principally derived from people arriving in England as a result of the Second World War. Although the church congregation had some connections with like communities in Manchester, Liverpool and Huddersfield, it had not achieved connection with descendants of nineteenth-century German migrants; nothing in the present church membership offered a sign of descent from earlier immigrants.

Despite this, in conversations and interviews I have come across several individuals who did have German ancestors, including some who insisted that their surnames had been revised in spelling, making them appear entirely English. Sometimes the adjustment was more a token; the brothers Carl and Louis Glauerdt illustrate this. They appear to have arrived in Sheffield from Aldenburg in Germany, about 1873, as cutlers. They had sufficient wealth to buy a good new house at Nether Edge. Carl took the name Charles. In Sheffield, they chose to spell their family surname without the *d*. At first, the brothers had a cutlery works in Cambridge Street, and then near Gibraltar Street. Later, they owned the Wallace Works in Furnival Street, and sold cutlery and edge tools marked 'Patriot'. All of Louis' children became English professional people, including one, Ludwig, who was on the teaching staff of the Applied Science Department of Sheffield's then new university. The First World War split the Glauert family. Charles had already gone back to Germany. The descendants of Louis became English professional people: teachers, lecturers and college fellows. Later their contribution was as technologists connected with bio-medical science, or aircraft engineering.

Some German families who had not become invisible by 1914 had a frightening period at the outbreak of war, in which their shops, homes and businesses were under danger of attack. The Germans had had the roles of friends and industrial collaborators (as well as competitors both for steel and cutlery). Even as Sheffield firms were gaining fame and wealth by their major contribution to the great arms race prior to the First World War, German connections remained in place. Their severance in 1914 was never made good. Since then the German connection has been almost entirely absent from Sheffield conversation.

WHAT NEXT?

It is very clear, even from the restricted study I have made, that the population history of the city is a large and complicated subject. It is a topic for a lifetime. Not only could the study on Sheffield be extended by completing the 1861 census, but also it could be built upon by working in detail longitudinally on later censuses, perhaps via electronic databases, detecting personal and family decennial linkage. There would be interesting topics to pursue on the back of such stacked up data. These might well include some of the questions posed at the start: how did the incomers and natives impact on each other? Did the mixing have effects on procreation? What are the local cultural consequences of a mixed Yorkshire, midland, Irish and German ancestry?

REFERENCES AND FURTHER READING

Begley, D.F. (1981) *Irish Genealogy: A Record Finder*. Dublin: Heraldic Artists [Reproduces R.E. Matheson's valuable Special Report of 1894 on Irish Surname frequencies as they were in the year of 1890].

Best, Geoffrey (1979) *Mid-Victorian Britain 1851–75*. London: Fontana [A data-rich account of living conditions].

Cannadine, D. (ed.) (1987) *Patricians, Power and Politics in Nineteenth Century Towns*. New York: St Martin's Press [Has chapters devoted to the Black Country, Bournemouth, Cardiff and Southport].

Clark, P. and Souden, D. (1987) *Migration and Society in Early Modern England*. London: Hutchinson.

Coleman, A. (1985) *Utopia on Trial: Vision and Reality in Planned*

Housing. London: Hilary Shipman [About the terrible fate of city initiatives in public housing after the Second World War].

Currier-Biggs, N. (1982) *Worldwide Family History*. London: Routledge & Kegan Paul [Interesting perspectives on the spreading of families across the world].

Drake, M. (ed.) (1982) *Population Studies from Parish Registers*. Matlock: Local Population Studies [Has lots of interesting methodological chapters on data handling in population studies including one on regression analysis].

Edwards, R.D. (1981) *An Atlas of Irish History*. 2nd edn, London and New York: Methuen [Has much interesting mapped information of early and modern Irish history].

Forshaw, J.H. and Abercrombie, P. (1944) *County of London Plan*. London: Macmillan [Fine example of a planning document. On such as this, house clearance and building, road layouts and other major initiatives were often based].

Holland, G.C. (1843) *Vital Statistics of Sheffield*. London: Robert Tyas [Local health and living conditions].

Laslett P. and Wall, R. (1972) *The Household and Family in Past Time*. London: Cambridge University Press.

Panayi, P. (1993) 'Germans in 19th-century Britain', *History Today 43*: 48–53 [Summarises aspects of German emigration and entry to Britain].

Pryce, W.T.R. (ed.) (1994) *From Family History to Community History*. Cambridge: Cambridge University Press and the Open University [Many articles about migration including some on movement into Britain].

Whiteman, A. (ed.) (1986) *The Compton Census of 1676*. Oxford: British Academy.

Wrigley, E.A. (1987) *People, Cities and Wealth*. Oxford: Basil Blackwell [Includes much on city populations and families].

Wrigley, E.A. and Schofield, R. (1981) *Population History of England 1541–1871*. Oxford: Basil Blackwell.

CHAPTER SEVEN

Labelled for Posterity

USING SURNAMES AS TRACERS OF FAMILY MOVEMENT

When I was about 14 years old, the class I was in at school in South Wales had in it a boy called Chard. I knew at that school another called Whatley and some more called Berrow, Dando and Hockey. I did not realise at the time, but these names had all been brought from Somerset in the previous sixty years, several of them being the names of places. The origin of one major segment of the recent Gwent population was on display.

Chapter 6 described some of the ways that census enumerators' books can reveal the building of town populations in the nineteenth century. Name patterns in the population too can be used to determine geographical origin, both for the period before the availability of the census books, and after, always provided certain aspects of naming in England are understood. Your town probably has a characteristic and fascinating selection of surnames, which says much about when and from where the present people were collected. This chapter is about searching for the origins of the present population, by name. The strategy is to discover name sets that start with the earliest (possibly fourteenth century), or failing that later, then go stepwise through the centuries to meet the present. This chapter tries to show how, by working in layers, one can detect first the early name set, then discriminate it from the incomers of the next 300 years, up to the data strong point of Carolinian times, and subsequently isolate the migrants of the industrial period and of recent time.

WHAT ARE NAMES FOR? THEIR IMPORTANCE IN SOCIETIES

Names are not just there as decoration. There are good practical and operational reasons for people having names. Communication between people is very difficult without using names, and so is the recording of business between people. In fact, the longer that communities and nations grow, the more refined their workings become and the more the demand for naming increases. As each individual's concerns move into larger and larger arenas, there is a growing need for distinctive naming. It must be effective and efficient; in a large community, as far as possible, each person has to be unambiguously identifiable. It became clear in Chapter 5 that one sometimes needs quite a lot of information to avoid confusing the records of two or more people.

The available 'given' names (forenames or sometimes 'Christian' names) such as Gareth, Marie, Mahmoud or Candy, are insufficient by themselves to unambiguously identify every person. Generally it is necessary to add further information: John son of James (or of Mary) are versions which make identification much more precise. Adding a grandparent's name would focus things even more. However, most nations have found it most efficient not to use this patronymic or matronymic method but to adopt a binary form of naming, in which one segment states the family (or other grouping) and the other is a specific given name. Extra specificity can be added by using a second given name or a nickname.

The use of binary naming is convenient as it allows the retrospective genealogical tracing of individual origins and the collateral mapping of relationships because the family name is hereditary. More important for our purpose here, the adoption of family names (surnames) permits the tracing of personal movement and of personal origin and thus population geographical origin, always provided that the way surnames arise, survive and die is well understood.

RESEARCH ON NAMES

In the light of both the intrinsic interest of names and of these possible research uses, it is not surprising to learn that the hereditary names of the English have been the subject of a great deal of research. Many names have been traced to their philological origins with the aid of early documents, and run to earth in earlier forms of the English language.

The results of research on names and naming has taken several forms. On the one hand there is literature about the mechanisms by which different names arose, for example P.H. Reaney (1967) *The Origin of English Surnames* and R.A. McKinley (1990) *A History of British Surnames*. On the other, there are dictionaries explaining the meanings or origins of individual names, for example P.H. Reaney and R.M. Wilson (1991) *A Dictionary of English Surnames*, and on a broader front, P. Hanks and F. Hodges (1988) *Dictionary of Surnames*.

Readers are referred to these various works for general accounts of the subject of surnames, and detail on individual names that interest them. This chapter and Chapter 8 are not about names as a subject in themselves, but rather about ways of using them as tracers of family movement. They are valuable in the study of all documented periods, but especially for those times before the census enumerators' books, and in a more complicated way during the past hundred years. Studies of the latter have to build upon established detail and understanding of the situation at earlier dates, which is where the discussion has to start.

TYPES OF HEREDITARY NAMES IN ENGLAND

It is useful to note that English surnames can be split into several categories: first, those which are personal descriptions, second, those which are occupations (and which may be regional terms for the same), third, those which are derived from personal names, fourth, those which derive from nicknames, fifth, some which are topographic in character (i.e. to do with landform), and finally, those which are the name of an actual place (a 'locus'), and which are called locative names.

THE CREATION OF AN ENGLISH GEOGRAPHICAL NAME PATTERN

The whole period over which hereditary names were adopted in England was a long one, exceeding 250 years. The great bulk of names was formed in the period 1250 to 1500, the dates of adoption varying from region to region of England. Out in society, it varied depending on social class. The landed families were naturally first to gain names to hand to their children – who were going to inherit. Perhaps the last to take hereditary names were small tenants and the serfs of northern England, some possibly becoming fixed even after 1500. Many of the last surnames to form were directly from given names.

Many of the locative names were established at the beginning of the name-forming period, before 1300. Many were of farms or hamlets, owners or major tenants taking the name of their own home. Although these can occur in parallel in two places, many are entirely descended from a single small locality. For this reason, various districts or counties can have their own unique selection of locative surnames. However, for reasons that are not entirely clear, locatives did arise more frequently in some parts of England than in others.

In addition to English locations, the names of Norman ones were imported to England through the many years of Norman arrival. In some landed families, these were hereditary before 1086, the date of the Domesday survey.

OTHER REGIONAL SURNAMES

Topographic surnames are not as geographically explicit as the locative names, but nevertheless they often had (and still have), regional characteristics. Some of these can be attributed to regional differences in the landform or in the descriptive words for landform, in different parts of the country. Thus Coombes is a name prevalent in the West Country, while Downes is commoner further north; Downer is concentrated in southern England. While many other occupational names are hardly regional, certain trade names were also of a provincial character, with different dialect trade words featuring in different regions. These are sometimes fairly obscure. The best known example of a set of regional trade names is the set for persons who cleansed and thickened cloth: Tucker (south-west), Walker (north) and Fuller (south).

Finally, many given names could be very widespread, as indeed could commoner nicknames. However, the particular style by which these became surnames was not necessarily the same everywhere, there being provincial versions of spellings and endings.

EVOLUTION OF THE NAME PATTERN

Spare though the last few paragraphs are, they are perhaps enough to make clear that a county or province would be likely to have gained by 1500 its own characteristic name set. This would have contained unique local names and also unique balances of names – characteristic mixtures, spellings and even absences – the starting material from which the modern set eventually grew. Several volumes devoted to detailed study of the surnames of certain counties have been prepared in the *English Surname Series*. Volumes available include accounts of names in Oxfordshire (McKinley 1977), Lancashire, Sussex, Suffolk and the West Riding of Yorkshire. These make interesting reading and show just how much character each county had and still has with regard to names.

The evolution of the modern name set was due to a great variety of factors. First of all, the survival of the rarer names was very chancy, since the original name holders might have been few in number, or perhaps have been single individuals. The success of the earliest marriages must have been crucial in deciding if a name would still be extant several hundred years hence. However, some of the rare names not merely survived, but prospered. Others died out. Of the surviving names, some spread geographically much more widely than others.

Many names have changed, differentiated into several distinct spellings, sometimes related to local pronunciation, sometimes via the way they were written in registers. Variants of spelling are frequently regional and different spellings may show proliferation to varying degrees. Even one letter can be a very significant difference. For example, the names Crook, Crooke or Crookes are common in England. Though spelt variously in the past, this topographic name, is now mostly spelt without an *e* or an *s* in Lancashire, where there are many hundreds of people named Crook, and with an *e* and an *s* in South Yorkshire whose surname derives from the village of that name. However, in the past the Lancastrians rarely used an *s*, though they sometimes used a final *e*. Sheffield people were loyal to their *s* through thick and thin even from before the year 1300. Small differences of spelling can be characteristic and of long standing, many withstanding the general stabilisation and tidying of spelling due to civil registration and by the Ordnance Survey.

SURVIVAL OF A GEOGRAPHICAL NAME PATTERN

Over the past few hundred years, several processes have contributed to a blurring of the original geographical name pattern. Rationalisation of name spelling has already been mentioned. Population growth and the migration of people into towns must also have had a marked though different effect. National emigration and immigration too have also occurred on a large scale, and must have contributed to change. Considering this list, it comes almost as a surprise to find that a selection of current national street directories, telephone directories and electoral rolls does confirm the survival of a national geographic surname pattern. The name spectrum of each city and each county still has a distinctive balance. No place is free of many names which also occur elsewhere, but all regions do have their own local names which are more plentiful there than elsewhere. Plotting the dispersion of some individual names on a national map leaves one in no doubt that a pronounced national pattern persists.

The many surviving early nominal lists, especially those from the fourteenth and seventeenth centuries, and the early parish records do allow us to build some parts of a picture of the early name dispersion for the majority of counties. We can confirm that the concentrations we see in the 1990s

189

do indeed relate to the early concentrations for these places. They are grown from the early lists which have been added to and embellished by immigration from self-selected regions.

WHY HAS SO MUCH OF THE ANCIENT PATTERN SURVIVED?

National emigration, while it has removed large numbers of people from England, has not changed the geographical pattern of those families that remained behind. People after all rarely decided on emigration just because of the spelling of their name or according to what category of surname they had. Thus, although losses were not evenly spread across the country (the south-western counties for instance, experienced a long drawn out series of departures), this process did not necessarily much disturb the geographic dispersion of the names among remaining English people. And immigration to England from abroad has simply acted to add some extra variety to the existing British name stock, though the amount of variety added is actually less than one might suppose due to the anglicisation of continental names after arrival (see for example Chapter 6).

Neither migration to other countries nor movement into towns much affect the spectrum of names left on the ground in the rural parishes, though some rare names can get entirely relocated into a town environment. For instance, nineteenth-century Birmingham grew by taking people from a belt of country across the middle of England; from Norfolk and Lincolnshire to Shropshire, Flintshire and Denbighshire. It created a mixture of folk and names in the greater Birmingham conurbation, but the patterns of names remaining in Shropshire and those other central English counties were not much changed by the process, though certain names were stripped out. By such means, many towns acquired inhabitants whose names reflected the name spectrum of nearby country settlements and smaller towns, as much movement to town was to the *nearest* town. The growth of towns may even be said to have acted to conserve the regional name pattern, by providing local 'sinks' to entrap the people who might otherwise have taken their names further afield.

THE LOSS OF SURNAMES

These days we are not generating new English surnames at a significant rate, yet we are losing them. Rare surnames or surname variants have been weeded out in considerable numbers over the whole of the past 600 years. A scan of some early tax lists will readily confirm this. Mostly this has occurred by chance. When the available pool of name bearers was small, two successive generations composed mostly of daughters, a few deaths from fever or tuberculosis, and the name could be extinct.

Other surnames have been lost because they were borne only by women in the first place. Some others were abandoned because they were too hard to spell or to write, or because later owners found them embarrassing to bear. Many of the people originally called Bollok now write it Bullock, and the Broadarses and Crookbacks generally go by blander substitutes.

Name loss even in quite modern times can be confirmed quite easily. For instance, recorded in nineteenth-century Sheffield, there were some dozens of people that went by the surname Blonk. Perhaps it was a variant of Blank or Blanc. At any rate, there is still a Sheffield street named Blonk Street, and there was formerly a Blonk Works and a Blonk Island in the River Don. Yet today, it is hard to find any locally resident Blonks. Even worse, there is hardly a Blonk to be found in all England (though I do know one in the Netherlands). You might say that we have drawn a complete Blonk! If they are not actually extinct, then the Blonks certainly appear to be an endangered species at least. The total English name stock is still changing, even if slowly.

RESEARCH USING LOCAL HEREDITARY NAME PROFILES

One of the great strengths of the census enumerators' books is that from 1851, birth places are given and hence nation-wide population movement can be studied. Indeed the census material has been extensively used to obtain data including movement data for governmental use. In the presence of such direct information like that used in Chapter 6, there is no need to recommend indirect methods such as those based on surname patterns to probe personal movement during the period 1841–91.

The years of birth of named individuals can be closely inferred from the census, thus it is possible to use those returns to relate surname patterns to place and date. Of course, in the cases of bearers of locative names from places other than the one described by the census book concerned, the movement implied by the name could have taken place at any time from just before the birth year, to five hundred years previously, since many English locative surnames were established before 1360. However, the census enumerators' books are a valuable resource for name-based research. They are a landmark to rank with the fourteenth-century tax lists on the one hand, and with the Hearth Tax returns on the other.

PROFILING A LOCAL POPULATION BY MEANS OF SURNAME ANALYSIS

In order to analyse a local population name-wise and gain insight into both the past and the present time, the first practical step is to identify the early local name set. You will need appropriate early documents, so the questions you have to answer are, first, 'What sorts of documents am I looking for?' and second, 'Do they survive for my town or county?'

You are looking for nominal lists from before 1500. The first sources to ask for are the Lay Subsidy Rolls of the period around 1330, and the Poll Tax assessments of the period around 1380. You should enquire about the availability of these at the county record office. You may be referred by the archivist there to the PRO, Kew.

Third, if any appropriate lists do survive, the next important question is 'Have they been transcribed into modern script, or even better, have they been published?'

The CRO is almost certain to know if any have been published. Published material, especially if it is also indexed, makes many things feasible that would otherwise be hard work and expensive of time. Note that the published versions are secondary sources (see Chapter 4), which could contain omissions and transcription errors. If you wish, or need to work from an original document, consider purchasing a photocopy, microfilm or microfiche copy so that you can ponder it in out-of-office hours. However, many of the county record societies have published at least some of their county's early tax rolls.

Finally, if none of these lists survive, ask the following subsidiary questions:

- Are there any (even brief) lists of local names of any other kind for the period before 1400?
- Do any Lay Subsidy Rolls exist for the period 1500–1600?
- If the answers are 'yes', again ask if they have been published.
- Do any Elizabethan Easter Books exist?

On the early nominal lists that you manage to collect, you will need to try to interpret each one of the surnames. First, you will want to detect and find the locus of the locative names. On fourteenth-century lists, the names may not all have lost their initial *le* or *de*. To help in your interpretations of locatives, you will need a good gazetteer, some detailed modern local maps, certainly some old maps, maybe some eighteenth-century ones, if there are any, and a local telephone directory. The *de (or del)* indicates a location; the *le* indicates an occupation. Other books you may find useful here are the *Domesday Gazeteer* (edited by H.C. Darby and G.R. Versey 1975), an atlas and index of ancient parishes and various name dictionaries. When you have identified the locatives, you will want also to amass (eventually) the local occupational names and regional topographic names, and add to them any other name which is particular to the locality. The result will be your first attempt at the early local name set. It is recommended that this is put up as a database using appropriate software (see Chapter 4) and perhaps also as a text file; this will allow it to be sorted and compared to later lists.

As well as obtaining a list of the locative surnames of your own region, it will also be necessary to get to know those of adjacent districts. This might mean going into nearby counties, or at least adjacent hundreds. Undoubtedly, you will find even on some early tax rolls, a short list of candidates for incomer status. The local locative names not only will be associated with places familiar as towns or parishes on the modern map, but also are often the names of small settlements or of single farms. This will be especially so in the counties of northern England.

Where both Lay Subsidy Rolls (e.g. 1327, 1332) and Poll Tax lists (*c.* 1380) survive for the same district, the name sets on the two lists can be compared. Both database and word processing software (see Chapter 4) can be used to compare lists. This can usefully be done twice, once by working with the original spellings and a second time by working with what you take to be the equivalent modern spellings. *Soundex* type software (see Chapter 4) can be used to link ancient and modern spellings. It will for instance offer modern spellings as appropriate to ancient names.

When comparison between 1327–32 and 1379–81 is possible, it yields some information about very early family movement. People were moving, even as they took permanent names. Reaney (1967) illustrates an excellent and interesting study from these types of sources in which he has demonstrated that many of the residents of later fourteenth-century London were either immigrants or the progeny of immigrants from East Anglia. Most other Londoners of that time were from the home counties or the East Midlands. Many of them were town dwellers before they ever arrived in London. They had moved from town to town, rather than from country to town, something noted and commented upon for a later date in Chapter 6.

In a study of a similar type, Richard McKinley (1990) reports on the nature of movement within the very large Lancashire parish of Rochdale. There, by 1379, 42 per cent of locative name-bearers were still living within the parish that contained the locus of their hereditary name. Furthermore, 90 per cent *in toto* lived within 10 miles of the original locus. Studies in progress on the Poll Tax lists for South Yorkshire (where 19,000 names survive) indicate that, in general, distances moved were similar to those in McKinley's account. There is, however, also a suggestion of asymmetry in the axes of movement into the Sheffield region, which persisted (see Chapter 6).

MORE NOTES ABOUT LOCATIVE NAMES

Studies of sets of local early names do show quite a lot of surnames which seem to be locatives whose loci have been somehow lost. The places concerned may have acquired new names, or they may simply have been abandoned as settlements many years ago. From our point of view, provided we can demonstrate where the loci were, these names are as useful as movement tracers as are any other of the locatives. But of course you do have to prove they are local. You may have to ask if the archivist at your county record office can recommend any very early documents that refer to settlements and place names. Sometimes it emerges that the locus still exists as a settlement under another name.

Some locative hereditary names that are currently present in England and Wales have geographical loci that are not in Britain, but in Normandy or another part of northern France. Examples are Devereux (de Evereux), Cambray and Kembrey (Cambrai), Grenville (Grainville) and, more obscurely, Westney or Wastnedge (from Gastinois). Some of these names will be mentioned again below; they are now unevenly spread across England. Being often the names of landowning families, they got moved about as the family changed abode or acquired new estates. Some Norman locatives have been principally associated with particular English locations, though some had several locations before 1400.

Norman arrivals continued for many years after the conquest, and new names were arriving all the time. Much later, in the sixteenth century when iron furnace skills were in demand, more people arrived from the European continent; this time the names they acquired indicated their broader area of origin: Marten Braband (1540), John Perygo (1524), John Veurne and Blasse Bryda (1560) are all persons listed on Sussex Lay Subsidy Rolls.

LATER POPULATIONS: LANDMARK SIXTEENTH- AND SEVENTEENTH-CENTURY NAME LISTS

After the years of the fourteenth-century tax lists, there were few suitable nominal lists compiled until after 1600. There were occasional lists, such as Elizabethan Easter Books and certain muster rolls. Cornwall, Devon, Somerset and Dorset, for instance, have fine sets of muster rolls principally for 1569. These have all been edited and published in the late 1970s in tiny editions by T.L. Stoate and another (Stoate 1978; Stoate and Howard 1977: consult the PRO or a CRO). Many other unpublished (and a few published) muster rolls are referred to in the compilation prepared for the Federation of Family History Societies (FFHS) by J. Gibson and A. Dell (1991). There are rare lists of a few other types available too. It is important to understand that they are of no use for our purpose unless they are likely to be well representative of the local population at that time; you will have to assess this yourself. Specialised trade or membership lists are unlikely to meet the criterion. In counties where fourteenth-century lists are rare or entirely lacking the muster rolls, some of which are from as early as 1539, may prove useful. However, gazeteers and maps will be very necessary during their use, since by that date much family movement had already occurred.

SEVENTEENTH-CENTURY LISTS

The first seventeenth-century lists of general use for obtaining name lists are the surviving Protestation Returns of 1642, which are held at the House of Lords Library. These can be useful, but they are not by any means comprehensive in coverage. Unfortunately the survival too is rather patchy, even within counties. Also available, mostly in the original, are certain lists of the 'Free and Voluntary Present' of 1661–2. These county lists sometimes have as many as 15,000 names, though usually the number there is many fewer.

Probably the firmest anchor point after fourteenth-century lists are the Carolinian Hearth Tax Assessments (usually 1662, 1663, 1664, 1670, 1672 and 1674). They are tax lists of wide cover and fairly generally available. Many of these have now been published, including those for Nottinghamshire (1664: 1674), Bedfordshire (1671), Derbyshire (1662–70), Dorset (1664), parts of Lancashire, South Yorkshire (1672), Oxfordshire (1665), Hampshire (1665) and Suffolk (1674). Others can be found on microfilm in county record offices.

By 1674, about 300 more years had elapsed since the Poll Tax. Name lists thus show the accumulated movement of about ten more generations on top of that which had elapsed between 1330 and 1380. It is not uncommon to find on the Hearth Tax Assessments persons whose names indicate that they are some tens of miles from their locus of origin. Movement between counties is commonly seen, though those who relocated large distances are generally still a small minority of the total population. For instance, the Nottingham Hearth Tax includes a few Welshmen, the Derbyshire list includes many men bearing Cheshire names, and movement into the West Riding of Yorkshire brought many holders of Derbyshire names. Occasionally, in the south of Yorkshire, some surnames from as far away as the Yorkshire Dales are notable.

OTHER NAME LISTS

For the eighteenth century the lists most likely to serve will be Muster Rolls. The booklet prepared by the FFHS gives information on availability of these lists in various repositories. However, there is no guarantee that such a list will exist, for a given place, that will fill the gap between the Hearth Tax and the early census books. After the series of census books, the post-1918 electoral rolls provide the next comprehensive list where personal names are attached to identified districts (see Chapters 4 and 5).

PARISH RECORDS FOR NAME STUDY

It is bound to occur to family historians that their stock resource, the parish register, might be exploitable as a source for local names. In fact for the period prior to 1650, for some areas of the country, the only records that are near to being comprehensive in coverage are the parish records of baptism, marriage and burial. Approximately 8–9 per cent of pre-1841 English parishes have records of vital events commencing in 1540 or before; a further 25 per cent of parishes have records commencing in the period 1541 to 1570. There is thus at least a one in three chance that a given English parish will have a substantial body of entries relating to the sixteenth century, although some parish records do begin distinctly later than the year 1600. In cases where no local Lay Subsidy Roll survives, the parish records from the 1540s may be the earliest name sources available. So are they useful for name analysis?

It must be said right away that they are far from being ideal sources. First, obtaining a sufficient sample involves taking baptismal entries for a block of years; this may be as long as a generation. One is then putting together many persons who were not all living at the same time. Second, a view of the burial register for the same parish often reveals a rather different selection of names, demonstrating the instability of the situation. Neither compilation is a list of residents. Finally, the raw surname list quantitatively distorts the surname situation, since one name may have many baptisms in the time period collected, while others have few or none. The names collected must therefore have attached baptismal numbers. Almost certainly, a cluster of parishes makes a better sample than a single parish. Even then, a consolidated list must be used with great circumspection. Chapter 8 illustrates one successful use of those sorts of data in eighteenth- and nineteenth-century work. In that instance, the census enumerators' books could be used as a parallel resource for part of the study.

TRACING INCOMERS

Previous sections in this chapter are about detecting and building the spectra of local names that exist at places at particular dates. The foregoing has been written with the tracing of personal movement in mind. Of course, there will be alien names on your patch, at almost all dates, including the earliest. You will want not only to recognise aliens, but also to find out whence they came. So how *do* you find out where they are from? The following is a tactic to be employed even for names taken from the earliest rolls. It is all about maps and numbers. Do you enjoy reading the telephone directory? Can you steel yourself to scan a set of them? If so you can try something for yourself.

First, decide which name you are studying. If it is from an ancient list make sure you are clear on what may be the modern form or forms of it. Second, locate a complete set of the telephone directories for England and Wales (there is probably a set in the local reference library). In these volumes count the numbers of *private subscribers* of the surname you chose (in each of its forms) in every book, and record the results separately. Third, find a map of telephone districts of England and Wales to trace or photocopy; there will be one at the back of the phone books. Plot upon it the numbers that you obtained. (For this work, telephone books issued from some years ago are more useful than current ones, since in those, the areas represented by each individual book overlaps less with its neighbours than is the case in recent book series.)

I have tried studying a panel of surnames. The directory series I had to hand was that for 1989. The first surname I studied was Creswick, and the results are shown in Figure 7.1. Creswick was a small settlement in Ecclesfield parish (West Riding of Yorkshire), the chief house being still occupied by the Creswick family as late as 1670. The original settlement is now swallowed up by housing estates in the eastern reaches of Sheffield. Currently, the Sheffield telephone directory has the greatest number of Creswick subscribers. This is followed in number by the Chesterfield book (an adjacent district). Most of the remaining Creswick entries are in the Derby or Leeds books. Well over half of the English and Welsh total is within a patch of England taking in Derby, Sheffield and Leeds.

A second example is provided by Bagshaw, a far more numerous name, which is a locative name derived from a settlement in north-west Derbyshire. In this case, the greatest numbers of subscribers are in the several directories covering Staffordshire, Yorkshire, south Lancashire and especially Derbyshire.

A third I tried was Pemberton, a Lancashire name, which also exhibited a well-clustered distribution, with its Lancashire locus included.

Figure 7.1 A telephone directory map of England and Wales showing the numbers of Creswick subscriber entries in each district.

The examples I give were really chosen as experiments. All three were names whose original locus was already known to me. The results confirm that some names, at least, still concentrate to a significant extent near their origins. It follows from this that *in the twentieth century any name which is highly localised either originated close by, or arrived at that locality early in the period of hereditary name use.* This sort of work is much facilitiated by access to the British Telecom National Directory CD-ROM. The results must then be plotted on a map of post-code districts.

EXPLOITING NAME CLUSTERING TO STUDY MOVEMENT

The result of the telephone search can be verified by moving back in time, and studying the early birth registration indices at St Catherine's House. The data for 1837 to 1851 are best (after this the registration district boundaries were changed). The data from the registry are plotted on a map of registration districts. If the telephone book result is really the remains of an ancient distribution, the registry results will almost certainly sharpen it. You should also be able to further confirm the national site of high name density by reference to county or city directories that should have a concentration of the name in question.

A NOTE ON WHAT MAKES A NAME CLUSTER

Really here we are in the business of detecting clusters. Studies of population movement using name data from national or regional lists depend much on deciding what makes a cluster. The experiments related above show that generally a cluster is likely to mean an ancient origin in the vicinity. But what qualifies to be taken as a cluster?

There are several ways of looking at this problem. One would be to take the supposed focus of the name and draw a circle around it. This could be chosen to contain, say, 50 per cent of the total name holders. If the circle proved to be smaller than some chosen radius (say 25, 50 or 100 miles), the name could be said (in our view) to be clustered in that region.

This approach has several practical drawbacks. One is that the focus of the name is not really being established, so it will not be clear where to centre the circle. Another is that the national population dispersion is in fact very uneven, making circles an inappropriate shape.

A better practical approach is to work in terms of the percentages of the national subscriber total per individual telephone book, or per patch of books. Now, if there are eighty books in the total test area, and assuming a constant average subscriber number per book, if 50 per cent of the national total of the name are in one book, then the other 50 per cent must be in the remaining seventy-nine. The relative density in the 'active' book is thus 50/1 as opposed to 50/79 in the rest of the books, i.e. 50 versus 0.63, which equals 79. (Here density = number of people with the chosen name per total head of population.) Seventy-nine is a very high ratio, but how high qualifies to be significant in our view?

Proceeding with the argument, 50 per cent of the national total in a patch of five directories would give a density ratio figure of fifteen instead of seventy-nine. This is still really a high ratio. If the patch is extended to fifteen directories, however, the ratio falls to less than three. Most of us would, I think, accept that fifteen is a ratio to take note of, whereas three is not. We accept fifteen as indicating a cluster, but three as being not convincing. In fact, three is far less convincing. Ratios of this sort can be simply worked out for any desired percentage of the national subscriber total, and for any directory patch size. I have done this for directory patches of one right up to twenty. The data indicate that a density ratio below five can be regarded as insignificant.

On this basis, 10 per cent of the national name total would have to occur within a single directory for significant clustering to be accepted. For 20 per cent of the national total, this may extend as far as a patch of up to three directories. For 30 per cent it is up to five directories. It is true that subscriber numbers do vary from directory to directory, but this will almost always not matter. In awkward cases, actual subscriber book totals rather than averages can be used for the calculations, though this is not generally necessary, despite the apparent crudity. Summarising, a cluster is defined as *>10 per cent of the total within one book; >20 per cent within three contiguous books; >30 per cent within a patch of five books.*

Finally, it is evidently possible for more than one part of the country to have a significant cluster for the same name at the same time. In such a case, follow-up studies must be used to determine if there is really more than one locus of origin. In instances where you find a supposed locus whose name appears several times in the gazeteer, it may be useful to examine your maps carefully for evidence of clusters involving all those regions containing the place name in question. Bear in mind that to define two clusters will require a bigger total of data than the defining of one.

TRYING TO FIND THE LOCUS OF A SUPPOSED ENGLISH LOCATIVE SURNAME

Sometimes, from the form and clustering of a name, it seems most probable that it is a locative surname that is or was in a certain district. Can the locus be identified on the ground? Of course it could be that the settlement that gave the name has long been lost. It is also possible that it is merely obscured. You may feel the need to search for it, since when it is identified you will be secure in the use of that name as a tracer. Here is an example of a real search for a locus.

The hereditary surname Yerbury (often pronounced *Yarbury*) became distinguished when it was borne by a successful family of West Country clothiers, who became established in broadcloth making in the first half of the sixteenth century. One later member of the family, Francis Yerbury, patented a particular style of broadcloth manufacture and with his subsequent wealth, built a very fine house at Bradford-on-Avon. Published pedigrees suggest that many (perhaps all?) of the bearers of the name, with its variants of spelling – Yarbury, Yearbury, Earbury and Erbury – descend from one Lawrence Yerberie of Batcombe, County Somerset, whose will was proved in 1516, and whose sons lived and prospered at Trowbridge in Wiltshire. Analysis of the birth registers at St Catherine's House shows that until the mid-nineteenth century the name was very concentrated in west Wiltshire and east Somerset, and from this fact, and from the form of the name (the suffix -*bury* means a fortified settlement) one might well suppose it to be a name of locative origin, with a locus in east Somerset or west Wilts. Where then is the place called Yerbury? It seems to be a little too far fetched to invoke the Yarburgh that is in Lincolnshire, though of course it *could* be the locus.

One suggestion I had for a site local to the concentration of the people bearing the Yerbury name was Yarnbury, an ancient fortified hilltop site in Wiltshire. This is a place where no one has lived for many years, but where sheep fairs were formerly held. Pursuing this suggestion via the surviving early taxation lists for Wiltshire proved disappointing, however. No Yerburys appeared in the early Wiltshire tax rolls. A second suggestion was Yarbury Combe, a site at Challacombe parish in east Devon. Again though, no surnames in early Devon lists supported this locus, and the locality hardly features at all in Devon land records such as the Feet of Fines. A search of early Gloucestershire and Dorset nominal lists (including muster rolls) was then made but no Yerburys could be sighted in those counties either. I was becoming convinced that it had to be a Somerset place.

I had already failed to find Yerbury in several gazeteers, so I made an exhaustive search of maps of the county of Somerset at various dates, and finally after some prompting, I did find in north-east Somerset a very small place lately called Yarborough, close by Banwell in Somerset. This tiny place is spelt Yarbury in some nineteenth-century records and from about 1990 has been known as 'Yarberry'. It is just a few miles from Butcombe and consists of only one eighteenth-century farm and an ancient long house, though when I visited the site, I was assured that there were stones from an even older house in a field at the back of the farm. This seemed altogether more plausible as the locus of the surname, it being within 10 miles of Frome where so many Yerburys had lived. The present owner of the farm insisted that the spelling 'Yarberry' had been recently adopted (and a sign duly erected), for certain strong botanical reasons.

Later, I searched the earliest accessible major tax roll for Somerset, the 1327 Lay Subsidy, which was printed in an edition of 1889. (Alas for an index!) A line by line search revealed two male taxpayers with the name Yerbury.

Researching another name: Gulledge

At first I thought that Gulledge was a topographic name. The word appears in ancient dictionaries as a term connected with old farm buildings. However, it seems from name dictionaries that this is a version of Golledge and Coolidge, renderings of a place name, Colwich, a small town in Staffordshire. Coolidge is well known as having been the name both of a US President and of a successful vocalist. The Golledge form is widespread in England, though not especially plentiful. Gulledge, the form spelt with a *u*, is far more uncommon. A recent telephone directory series shows significant numbers only in the Taunton, Avon and Mid-South Glamorgan books. Many if not all of these persons, plus those at Illinois, USA, seem from family tracing to be descendants of one Henry Gulledge of Martock, Somerset, who was married, widowed and remarried there in the 1740s. This variant of the Colwich name seems to have arisen from incomers to Bristol via Severn water traffic, some of whom are documented in early apprentice records, to come from Colwich and places in that general area. As far as late-eighteenth and nineteenth-century movement is concerned, the name Gulledge is, for practical purposes, an indicator of an origin in central Somerset. But where did Henry Gulledge of Martock come from?

Care is required in studies of names in the vicinity of large medieval centres of trade. (Bristol was, after all, at one time, a great port and England's second city.) Many people would have come large distances to such a city; from thence their names may have been spread about the adjacent country, and in Bristol's case, the Empire. In the process, the names brought to the city may have been metamorphosed.

OCCUPATIONAL NAMES: BOWERMAN, NEATE AND MELL

Many hereditary names other than English locatives have rather particular geographical distributions. This means that they may prove exploitable in movement studies. It is necessary however to study the individual names closely to find out if they are of use in this respect. Here are some findings on a few occupational names.

Bowerman is a name closely related to the much commoner Bower or Bowers, a bower being a wooden construction. The occupation appears to have been the looking after (or living near) the bower. An analysis of telephone subscribers reveals the rather surprising fact that the name Bowerman is generally thinly spread around England (on average about six subscribers per directory south of Birmingham, one or two only per directory north of that city). A few southern areas have marked clusters of the name. Oxford and Banbury have seventy-three Bowermans between them, and there is the fairly usual concentration in the south coast resorts. A further concentration is in the area containing Bristol and Taunton.

The concentration of a name in south coast resort towns is generally to be disregarded as a product of the wide gathering into those places. We are thus left with the suggestion that the name Bowerman is one which originated primarily in one or at most two localities in central southern England. The pattern is partly confirmed by a study of older Oxford street directories, which contain many Bowerman entries, and by the birth entries at St Catherine's House 1837–51. As a tracing name Bowerman is almost as good as a locative name. Its relative Bower (or Bowers), on the other hand, is not.

Neate is an old word meaning an ox or cow, so the surname means a herdsman or a tender of cattle. You might reasonably suppose that such a name would have arisen all over England, where cows were kept, since this appears to be the case with some other occupational names. However, Neate seems to have become a surname only in one locality in Wiltshire. It is thus, unexpectedly, rather useful as a marker.

Mell is one of a very few names that have been studied in great depth, it being the subject of an excellent small book by J.D. Porteous (1988) *The Mells*. While the meaning of the name is not wholly clear, there being several possible origins, perhaps the likeliest is 'meal' (i.e. ground cereal). Porteous' analyses began with the telephone directories and went on to parish registers. He paid particular attention to migration, concluding that the name had originally been strongly concentrated in the 'Humberhead' area and that the great majority of the Mells in Britain and abroad have spread from that marshy part of the country. It is not a locative name, nor even a name with a clear meaning, but it is a name associated with a particular district of England.

TENDENCIES OF MOVEMENT

An advantage of generating name sets for places and times is that one can extend the study of aliens by asking if they were part of any group or general movement. If you detect one incoming name from a distant county, it is natural to look to see if there are others from the same place. Remember, if you see several locative surnames from the same general region, locatives being only one part of the name pool, the ones you have noted are almost certainly accompanied by other less visible incomers with non-locative names. Only you can decide what number makes a significant trend in your study, but I begin to get interested when I have three incoming locatives from the same region.

THE SITUATION WITH REGARD TO CERTAIN VERY COMMON NAMES

Even very common names, if studied for the country as a whole, may give a pattern of occurrences containing valuable specific or general information, though they are not tracers for studying specific family movement. A friend studying the surname Gent discovered that it was wide in distribution, but that it had an especially high density around the Erewash valley in Nottinghamshire. However, even in the early days of civil registration (1837–50) it was already very well spread across England, and almost certainly originated at multiple sites. When he followed it through the nineteenth century using General Registry Office birth data, it was revealed as clustering increasingly in the towns. Evidently, such a widespread marker name can be used to some extent, as a means of tracing very general population movements.

The common patronymic name Bennett is another that gives revealing results from a telephone directory study. The current total of private telephone subscribers named Bennett exceeds 25,000 in England and Wales. They probably represent a national total of more than 100,000 Bennett inhabitants. When the regional subscriber totals are plotted on a map, one notices large totals in Liverpool, Birmingham and the Staffordshire towns, and in the south coast resort towns (which contain a rich medley of names, mostly twentieth-century arrivals). Indeed, no district is without its Bennett representatives. However, the most interesting finding is the way that the Bennett frequency, which is high in the west of the country, including Wales, falls off as one moves east. Devon, Cornwall and Somerset are especially rich in Bennett families; indeed, unlike other areas, they also have families called Bennetts and Bennetto. This all suggests that the personal name Beneit must have been richly popular in the west some 600 years ago.

THE EFFECTS OF EARLY MODERN TOWN AND CITY GROWTH

The mention of town growth brings me to an important point. National population growth and the aggregation of the population into towns had some very curious results. As well as conserving the local concentrations of some local locative names, it also conferred a local status on certain other names. Thus, Westney (Wastnage, etc.) is first documented in the Staffordshire Pipe Rolls (very ancient tax rolls) of 1165, and is listed also in the Pipe Rolls for Lincolnshire of 1191, while in 1249 it is cited among the ancient deeds of Leicestershire. Established at Headon in Nottinghamshire by 1330, it is reported there frequently until about 1690, in connection with land holding in the vicinity of Todwick, Yorkshire, a place about 7 miles south-east of Rotherham. The national telephone directory total for England and Wales is 183 subscribers, of which 42 per cent occur in the Sheffield directory. For tracing purposes from 1660 onwards, it is a Sheffield name. For fourteenth-century purposes, however, it is a Nottinghamshire name. If the city of Sheffield had not grown in the way that it did, when it did, this name may well have concentrated itself elsewhere.

Norman names of this type, that entered England at or not long after the Norman invasion, had the greatest of chances to spread and relocate. They were perhaps hereditary before other English names and, attached to members of the new aristocracy, had many opportunities to move with the acquisition of new land. Cambray, which is mentioned in Domesday in connection with land in Lincolnshire, Rutland and Leicestershire, was in Huntingdonshire in 1199, and by 1312 had reached the Shropshire/Radnor area. In the last 400 years, however, bearers of the Cambray name have appeared mostly in Gloucestershire and Oxfordshire, and most current Cambray telephone subscribers (who are not very numerous) are in the west of the country, within reasonable distances of Gloucester.

On the debit side, population accretion by towns has resulted in some areas being depopulated. If there was no strongly growing town in the vicinity of a name locus, the name could become much depleted in its area of origin, sometimes entirely cleaned out. Gravenor (a name quite distinct from Grosvenor) is a locative name derived from a small settlement in the Shropshire parish of Claverly. The late 1980s telephone directories show no Gravenors at all in either of the volumes covering the county of Shropshire. Only Gwent and Glamorgan, which amass eighteen between them, plus Liverpool with thirteen and Warrington with fourteen, have significant numbers today. Yet the records of the Shropshire parishes of Claverly, Clungunford and Stanton Lacy are rich in Gravenors in the eighteenth century. The rise of iron making in south-east Wales between 1740 and 1800 drew in families from other places. Shropshire was an old iron making centre and workers were drawn from there, perhaps carrying valuable technical experience. The Gravenor name appeared in Brecknockshire and at Abergavenny in the north of Monmouthshire in the 1740s; further families arrived there in the valley heads and at Monmouth town later in the century. The Gravenor surname, now rather uncommon, but widely dispersed, redistributed itself from Monmouthshire to Yorkshire, to the south of England, to Australasia and North America. It constitutes a useful Shropshire tracer only up to about 1770, though its true origin there is beyond any doubt. Interestingly, as late as 1945, two elderly Gravenor sisters kept a sweet shop in Morgan Street, Tredegar, Monmouthshire. They were able to tell their customers, even then, that 'our family originally came from Shropshire'.

STUDYING RECENT MOVEMENT

It will be clear by now that in the early days of surnaming, even though it was a minority of people who moved far, by the time the first parish registers were compiled (post-1538 or often post-1558), some families had already moved a long way. As studies are brought forward towards the present, it is increasingly necessary to take into account previous movement, something we planned to do relying on the Hearth Tax Assessments, muster rolls, and nineteenth-century name sets from the census enumerators' books. Over this very long period, secondary or even tertiary movement may have become significant. For example, the names Evans and Jones were among those introduced into Norton near Sheffield, when the Earl of Shrewsbury imported lead workers from Somerset, before 1600. These names had presumably entered his Somerset estates from Wales, sometime just previously. In the Norton references, Evans is often spelt 'Evance' giving some credence to the thought that a Welsh accent was still evident among the arrivals at Norton.

Despite the increasing complication posed by previous and stepwise migration, family movements between 1750 and 1950 can be studied by establishing the early name spectra in the supposed source locations. The total of names in all the sites will of course contain autochthonous ones (autochthonous: literally springing from that place), plus those accumulated by in-migration. The important thing is to obtain the spectra of names from each of the localities of interest at the relevant dates.

One is bound all through the process to be particularly interested in locative names even though they will comprise only part of the panel of names in the study. If you think you have spotted one or two locative names characteristic of locale A, now at locale B, then you should look for other names which would confirm the migration of families from A to B. Some of the commoner of the names at A would be expected to turn up at B, if any sizeable movement of people had occurred. Names that might be used in this way could be nicknames, occupational names or topographic names. In a city like Sheffield, having established the early name spectrum and that for the sixteenth century, one can distinguish fairly clearly in parish record and census the name pattern of early incomers from Cheshire and north Derbyshire such as Hattersley, Mottram, Hadfield, Charlesworth, Dukinfield and Hollingworth, from the much later arrivals from Lincolnshire such as the Mackinders, Tetneys, Brocklesbys and Bucknalls and particular journeying groups such as the Irish.

NAMES AND THE MATTER OF RECENT MOBILITY

In Chapter 6 I gave an account of some ways that census enumerators' books can be exploited to analyse the origins of the residents of a chosen place; for the period 1841 to 1891 these must always be a preferred source. They are especially useful since they permit analysis of the patterns within a town or city, comparing street with street, and district with district. For nineteenth-century studies on immigration and town growth, no other source competes in value with those books.

However, the hundred-year rule, applicable in England and Wales, leaves a small, uncomfortable (but intended) gap between the earliest memories of old people and the persons listed in the last census released to public use, and denies us, as yet, a study of the daughters and sons of the twentieth century. This is awkward because there was much movement and interesting industrial and civic activity in the period roughly between 1880 and 1914. This involved the building of larger industrial units than had been in place before, and attendant population movements and house building. Heavy industry was getting heavier. The large numbers of houses built lengthened the radii in many towns and cities causing them to spill into surrounding rural parishes. But oral evidence apart, how is it possible to study the origins of all these new people? We must not forget either the large-scale movement of people between 1920 and 1940, first related to the need of returning soldiers for jobs, and later associated with the demise of heavy industry. Oral research confirms that in many towns and cities a large proportion of residents is the product of movement inside the past hundred years (see also Chapter 6).

NAME SETS IN THE TWENTIETH CENTURY

As I pointed out in Chapter 3, an electoral roll is much inferior to the census book as a source of personal detail, because it gives no birth places, relationships, ages or professions. However, in making a name set we are not looking for personal detail. After 1918, electoral rolls were produced regularly at least annually, sometimes twice yearly until the present, excepting only for interruption by the Second World War (see Chapters 3 and 5). For name-based analyses of adult population movement these rolls give outstanding opportunity. They permit a comparison of 1920, 1930 and 1940 name patterns with those of the adult entries on the 1891 or 1881 census. Those in turn can be compared to earlier lists. The general availability of microcomputers for name sorting and list comparison greatly encourages this sort of data comparison by which early sets of names are serially subtracted from the recent name set. It was by using such means that I was able to confirm the source of the group of Somerset names that I mentioned at the start of this chapter.

REFERENCES AND FURTHER READING

Darby, H.C. and Versey, G.R. (1975) *Domesday Gazeteer*. London and New York: Cambridge University Press.

Dickinson, F.H. (ed.) (1989) *Kirby's Quest for Somerset: Exchequer Lay Subsidies 169/5*. London: Somerset Record Society.

Gibson, J. and Dell, A. (1991) *Tudor and Stuart Muster Rolls*. Plymouth: Federation of Family History Societies.

Hanks, P. and Hodges, F. (1988) *Dictionary of Surnames*. Oxford and New York: Oxford University Press.

McKinley, R.A. (1977) *English Surnames Series III The Surnames of Oxfordshire*. Leopards Head Press.

McKinley, R.A. (1990) *A History of British Surnames*. London: Longman.

Porteus, J.D. (1988) *The Mells*. Saternalia, BC: Saturna Island Thinktank Press.

Reaney, P.H. (1967) *The Origin of English Surnames*. New York: Routledge and Kegan Paul.

Reaney, P.H. and Wilson, R.M. (1991) *Dictionary of English Surnames*. London: Routledge.

Stoate, T.L. (1978) *Dorset Muster Roll, 1539, 1542, 1569*. Almonsbury: T.L. Stoate.

Stoate, T.L. and Howard, A.J. (1977) *Devon Muster Roll for 1569*. Almonsbury: T.L. Stoate.

CHAPTER EIGHT

Tracing the Welsh

MOVING OUTSIDE ENGLAND

Believing we have got some workable methods for studying family move-ment within England, it would be natural to hope that we could import the ideas, adapted as appropriate, into other parts of the British Isles. While the census-based methods of Chapter 6 must be applicable in Wales, Scotland and Ireland, it is important to ask how far name-based methods apply. In fact, the three Celtic lands are, in terms of personal records, quite distinct from each other. It not being possible to consider all three provinces, I have chosen Wales.

WHAT IS WALES?

For the purposes of this account, Wales is a geographical entity that in-cludes all that country defined in the new (1974) counties of Dyfed, Gwynedd, Powys, the Glamorgans, Gwent and Clwyd. These comprise the territory of all the counties established by Edward I, and also of those that came into existence by the Acts of Union of 1536 and 1542. The latter in-clude Monmouthshire, a county that for about 400 years was in an anom-alous situation with regard to the administering of English law. Some of the sixteenth-century county creations were made out of patches of Anglo-Norman Marcher and Royal Lordships. In the 1974 local government changes, some attempt was made not only to tidy and redefine the map, but also to reintroduce certain ancient names, replacing sixteenth-century shire names. Some of the shires such as Brecknock and Radnor were conjoined to make new counties. Glamorgan was split up. Gwent county was made almost exclusively out of Monmouthshire. This, like other counties new in the sixteenth century, had been originally created from various Anglo-Norman lands. Here they had covered the ancient Welsh kingdom of Gwent.

Most of the area of Wales thus defined, until perhaps 250 years ago, supported people who almost exclusively spoke the Welsh language. The language (now spoken by about 20 per cent of Welsh people) shows up clearly in place, church and field names, such Welsh names spreading even a little into Shropshire and Herefordshire. The Welsh language has very ancient roots and a rich literature, including histories, prose, poetry and genealogies.

The native Welsh people had had until 1292 their own system of law, including procedures for partible inheritance of land. Formerly too, they had their own Celtic Christian church. However, following the conquest by Edward I, the land, March or shire was subjected to a process of 'Normanisation'. Anglo-Norman style manors and lordships were created, often using the previous local Welsh boundaries. Although apparently absorbing many new words (English, or French via English), the Welsh language of that time largely survived this process, growing into the modern version of Welsh. In some ways it could be said that the Normans made a much less comprehensive job of subduing the Welsh, than they did of subduing the Saxons. Where the Saxon lordships, land tenure and culture were largely obliterated, in Wales the indigenous culture was dominated and modified. However, local Welsh princely activity did persist until near 1300. Especially where there was higher ground, there was a tendency for the Welsh to keep cultural influence within a lordship system, whereas on the better lowlands, things were more Normanised, and later more rapidly infiltrated by the English language. However, the influence of Welsh lords and princes persisted until after 1400. In Wales, the Normans were inclined to a degree to make alliances and marriages.

The territory of Wales before the Acts of Union was then a kind of rump end, a portion of incompletely absorbed but colonised southern Britain. (For an account of medieval Wales, see David Walker 1990.) It was only after the legal changes of the 1530s and 1540s that Wales become assimilated in the sense of taking up certain English ways, laws and styles of administration. The pre-1974 Welsh shires were imposed as 'English style' units, based upon groups of earlier Anglo-Norman lordships. To an extent therefore these rested on very ancient boundaries that had not been redrawn by any Angle or Saxon.

WHAT IS MEANT BY WELSHNESS?

The Welsh do not have a different passport from the English. They carry the same small reddish book, with the same Arms on the cover. Her Britannic Majesty's Secretary of State requests and requires for them the same rights of passage as for English citizens. Yet, when asked to state their nationality, many will say Welsh before they say British, and would not think of saying they were English, though sometimes compelled to endure the idea through the innocent tactlessness of foreigners! So what, in their own view, makes them Welsh?

They were perhaps born on that piece of territory ('the Principality') or were of parents who were born there. Maybe they claim a long genetic connection. Possibly they have a tie of language, music, liturgy, politics or romance. Whatever the foundation of their assertion, it is about 4:1 against them being bilingual Welsh language speakers. (There are almost no monoglot Welsh left.) Perhaps one still has to add that they are Welsh by conviction. However, it is necessary to tread with some care here. Welsh identity as a nation is a relatively recent thing, perhaps little more than a hundred years old. Before that concept was born, it was possible for people to be Welsh by residence, custom and language, yet to carry inside themselves little imagining of a Welsh nationhood. However, if one refers today to a person as Welsh, there is a nation recognised by others, for them to belong to.

In the light of all this, if I write in this chapter of the Welsh of some earlier time, say the year 1700, I evidently cannot be writing of a nation. I am writing really of the natives of the territory we have been defining. They were certainly not English, just as their forebears had not been Saxon. At a date like 1700, they were very probably Welsh language speakers. I use the word Welsh to mean a member of a culture, which has roots in a territory, a language and a society. But I do not necessarily use it to mean a member of a nation in the present-day sense.

MEETING AND MIXING

The grass-roots conjunction of the English with the Welsh over the past 250 years has been, above all, a meeting and mixing of two cultures. When any two cultures mix, the long-term results can be very complex. One may impress its laws on the other, or offer a dominating language. It may buy into the local landownership and positions of power. The other may respond with subtle changes, adjustments and rejections. In parts of Wales where the English entered in numbers, the Welsh did not become English. Rather,

Welshness adapted (and still adapts) linguistically and behaviourally. It continued and continues to exist, a contemporary thing, but always differently. To a degree incomers were and are 'Welshised'.

Following industrialisation (generally by English capital) the pattern of Welsh life was much changed. There was a gathering of people into towns, the creation of valley communities of heavy industry. These and the places in less industrial areas took up non-conformism on a major scale, the chapels latterly becoming the seed beds of political radicalism. Some political, cultural and religious dissent took the form of emigration. There has been a steady flow of Welsh into England, but also moves at some times to places in the Americas.

WHAT IS MEANT BY A WELSH NAME?

The history of Wales is thus a complicated story of old ways, of separation, annexation and persistent 'otherness'. Welsh people's names reflect their history. The Welsh had their own names, but with the Normans dominant, some Welshmen changed theirs, and many others gave their children biblical or non-traditional Norman names: Hugh, Robert, William, Roger, Beneit, Henry, Humphrey or Herbert, rather than the Welsh Hywel, Maredydd, Morgan, Rhys, Owain, Gwalchmai, Siencyn, Iowerth, Llewellyn, Leyson, Cadwalidwr, Gruffydd, Ieuan, Hopcyn, Dafydd and so on. Where Welsh given names remained in use, they evolved with passing of time, choice and usage reflecting changing fashion. There were adjustments in spelling and pronounciation of the traditional Welsh given names. Siencyn became Jenkin or Jankin, Rhys became Rees, Maredydd became Meredith, Hopcyn turned to Hopkin and Owain to Owen, Howell replaced Hywel. Perhaps these spelling changes reflect the presence of the evolving English language alongside the Welsh. Even the Normans' names became adjusted to Welsh language sounds. Not Roger, but Rosser, originally pronounced 'Roshier'.

The Welsh social system meant that individuals were identified as the child of a named person, man or woman. Thus Ieuan the son of Dafydd was referred to as Ieuan ap Dafyydd. Tegwyn, Dafydd's daughter, would be called Tegwyn uch Dafydd. There were many instances where, to be absolutely specific, two or even three *ap*s or *uch*s would be required, as in the example of Ieuan ap Howell ap Ieuan ap Rered (Newport Lordship 1465), who is one of a large number of individuals referred to by this style in lordship records, assize rolls and other documents in Wales.

The binary naming system formed in England in the fourteenth century (see Chapter 7) was adopted only slowly among the Welsh, mostly beginning among the nobility after the battle of Bosworth in 1485, when the Welshman Henry Tudur became King of England. Some Welsh nobility took surnames as a definitive act. In the case of others, their naming went through an intermediate stage. William Herbert of Trebus-godlyn was base son of John ap Gwilym Herbert (killed at Banbury 1469), who himself was base son of Sir William Thomas of Raglan. The ordinary people, under pressure of English law following the Acts of Union, took up the binary surnaming process, beginning some 200 years later than its adoption in England. The conversion was patchy and not complete, even by 1700. For example, at Llansannan in Flintshire (Clwyd) between 1660 and 1700, 25 per cent of baptismal entries are still recorded using the ap style. The process of change was very uneven. Within the same lordship, it is possible to see in one manor, especially if it was in hill country, the ap naming almost exclusively employed, even after the time it came under English law, while in another adjacent lowland manor of the same lordship, surnames were the rule. The surnames finally adopted were often in the first instance the father's or grandfather's given name, sometimes with the ap absorbed or sometimes in the English form. Hywel ap Rhys might thus have become Howell Rees or Rice, Howell Price or perhaps even Howel Preece. Surnames in the ap (ab) form which became common include Price, Powell, Bowen, Bevan, Bellis and Prosser.

The Norman given names gave rise to their ap forms also: Pugh, Probert, Proger, Pritchard, Parry, Penry and some others. However, the alternative English style names – Hughes, Roberts, Jones, Williams, Davies, Richards, Herbert, David and John – are especially common.

In some areas, as the surnaming process gathered pace and force, and under pressure to take a name in place of a complex set of *aps*, it was common to adopt the name Jones or Davies. When this happened, all the children of the same man did not necessarily adopt the same hereditary name.

LOCATIVE NAMES IN WALES

It is not hard to see why locative surnames were going to win only a small place in the scheme of things in Wales. In England people first asked where you came from. In Wales their first question was (and often still is): who is your father?

There are some locative surnames in Wales, however, such as Kemeys (the anglicised form of Cemais, two places in Monmouthshire), Hanmer (Flintshire), Conway, Hargest (Radnorshire), Pennant (Flintshire), Powis (Powys), Gwinnett (Gwynedd), Carne (Monmouthshire) and Prendergast (Pembrokeshire). There are, naturally, more than this, but the numbers of individuals carrying them is small, and the total of such names is also small. As I shall describe later, locatives can on occasion be used for tracing Welsh movement into England, but their use is not an approach that can in any way be depended upon.

WHAT ABOUT OCCUPATIONAL AND DESCRIPTIVE NAMES?

Personal descriptive surnames in Wales include the Welsh words for proud (Balch, Baulch), small (Bach, Batch, Baugh), red (Coch, Gooch, Goodge, Gough), thin (Faen, Vain, Vayne), beautiful (Teg) and fat (Tew) and English speaker (Sayce, Seyes). Again these names are not numerous enough to be very useful, but like the few locatives, they may be useful to confirm a Welsh connection when you are lucky enough to find an example, but not much more than that. On the other hand two descriptive names are very common and unmistakable, Vaughan (meaning younger) and Llwyd, Lloyd or Floyd (meaning grey, presumably grey-haired).

OCCUPATIONAL NAMES IN WALES

A very few surnames originating from the Welsh language are occupational names. The Welsh words for baker, carpenter and butcher do not feature as surnames. The common English trade names became adopted in Wales, in some areas at least, quite early (pre-1500); it is possible in some of the modest number of surviving early parish records to see a process of English trade name adoption.

At Caerwent in Monmouthshire, for example, the baptismal register shows the following sequence of baptisms:

17-4-1579	to John Thomas alias Painter
13-2-1580	to John, painter
3-2-1582	to John Painter
16-10-1583	to John Painter

and likewise in 1587 and 1589

Also in these records are numerous other instances of aliases:

William Conart alias Glazier 1588
Moris Robert alias Tyler 1593
William Thomas alias hupper 1572

In these instances, the English trade word has arrived, but not necessarily the usage of the English language in a complete or exclusive way. Almost

214

certainly no English person named painter, glazier, tyler, miller or hooper has put in an appearance. Proving that these names had become hereditary at that time would be a difficult follow-up task.

CHOOSING PATRONYMICS AND OTHER WELSH NAMES AS TRACERS

Wales is a province of many hills and many valleys. The southern coastal plain apart, the land is not easy to cultivate, but over the centuries, most of Wales proved to be excellent terrain for guerrilla warfare, and thus to be eminently defendable. Infiltrated though it has been, much and often, its population has remained quite small (about 3 million) and, the periphery apart, rather thinly spread. The features of landform that kept it culturally unassimilated into England are the same ones that kept it thinly populated, and still do, even in the twentieth century.

British Telecom directories divide Wales into six areas, two of which (North-East Wales and Mid-Wales) include sizeable towns on the English side of the border. This fact, and the considerable size of several of the areas, limit the quality of distribution data which can be easily gained by name analysis using telephone books. Detailed study would involve the splitting of some of the areas, segregating the contents, entry by entry. This would be quite a substantial task, unless one was able to work from the British Telecom National Directory CD-ROM and plot data on post-code maps. Several interesting and informative things can be done, however, without resorting to heroic measures.

POSSIBILITIES

One prime target of this book is promotion of methods for studying local and regional history in England. An aspect of this is the extent to which the Celtic nations have contributed to the populations of English places (see also Chapter 6). An obverse interest would be studies of the infiltration of English or other peoples into Welsh places. In fact, operationally, the two lines of investigation are closely connected and not entirely separable.

To take an example, if we are interested in the extent to which people (from any part, or from a particular part of Wales) contributed to the growth of the population of some English city, such as Leeds or Sheffield, then we would need to identify test or marker names which permit us to follow the process. But we can pick those names only after we are in possession of certain prerequisite information, namely the frequencies of various hereditary names in Wales as a whole, the relative frequencies of various names in different parts of Wales, and the frequencies of the same names in England and its districts. We might need these classes of information for several different dates.

Since Wales has been infiltrated over a long period by people carrying English names, and not equally in all parts either, we cannot take the whole set of current names in Wales as being simply a spectrum of Welsh names, as they may have been at some stage in the past. We need name occurrence information for some earlier times than the present. Perhaps a period before the major advent of industrialisation in the middle of the eighteenth century would be something to aim for. Evidently, we are restricted in how early we can go, by lack of records, and by the lateness of surname adoption.

I first set off to obtain these data by taking the pre-1800 parish baptismal records of a selected set of parishes scattered across Wales. They were ten in number and I abstracted from them and consolidated a list of surnames. At dates before major English infiltration, such an exercise yields only about 130 different hereditary names. Among them though are about 20–30 rare, often unique instances of English names. I found locatives such as Burchinshaw, Carlisle, Langley, Salusbury, Dryhurst and Hanbury, and other English names such as Rodman, Hussey, Newman, Byrd and Falconer. Where there was doubt about the provenance of a name, it was taken to be not Welsh if it did not appear in Morgan and Morgan (1985) *Welsh Surnames*. The evidently non-Welsh names were eliminated from the consolidated list. After consultation of various accounts of Welsh names, a further name group was added to the 100 or so that had been retained, finally giving 120 surnames in all.

The frequency of each of these names in each of the current Welsh telephone directories was then collected (see Figure 8.1). These were tabulated in a computer at the University of Sheffield, and a rank order compiled for each directory and for the total directory entries for Wales. Using the rank order of sums, each district of Wales was tabulated for name frequencies. It should be noted, first, that some data from Chester and Shrewsbury were unavoidably included (though this is not damaging to the purpose), and second, that these are not necessarily the 120 currently commonest surnames overall in Wales. Smith, for example, if inserted into this list comes in thirteenth, while another common and very English name, Green, would come thirty-eighth and Gray (or Grey) seventieth. We must also realise that several names such as Roberts and Ellis, very common in Welsh documents, are also common names in England. But again this does not undermine the purpose. The top 100 in the final ranking are shown in Table 8.1.

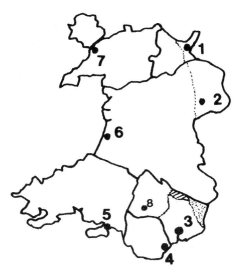

Figure 8.1 A redrawn portion of the map of telephone subscriber districts showing the coverage of the Welsh books. The numbers represent the following towns: 1 Chester, 2 Shrewsbury, 3 Newport, 4 Cardiff, 5 Swansea, 6 Aberystwyth, 7 Caernarvon, 8 Merthyr Tydfil. The stippled area attached to Gwent contains the Dean district of Gloucestershire.

WHAT DOES SUCH A LIST TELL US?

The detailed significance of the relative numbers apart, we have to ask two questions about the list. First, to what extent is the new list representing the names that the Welsh people carried just after surnames were generally established in Wales? Second, how good a picture is the list of the name pattern before industrialisation?

There are three ways to seek answers to these questions. First, one can take a group of parishes or a large parish, preferably the former, chosen without bias, and extract all the names therein for the period, say 1680–1750. These can then be compared with the list shown in Table 8.1. The result of such an exercise for a group of Monmouthshire parishes shows that the occurrence of the top fifty names is persistent. They are very coincident with those in Table 8.1. However, the rank order of relative frequencies does not coincide, principally because the surname Morgan is so much more common in south-east Wales than elsewhere, whereas Roberts, Owen and Ellis are less common there than they are in the north of the principality.

Second, we can look for some reference listing of Welsh-born people, of

Table 8.1　Surnames of telephone subscribers in Wales, 1986 (thousands)

1	Jones	60.57		51	Nicholls	0.99
2	Williams	37.81		52	Daniels	0.99
3	Davies	36.76		53	Nicholas	0.95
4	Evans	24.66		54	Preece	0.93
5	Thomas	22.97		55	Prosser	0.81
6	Roberts	17.14		56	Edmunds	0.79
7	Hughes	13.38		57	Wynne	0.75
8	Lewis	12.96		58	Gough/Goff	0.73
9	Morgan	11.70		59	Herbert	0.64
10	Griffiths	10.90		60	David	0.64
11	Edwards	10.33		61	Beynon	0.63
12	Owen	8.85		62	Arnold	0.56
13	James	7.66		63	Charles	0.55
14	Morris	7.50		64	Gittins	0.53
15	Price	7.50		65	Griffin	0.51
16	Rees	7.30		66	Rosser	0.50
17	Phillips	6.34		67	Mathias	0.48
18	Jenkins	6.23		68	Probert	0.45
19	Harris	5.79		69	Anthony	0.43
20	Lloyd	5.64		70	Gwilliam	0.40
21	Richards	5.51		71	Rickett/ard	0.37
22	Powell	4.72		72	Giles	0.36
23	Parry	4.49		73	Protheroe	0.35
24	John	3.65		74	Phelps	0.35
25	Watkins	3.39		75	Gwynne	0.32
26	Howells	3.25		76	Roderick	0.30
27	Pritchard	3.14		77	Bellis	0.29
28	Rogers	2.71		78	Meyrick	0.29
29	Matthews	2.37		79	Mansel	0.27
30	Rowlands	2.35		80	Rice	0.26
31	Humphreys	2.22		81	Trehaerne	0.25
32	Pugh	2.19		82	Michael	0.25
33	Ellis	2.17		83	Eynion	0.25
34	Bowen	2.17		84	Elias	0.24
35	Hopkins	2.04		85	Havard	0.24
36	Martin	1.91		86	Pullin	0.22
37	Bennett	1.86		87	Paul	0.21
38	Bevan	1.69		88	Abraham	0.21
39	Pearse	1.65		89	Cadwalidwr	0.19
40	Adams	1.61		90	Leyshon	0.19
41	Walters	1.59		91	Jarrett	0.18
42	Llewellyn	1.50		92	Picton	0.16
43	George	1.45		93	Gething	0.13
44	Simons	1.32		94	Gronow	0.12
45	Vaughan	1.31		95	Onions	0.12
46	Reynolds	1.25		96	Powys	0.12
47	Andrews	1.19		97	Craddock	0.12
48	Davis	1.17		98	Sayce	0.12
49	Meredith	1.07		99	Prytherch	0.12
50	Lawrence	1.02		100	Gwyther	0.10

The top hundred Welsh names (selected as described in the text) in thousands, totalled from the six British Telecom directories for Wales in 1986. In most cases all variants of spelling are combined, e.g. Pierce, Pearse, Pearce.

certified Welsh ancestry, and study the occurrence and frequency of names among them. The *Welsh National Dictionary of Biography* is a possible source. However, this is an intimidating twenty-seven volumes, too large a source on which to start. Instead, I used T.R. Roberts (1908) *Eminent Welshmen*, which contains some 2,000 named persons. From these I eliminated those born abroad. The remainder, 1,896 in number, were ranked according to name frequency. Of the list thereby produced, twenty-six names of the top thirty coincided with names in the top thirty from the recent telephone directories of Wales. The commonest names were even in the same rank order of frequency.

Only four names, Herbert, Vaughan, Ellis and Wynne, sited low down in the modern list, yet reached the top thirty in Roberts' compilation. They displaced Watkins, Pritchard, Rogers and Matthews from the modern list. The correspondence overall was thus extremely good.

Finally, it seemed possible to study some early Welsh name lists, where such exist. These could inform if the names commonest on recent lists really were so in earlier times. The earliest extensive list of names for some Welsh counties are muster rolls. For example, the oldest large listing of men of the County of Monmouth that I could find was the muster roll of 1539. This exists only in the original, at the PRO, inscribed in Tudor secretary hand. I needed help to interpret and transcribe relevant parts of it. However, the result was less helpful than I hoped. Many men listed thereon proved to have names in a rather degraded version of the ap style thus:

David ap Ieuan ap Griffith
Thomas ap Ieuan Gronow
William Bean ap Rise
Lewis Thomas ap Jeuan ap Gwylim

The confusion was increased by the curt abbreviations which were used. Evidently, despite its location near the border with England, hereditary family names had not fully taken hold in rural Monmouthshire in 1539, three years after the first Act of Union.

The muster list for 1601–2 for the county fortunately presents a tidier picture. In its preamble it points out that listed below are men called to sail to Bristol for service in Ireland: names, surnames and addresses. A count of these showed that of 185 men, 15 had English names, often trade names. Overall, the proportion of patronymics was 90.3 per cent. Of these about one in eight were William(s) and one in seven John(s), presumably a precursor of Jones. The other commonest names were David, Thomas and Morgan. This list was encouraging, but not really extensive enough for my purpose.

The next extensive early lists of personal names I could find for the county were the much later Hearth Tax Assessments for 1662, 1663 and 1664. These too were available only in the original at the PRO. On these documents, more than 95 per cent names are given in the binomial manner. A check against the earliest parish records for some parts of the south of the county has indicated that the names, where they could be checked, were indeed hereditary.

I was satisfied also to see that the commonest names on my Telecom list featured strongly as well on the Hearth Tax Assessments. On the 1663 list Thomas, Williams, Morgan and Jones were the four commonest surnames. There were certain differences in the frequency rankings, due presumably to the local nature of the Hearth Tax listing I used. There were the very low numbers of Davi(e)s and Evans entries and a rather plentiful supply of Morgans.

For almost all Welsh counties, the Hearth Tax is likely to be the earliest reliable, extensive list of personal names appropriate for use in movement tracing, although for some places earlier muster rolls also may be useful. A study of the Hearth Tax lists for Monmouthshire makes clear that English penetration was, as yet, of modest amount. In Usk Hundred for instance, about 9 per cent of local taxpayers had English descriptive or locative names. In the borough of Newport, the figure was higher, at 16 per cent. At Newport though, some of those English names had been present in the lordship records long before the 1660s. Thus even as late as 1663, southern Monmouthshire was, apparently, very largely the home of people of Welsh ancestry. That English incursion that had occurred took place during a period when surnames were not yet fixed in Wales. There was, I think, no time when a local Welsh community was described by hereditary surnames of Welsh patronymic or Welsh descriptive origin, uncoloured by the presence of English names.

USING THE NAME FREQUENCY DATA TO STUDY POPULATION MOVEMENT

A Welsh district whose surname pattern was unmodified by English penetration would exhibit at least 90 per cent of the membership (or baptisms) in patronymic surnames. In the Hearth Tax Assessment at Usk Hundred, when the thirty-two English names there are removed, 98 per cent of the taxpayers have patronymic surnames, the small remainder being men called Vaine, Tegg or Kemeys. In some places the figure is lower than 98 per cent due to the presence of common descriptive names such as Lloyd and Vaughan, or more occasionally, Seyes (or Sayce, an English speaker), Coes, Goff or Prisk. Of the high figure of 90 per cent, above 75 per cent is accounted for by the names in the top thirty from our Telecom contemporary list. This figure falls when English people arrive, because patronymics make up a much smaller part of the English name spectrum. We can have a sort of rough and ready 'Index of Welshness' which we can set at 1.0 if 75 per cent of the baptisms in the local register or names on a nominal list are in the top thirty names. As I pointed out above, some English families were already well settled by the time the Welsh had got into the process of binary naming. The very earliest surname lists available tend therefore to have small numbers of English names included. It is sensible though to use those earliest lists as one's starting points.

The arrival of the English at Caerleon in Monmouthshire

Like many Welsh towns, Caerleon's beginnings were as a Roman fortress, Isca Silurum, the Welsh of those times having a culture that did not construct major towns. Caerleon thus has a very early documented history. The town has long been a mecca for antiquarians and a focus of archaeological research. Many of Britain's eminent archaeologists have studied and written about the Roman site there.

The town also has a place in chronicles and in legends. Geoffrey of Monmouth told rich tales of it, raising images of a city fabulous and gold-roofed. The Roman amphitheatre had a dual role: the finest archaeological feature of its kind in Britain at least, and a focus for Arthurian legend. The romance of all this was strong enough reason to draw nineteenth-century poets and story tellers to the town. Naturally, to natives, literary tales, Roman remains, excavations, museums and pottery shards in the garden were and are everyday facts of life. Yet the streets, older houses, public houses and town square are products of another history altogether. In the shadow of the Emperor Augustus and of Arthur, this is usually entirely overlooked. Writers of eighteenth- and nineteenth-century guidebooks, enticed to Caerleon by legends and a hunger for artifacts, sometimes left deeply disappointed, describing the town in such words as *'a very inconsiderable place'* or *'composed of but two streets of poor houses'*, though one does point out that the local tin works are extensive and remarkable.

THE POPULATION HISTORY OF CAERLEON

I spent my childhood in the town. Many of my school companions had names which were unarguably English: Stamp, Broome, Knowles, Bound, Giddings, Green, Cox, Wood or Greenland. Others had names that I might now suppose to be Irish, though I did not suppose it then. Yet other class-

221

mates were called Lewis, Davies, Pugh or Jones. Whatever we were all called, in a very uncertain kind of way we usually identified ourselves as Welsh. Very few of us heard much of the Welsh language other than occasionally on the radio.

I have never had to hand the telephone directories applicable to the 1940s, the years that I am talking about, but I do have some much more recent ones. They suggest that in the mid-1980s the Caerleon exchange had about 36 per cent of residents with patronymic surnames. Whatever it was like in earlier time, in terms of its 'gene pool' in the 1980s, it was less than half Welsh. Later in my life I took time to study the matter of Caerleon's population history, stimulated to do so by a remembered remark of my father's.

Father was a political activist. He was a socialist by religion. This was not an easy thing to be in Caerleon, which had in its recent past (when he was a young man) a strong connection with the countryside, gentry houses, estates, hunting and farming. He certainly lost more elections than he won. On the occasion of one of his victories he explained to me that he *'always had more chance in the South Ward, where the real old Caerleon families are'*. I knew the South Ward contained the oldest surviving houses of the town, but why should their residents be more willing to vote for him than residents of other wards? What did he represent for them? Is there such a thing as a *'real old Caerleon family'*?

I did two things to try to answer these questions. One was a name-based analysis of Caerleon population history. The other was a study in depth of my father's genealogy.

Name analysis at Caerleon

I considered several possible sources of names, but the only one that provided data over a long enough period was the Church of England parish baptismal record, which commenced in 1695. Both the original and bishop's copies reside at the National Library of Wales. Even aware of the drawbacks inherent in parish records as name sources (see Chapter 7), I decided to use them. I divided the material into twenty-five year blocks covering inclusively 1700–24 up to 1875–99. For each block I collected:

- a complete list of surnames
- the number of baptisms to each surname.

I was then able to plot graphs of

- total surname number against time
- total baptisms against time

- percentage of patronymic baptisms against time
- total number patronymic names against time.

It was soon clear that before 1750 the local population carried very largely patronymic hereditary names. These totalled about fifty and they accounted between them for about 90 per cent of all baptisms. (This compared with a figure of 92.5 per cent patronymic taxpayers on the 1663 Hearth Tax Assessment for the Hundred of which Caerleon is part. The 1663 tax roll has fifty-two patronymic surnames and three other Welsh names.)

The fifty names from the baptismal register were very coincident with the top fifty names described earlier for the Index of Welshness, though they were not identical. They were also very similar to the names on the Hearth Tax. A local characteristic of both tax and baptismal lists was the presence of significant numbers of persons called Thomas, Jones, Morgan and Williams and minute numbers of Evanses or Davieses. The surnames Charles and George were consistently present. George is forty-third in the modern list and Charles does not appear in the Welsh top fifty.

Two periods of family influx were detected on the graphs. The first period was 1750–74 (mostly 1750–60). In this period the patronymic percentage was lowered to near 80 per cent by the arrival of men and families with alien names. These proved on surname analysis to be from the West Midlands of England. They were metal workers arriving to work in or live alongside a new iron forge and tin works (see Chapter 9).

The second influx (1800 onwards) came after a period of return to high patronymic indices about 1790, which perhaps signified a temporary decline in fortunes at the local forge. From 1825 onwards the number of English names rose steeply, so that after 1850 the Welsh were outnumbered by English arrivals (Figures 8.2 and 8.3).

However, the matter is more complicated than that. Some of the incomers were not English, but Welsh from further west in Wales. These were, naturally, a hard segment of the incoming population to track using names. However, the census returns and the increased incidence of names such as Davies, both support the view that some incomers did come from further west in Wales (though not necessarily in a single move).

The percentage of patronymic baptisms fell yet again late in the nineteenth century, as a result of a period of tin works and forge closure (see Chapters 2 and 9). The loss of personnel from the parish at that time seems to have been more from among those of Welsh origin, than from among the English names.

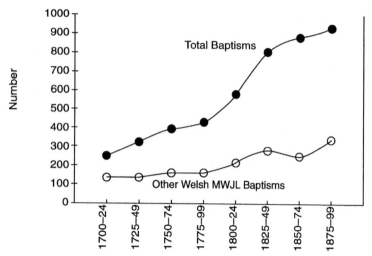

Figure 8.2 Total baptisms and baptisms of four common patronymic surnames (Morgan, Williams, Jones, Lewis) at St Cadoc's Church, Caerleon, plotted in twenty-five-year blocks.

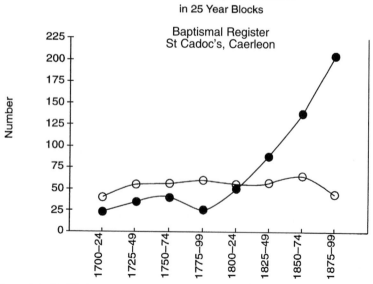

Figure 8.3 In filled circles, total numbers of surnames per twenty-five-year block. Plotted in open circles numbers of patronymic surnames in the same blocks. Both data sets from the baptismal registers of St Cadoc's Church, Caerleon.

Father's genealogy

The result of the genealogical search on my father yielded the information that on his father's side he was descended from people who were very local – within a radius of a few miles. The names are exclusively patronynics: Williams, Morgan, Jones and Jones again were his grandparents' names. Those identified in the next generation back were Thomases and more Williamses. This takes the line back to persons born in the period between 1740 and 1770, a time when, locally, industrialisation had hardly begun.

The work that the ancestors did, where known, was farm labouring, barrel hoop making (a greenwood trade) and later, iron rolling for tin plate production. Grandfather's uncles and cousins were all either tin plate shearers, doublers or rollermen on the one hand, or, on the other, woodmen who cut their own in the coppices, making hoops to be sent for packing Irish butter or Staffordshire pottery. Father's father thus connected via an unbroken line with the time when the district was not industrialised. If it could be said at all that there was an autochthonous people, then father's father was surely one of them.

Father's mother Agnes McNaught Jarrett had a different background. Her family were incomers. They were not, however, recent incomers. Her Jarretts arrived about 1829, though the name had entered the district about 1760, probably from Shropshire, in the first wave of West Midland iron workers. Grandmother's family then were the opposite to grandfather's; they were incomers brought to the town by early industrialisation, some at the founding of the forge about 1760, others at the re-equipping and expansion of the same works between 1800 and 1810.

As a couple, my father's parents represented most of the geographical and occupational strands of descent of the Caerleon population of the late Victorian times. The grandparents and their wider families were generally residents of the older stone houses of the South Ward. These had been home to much of the workforce of the forge and plate works: tinmen, behinders, doublers, shearers, rollermen, hollowfiremen, forgemen, puddlers, washmen and packers, and before that the people of the pre-industrial age. If any aspect of the town's business was missing from father's descent, it was only river life. The family had no boatmen, wharfmen or fishermen.

Father was seen at least to some extent as inheriting grandfather's public role and authority. Grandfather had been a very respected chapel elder, a Liberal political figure. Both father and son could have been seen, I believe, as representing the ancient roots of the community.

Further genealogical studies

If the above tentative conclusion is accepted, it makes an explanation only if the rootedness of the family was to an extent unique among the town people. Were there many other families still living there with the same deep local roots?

To test this, a panel of further local nineteenth-century families was selected for genealogical study. They were chosen mostly by name, some patronymics, some not. The names included Williams (four more families), Jones (three families), Charles, Green, Boddington, Morton, Poulson, Davies (three families), Gray, Jarrett (two families), Gravenor, Banner, Waters, Jenkins, Butler (Bootler), Winmill, Crockett, Ablart (two families) and Gething.

Space does not permit a detailed account of the results of all of this. But they can be summarised as follows: of all these names only Green, Waters and some of the Jones, Jenkins, Davies, Williams and Morgan go back to eighteenth-century Caerleon, though all did not come through to the twentieth century. The Green line looks to be the most convincing genealogy, stretching to the seventeenth century, though there is one unproven step. Father's family were twice married into the Greens. The Greens and Morgans were linked by marriage too. The surname Waters (really the patronymic Walters) goes back a long way in the general area also. Evidently, father's family is not unique there in stretching back from the twentieth to the eighteenth century, but it does comes from a rather small core group.

Some of the town Williams, Jones and Morgan lines trace back to a point well previous to 1800, where one loses them in a veritable jungle of common names. In south-east Wales, the nearest things to a genealogical 'black hole' are the names William Morgan and John Jones! Many families trace back to one or two men with these names sooner or later. They are the quintessential *Men o' Gwent*.

The Caerleon population now

In 1962 a large steel making operation was transferred from Ebbw Vale to Llanwern near Caerleon. This now assaults the eye of any one standing on Christchurch Hill and looking out to the River Severn. Many of the hundreds of associated incomers were 'valleys Welsh'. However, in 1969 the great bridge over the Severn was inaugurated. Now commuting to work across the bridge is commonplace. The families of people working in the Bristol area often live in Gwent, making demand for houses in the south of the county considerable. Since the early 1980s, several housing estates have been built on the edge of or actually within the old streets of Caerleon. An analysis of the surnames on the portions of the 1990 electoral roll covering those new estates, indicates that these new residents as a group are even more English than the 1980s community. The incidence of patronymic names is as low as 25 per cent. Even so, houses in the streets of old South Ward offer figures distinctly higher than that.

MORE ABOUT SOUTH GWENT

As far as the south of Gwent county is concerned, even this creation of a large commuter belt, which serves Cardiff as well as Bristol, does not destroy the deeper roots. If one turns from the 1990 electoral roll to the Yellow Pages for Cardiff and South-East Wales, the portion listing local farmers proves most interesting. More than 60 per cent of local farmers have patronymic names, with Jones, Davies, Evans, Jenkins, Lewis, Morgan and Williams featuring strongly, well supported by Bevan, Bowen, Edwards, Griffiths, John, Powell, Price and Pritchard.

Many of these families have been at the same farms for several generations. Furthermore, the farms themselves frequently retain their Welsh names, as do their individual fields. Long threads of connection run almost unnoticed past the integral garages, between the lines of shiny cars, and lead not only to the pre-commuter past, but also to the pre-industrial past.

WELSH DISPERSAL BEFORE 1700

Many English parishes or hundreds have surviving tax lists from the first third of the fourteenth century. A scan of those lists (a good example is the Nomina Villarum of *c.* 1316 for Somerset) sometimes reveals Welsh names. Thomas ap Adam of Whitstone, Somerset, for example, is in that 1316 list. In 1332 David and William le Walyshe were taxpayers in Wiltshire. There are references to Wales in fourteenth- and fifteenth-century West Country wills, which make it clear that wealthy people owned property either side of the Bristol Channel, and that crossing the water was, if not commonplace, certainly something one did if it was necessary. Those wills indicate clearly the input of wealth from the English side of the water to pay for building, bridge repair and things of that nature in Wales.

From both north and south of Wales, early arrivals in England were commonly called 'welch', 'walsh' or 'welchman', or le Wallis or le Walyshe. See for example the Walshman family, which features in documents of Elizabethan Manchester. Some of the arrivals thus called could have appeared as early as the time when the English themselves were still adopting binary naming. They became, all of them, holders of descriptive English surnames. Presumably the receiving communities did not know Wales well enough to distinguish different places within it. Of the ap and uch names of the early Welshmen and women, one sees very little evidence. The distinctively Welsh name that survives best from among the early arrivals seems to be Powel. Whether this is for linguistic or other reasons is not clear.

By the time the 1569 muster rolls were being compiled in the southwestern counties, the presence of modest numbers of Welsh people was usual, about 1.5–2.5 per cent of the total males. Near the Severn coast and in parishes by the navigable rivers in Somerset, there were sometimes as many as 8–10 per cent men with Welsh names, suggesting the use of direct passages across the Severn estuary in small boats. Men with unarguably Welsh names such as Morgan, Powell, Griffiths and Price are not hard to find in the Devon, Somerset and Dorset muster lists. There are plenty of Williamses, Joneses, Lewises and other 'top thirty' names too. Even the Williamses and Joneses seem to be almost all genuinely Welsh people (new arrivals or descendants), since at that time counties remote from Wales show very few, if any, people who bear even those familiar names.

Interestingly, in the sixteenth century, although the Welsh can be found early in Shropshire towns, and even places far across England (such as Norwich) had a few straying Welsh (on the Norwich Census of the Poor in 1570, there are present three Joneses and four Powels, one of the last named being stated to be from Wales), some counties such as Staffordshire, which are close to north-east Wales are very poor in Welsh names. For example, the family listing of the Archdeaconry of Stafford made in 1532–3, which has a total of roughly 50,000 named people, includes only about 70 people of putative Welsh origin. The name-based evidence of early Welsh migration into England, is necessarily fragmentary, but it seems to indicate primarily movement to the south and, especially, to south and east. It can generally be said that the current goes ultimately towards London, though not to the south coast.

WELSH EMIGRATION STUDIED USING SEVENTEENTH-CENTURY LISTS

The Hearth Tax Assessments for the 1660s and 1670s for English counties have survived in considerable numbers, and many of them have been published (see Chapter 7). These lists, together with sundry other seventeenth-century nominal rolls, such as the Free and Voluntary Present and the surviving 1696 Marriage Tax lists, allow the study of Welsh egress to be continued on a firmer basis in the seventeenth century.

Generally, lists for counties such as Nottinghamshire, Yorkshire, Derbyshire and Suffolk, which are either rather remote from Wales or apparently off the main arteries of movement, had Welshness Indices of below 1 per cent, indeed sometimes below 0.5 per cent. Even the city of Nottingham, for instance, which does boast the occasional 1674 resident called Rice Jones or Robert Howell, has overall fewer than a hundred holders of names in the top thirty test group. In contrast to this, the Hearth Tax for Worcester city for 1678 shows nearly 13 per cent Welsh names. The 1608 Gloucestershire muster roll has 6 per cent and the Bristol listing of 1696, at least 20 per cent.

The Welsh name data in England are as yet very incompletely exploited, much remaining to be done from unpublished seventeenth-century tax rolls, and one must beware of complexities that may arise from comparing data from documents of different types and dates. Furthermore, the lists thus far exploited do not cover all of England. However, they do all have the individual advantage of being extensive and hence constituting comfortingly large samples. To mention two, the 1696 list of Bristol inhabitants has 16,500 persons, and the Gloucestershire muster roll (mentioned above) about 18,000. It would be difficult to envisage how such large samples could be namewise unrepresentative of their regions.

The indications so far are that the Welsh movement detectable on seventeenth-century lists is via towns and of a similar directional pattern to that indicated in earlier documents, implying the maintenance and strengthening of the old patterns of movement into England. Will books, court rolls and other documents for Oxfordshire, Berkshire, Buckinghamshire and the Thames Valley exhibit enough references to people with south-east Wales names to support suggestions that when the mobile or descendants of the mobile moved further, on balance, that movement took them nearer to London. In that geographical direction, one can find locative surnames (presumably late-forming ones), such as Munmuth, Hayterell, Mager, Kymmin, Kerdyff, Raglan, Abergayney, Langstone, Skinfrith, Ewyas and Londaff. The new London Welsh of the 1930s who caught the train that ran from Pembroke Dock to Paddington were really following a time-honoured route.

AN IMPORTANT MATTER OF MECHANISM AND INTERPRETATION

It is worth saying at this point that personal geographical movement can be viewed like a chemical reaction, as a reversible process. At any given moment, individuals (like molecules) potentially might move in any direction, including moving back whence they came. What is noted as human population migration is the result of the *balance* favouring relocation in a certain direction. (Famous papers by E.W. Ravenstein (1885, 1889) asserted this matter of reversibility more than a hundred years ago. See also the text edited by W.T.R. Pryce, 1994.) In order for the balance to favour one regional accumulation or another, there has to be some underlying regional distinction. This could consist of the income potential of individuals, the chances for acquisition of space for families or perhaps differences in the congeniality of the religion or culture.

Analyses of taxation assessments have illustrated how, even in the time of the fourteenth-century Poll Tax, there was in general a diminishing gradient of wealth passing north and west from London. Even if the gradient was very slight, it would have been quite sufficient to ensure, over time, the steady accumulation of persons in the south-east quarter. The fact that people may have moved primarily from town to town does nothing to invalidate the suggestion. In much more recent times, some steep gradients have arisen by the serious loss of earning opportunities in some areas, thereby making other distant ones relatively wealthier.

USING NAME FREQUENCY DATA TO DETECT THE ARRIVAL OF WELSH PEOPLE IN ENGLISH TOWNS

Having established a picture of the name listing for Wales after surnames stabilised, we have created the knowledge base which we can draw upon to detect Welsh arrivals at specific places in England, in the years after 1700. The total Welsh name set we have identified includes 120 names in all. Mostly, so far, we have worked with the commonest thirty. It is now necessary to isolate an appropriate test set.

Some of the commonest Welsh names such as Jones and Williams may have arisen to some extent independently in England, and to be on the safe side, these names must be disqualified from our purpose. Davies (with the *e*) offers a little more hope, since it is mostly a west Wales name, whereas the English Davis was generally without the *e*, but it is not a tracing name that one feels confident about. In the same way, we would reject Thomas, the biblical name, and the Norman names, Hughes and Roberts, which were in early use in England. Roberts is common in the Hearth Tax Assessments for Yorkshire, Derbyshire, Nottinghamshire and other northerly counties. We thus have to forsake most of the commoner names on the top thirty list.

The names of most use to us are the commoner Welsh language names: Evans, Lewis, Griffiths and Morgan. Owen must be discounted, because it arose in England separately from the Owain of Wales and was commonly present in England in the fourteenth century. To be added to the useful list are Vaughan, Lloyd (and its earlier form Llwyd), Rees (Rice or Rhys), Rosser, Griffin and Gittins, as well as all the ap forms: Bowen, Preece, Parry, Pritchard, Pugh, Bevan, Beynon, Bellis, Prosser, and the rarer Probert, Protheroe, Prytherch and Pullin. One should not overlook either the rare names: Gwalchmai, Cadwalidwr, Eynion and Leyshon. These are all names either of Welsh first name origin, or are ap forms and hence are Welsh in another way. The arrival of several of the names from this list together at an English place is strongly suggestive of some sort of Welsh influx.

But we can take this further. Some of the names are much commoner in some parts of Wales than in others (see Table 8.2). Graphs plotting the frequencies of various names in the set of 120 for one region against for another, allow correlation coefficients to be calculated, and confirmation that the different geographical regions of the principality do vary in their name spectra. The largest difference is between north-west and south-west Wales.

Looking at individual names, Morgan is mostly a south Wales name. Lewis is much less common in the north than the south. Jenkins, David, Bevan and Llewellyn are strongest in the south and south-west. Beynon is more common in the south-west of Wales than in other parts. Wynne is far more common in north and mid-Wales than in south Wales. Bellis is almost exclusively a north Wales name. Gwynne is a south and mid-Wales form. Gittins is much more common in north-east and mid-Wales. Preece is really common only in mid-Wales and Gwent. Mansel is very much a mid-Wales name. Evidently, it is possible to make up panels of names that represent one region of Wales more than another.

From all of this it is not hard to see that it is possible not only to detect Welsh penetration in England, but also, given enough data, to make tentative guesses as to where in Wales the people originated.

THE WELSH IN NINETEENTH- AND TWENTIETH-CENTURY SHEFFIELD

To try this out on Sheffield inhabitants, lists of residents were taken from various Sheffield city directories. These were White's 1841, 1871 and 1902, and Kelly's 1934, 1954 and 1968.

Of the original unedited test list of Welsh names, the 1841, 1871 and

Table 8.2   Frequencies of certain Welsh surnames from five telephone directories, 1986 (thousands)

	North-west	North-east	Mid-Wales	Swansea and south-west	Gwent
Bellis	0.05	*0.22*	0.01	0.00	0.00
Beynon	0.00	0.00	0.01	*0.57*	0.04
Davies	3.28	4.09	5.86	*20.09*	3.45
John	0.08	0.08	0.17	*3.06*	0.25
Morgan	0.40	0.42	2.00	*6.84*	2.04
Preece	0.02	0.02	*0.46*	0.23	0.20
Rees	0.21	0.20	0.51	*5.76*	2.04
Roberts	*6.16*	4.95	2.27	2.98	0.78
Wynne	0.19	*0.32*	0.16	0.06	0.03

Regional subscriber totals in thousands in certain Welsh names, computed from five British Telecom directories for Wales in 1986. The Cardiff telephone book was omitted. Values of particular weight are in italics.

1902 Sheffield directories showed Roberts, Ellis, Jones, Rodgers and Bennett to be common. All of these names are poor guides to Welsh penetration and are among those we would have rejected for use. Of the ap names, only Price, Powell, Parry and Bevan were represented at all, a total in White's 1871 directory of some thirty-two people. This suggests the most minimal Welsh presence, a conclusion backed up when it is noted that people named Bellis, David, John and Preece were entirely absent, while the common Welsh names Morgan and Lewis had only a handful of representatives.

A study of the 1861 and 1871 censuses for the city confirms that Welsh-born people average only about one person per thousand of population at that time. The substantial occurrence of Ellis, Roberts and Bennett names is quite out of tune with this, and confirms that the presence of these names in Sheffield is unconnected with Wales. It is curious, however, how such local high frequencies in England are geographically adjacent to high frequencies of the same names in north and mid-Wales. The case of Ellis at least is probably just a coincidence, since the name in Wales may sometimes have a derivation from the Welsh Elisedd, or from Elias.

By 1934 the situation in Sheffield had changed. The numbers of many of the Welsh test names were increased. The Davieses outstripped the Davises, the Morgans were present in force, as well as persons called Watkins, Parry and Lloyd; there were even small numbers of the much less common Bellis, Powys and Gwinnett names, plus some persons called John and Rees. The Welsh had certainly arrived in the first third of the twentieth century. Many of the people named were professional people and skilled workers. For instance, some of the top posts in the university (founded

1905) were held by Welshmen. The balance of the Sheffield Welsh name set in 1934 is suggestive of a principal origin in north and mid-Wales.

By 1954 the situation had changed further. Compared to 1934, several Welsh names had selectively increased: Price, Rees, Griffiths, Morgan, Davies, Meredith and Hopkins. The balance of this string of names is very much in favour of south Wales. This perhaps relates to the large-scale emigrations from south Wales in the late 1930s and to a generally increased mobility in the coal and steel industries, and possibly among railway staff, after the nationalisations of the period 1945–51.

SOME OTHER MAJOR ENGLISH CITIES

I have heard it said that every major English city has acquired its Welsh presence over the past 100–150 years. This may be literally true, but Sheffield certainly gives no impression of being a place that the Welsh favoured. One would hesitate to describe the Welsh presence in Sheffield in either of the past two centuries as constituting a community. Some other English towns and cities, though, did gain significant Welsh communities.

I have mentioned London. Then there is Liverpool. The growth of that city during the Victorian era was spectacular. The parish grew from 77,000 to 258,000 in the fifty years following 1801. The whole city had reached 552,000 by 1881. The north Welsh arrived in Liverpool in a steady stream at least from about 1820; even at the 1881 census there were 18,000 Welsh-born residents. Indeed, these incomers were so constant a feature, and had such skills to sell, that they became not only a community within a community, but also took a large part in the construction of the very fabric of the Victorian city. They have probably even influenced the city people's accent. In the later nineteenth century, Liverpool was possibly the most popular British destination of the emigrant Welsh.

The incomers were able to establish their own religious culture in Liverpool and using this base, offer a point of anchorage for even newer incomers, who would be influenced to take lodgings near the chapel, in Welsh speaking lodging houses. This process (and a comparable one which operated in London, especially around the rail heads) is well documented, as are various aspects of business and employment of the Welsh in Liverpool. One thing that appears to stand out is that in both Sheffield and Liverpool, the Welsh who were settling were people with saleable skills or education. They were able to enter local society at a variety of levels. Welsh ghettos did not form.

Name-based studies on Liverpool of the sort that I outlined for Sheffield are really rather superfluous, unless they can give useful extra information about the sources of the Liverpool Welsh. Preliminary studies of nine-teenth-century Liverpool directories and censuses are entirely consistent with the view that the great majority of incoming Welsh were from the north of Wales. It is worth pointing out that some of the descendants of these people have in recent decades been relocated within England, while many remaining in Liverpool are well-integrated enough to be largely un-conscious of their own Welsh ancestry. In the nineteenth century, a com-mon onward path for Welsh people entering Liverpool was to New York or Quebec. Liverpool was not very obviously on the way to anywhere else on the English mainland.

SURNAMES AND PLACE NAMES OF CORNWALL: A NOTE

It is important not to conclude a chapter on tracing the Welsh by means of their hereditary names without discussing, at least briefly, the matter of Cornish names. In particular, it is important to be clear about the degree of confusion that is possible between Welsh and Cornish names.

The pre-Saxon people became divided by water more than a thousand years ago. The language and culture in Cornwall has thus had many years in which to evolve separately from that in Wales. Unfortunately the lan-guage which was used in early medieval Cornwall was overwhelmed by English and suffered a decline perhaps 500 years ago. Although there were some speakers of a Cornish much more recently, it is not easy now to be sure what form the language latterly took. Certainly though, the place name elements are very consonant with Welsh. Presumably the ap form of naming applied in some form to the end. But what personal names were in use in the last of the days when Cornish was the predominant language of the peninsula? Which current names in Cornwall came in from Wales over the last few centuries? The 1327 and the 1523 Lay Subsidy Rolls for Cornwall offer some evidence. Several later lists such as the 1569 muster roll for the county help one also to build a picture of the Cornish name stock.

There are numerous hereditary names in Cornwall which are unique Cornish locatives, and some other locatives there which are confusable with places or families in Wales (e.g. Carline, Carlyon, Prisk, Pill, Tredinnick, Carne, Magor, Trewin). There are also surnames that are co-incident with Welsh ones (Bevan, Rees, Powell, Tudor, Sayce, Morgan, Floyd, Cadwallader) and patronymics of the biblical or Norman types (Richards, Rogers, Williams, Thomas, James and Bennett). In addition, there is a group of personal names of characteristic Cornish form (see below).

The scope for confusion with certain Welsh names is considerable. Indeed, there are some interpretations of the occurrences of names such as Carne and Caerleon in Morgan and Morgan, *Welsh Surnames,* which could quite reasonably be taken to be Cornish incomers rather than the recent Welsh natives that those authors assume.

For tracing personal and family movement out of Cornwall, one would have to rely, I think, on the unique locative names and on certain characteristic forms of personal name. Due to the large-scale outward movement of Cornish people, some of these are currently borne only outside Cornwall. Thus, the useful locatives are those such as Penglaze, Penhaligon, Polgrean, Polwhele, Nankervis, Nancarrow, Trevanion, Trevaskis, Trewartha and many more. And the characteristic patronymics are Bennetto, Jacka, Jago, Jose, Kitto, Clemo and some others.

REFERENCES AND FURTHER READING

Curtis, T. (ed.) (1986) *Wales, the Imagined Nation: Essays in Cultural and National Identity*. Bridgend: Poetry Wales Press.

Morgan, P. and Thomas, D. (1984) *Wales: The Shaping of a Nation*. Newton Abbot, London and Vermont: David & Charles.

Morgan, T.J. and Morgan, P. (1985) *Welsh Surnames*. Cardiff: University of Wales [Well-researched dictionary of surnames in Wales].

Pryce, W.T.R. (ed.) (1994) *Studying Family and Community History, Volume 2, From Family History to Community History*. Cambridge, New York and Melbourne: Cambridge University Press and the Open University.

Ravenstein, E.G. (1885) 'The Laws of Migration', *Journal of the Royal Statistical Society* **48**: 167–235.

Ravenstein, E.G. (1889) 'The Laws of Migration', *Journal of the Royal Statistical Society* **52**: 214–301.

Roberts, T.R. (1908) *Eminent Welshman: A Short Biographic Dictionary of Welshman, Volume 1*. Merthyr Tidvil: Educational Publishing Company.

Rowlands, J. (ed.) (1993) *Welsh Family History*. Birmingham: Association of Welsh Family History Societies/FFHS, Birmingham [Has much useful review material concerning the tracing of Welsh families].

Walker, D. (1990) *Mediaeval Wales*. Cambridge and New York: Cambridge University Press.

Williams, Gwyn A. (1985) *When was Wales?*, Harmondsworth: Penguin [A book that many Welsh people would like many English people to read].

CHAPTER NINE

Getting it Together

PEOPLE IN ASSOCIATION

Some people do point out that they live well enough by themselves, and a few even say that there is no such thing as 'society', but the usual human condition involves group membership, or perhaps more accurately, membership of several distinct but overlapping groups. Even if we do not share a home, one group we probably belong to is a genetic family. Others we join early, without having the option, are school classes. Some sorts of membership are optional; we can choose to be a girl guide or boy scout, join a riding club, or (later in life) be an active member of the Liberal Democrats.

Chapters 6, 7 and 8 address one fundamental aspect of local history – the evolving nature of the local population. Its change and growth are closely associated with urbanisation and industrial development of the place, and of its region. But such growth and change is not merely a matter of human numbers or of area of occupied land. As towns grow in size and population, they also grow in social complexity. An increase in the number of people is associated with differentiation of the place into distinct town districts, and with the genesis of many kinds of associations of people. Growing towns develop the social structures and institutions required for social administration. They also gain some which arise as spontaneous products of the coming together of people. The total of structures developed can be bewildering large. A listing has to include workplaces, especially since some of them are pivotal in the life of the community. A village, town or city is an organic entity made up of innumerable jostling, overlapping associations. It depends on a myriad of interactions between its people who, in coming together, make all their various social productions. It must be remembered too that all takes place amid a fabric of built streets, and beneath the influence of social systems, that the town people both inherit and modify.

RESEARCHING SOCIAL STRUCTURES

Evidently, study of local social units and structures is really study of that layer of societal detail upward from that of overall population. It is the level of names and locations at which much written local history is directed, a body of inquiry of significance and subtle variety. Clubs, lodges, schools, branches, congregations, teams, sisterhoods – they are all discrete entities or groups that may be identified by name. Each may be discriminable too by its specific records, its location and its premises. The individuality of their life ensures that they do remain long in local recall and that they stay especially in the shared memories of their members, their buildings serving also as enduring reminders. The attributes of local associations mean that they lend themselves especially well both to research and to history writing. It is thus unsurprising that so many small histories are devoted to institutional topics.

A choice of units to study

It would be a demanding and interesting exercise to attempt a complete listing of all the social structures, units and associations that existed in one large city. One might commence by first creating a list of headings – all *types* of associations. There are, after all, groupings required to exist by law, some standard ones that exist in all towns, spontaneous local recreational units such as sports clubs, which often parallel those in other towns, and as well, a few almost unique associations. Some town institutions have written standing orders, some assiduously keep minutes or lists out of habit, or perhaps because of a legal requirement to do so. Others do not. There are some which by preference are open organisations, others which are secretive. Formal or informal, documented or otherwise, the activities of any one can be either quite profound, or more frivolous by far. Some could be described as the daily bread of the place. Finally, there are as well all of these, informal, habitual, recordless groups and connections, operated just by word of mouth – obscure consensus fellowships.

While I think it unlikely that either the reader or I will ever have completed for our town the list talked of in the last paragraph, nevertheless, we all do evidently live in or near places which have a very large number of associative features. We could choose to study the past of any one of them. Our personal selection from them might be influenced by a number of factors, including our own, or at least a family involvement, the wishes of a group or club itself to be studied, and the existence or otherwise of relevant written records. We might also have a personal preference for an organisation whose business has a technical or trade dimension, perhaps with a terminology of its own.

In choosing, it is always important to have in mind one's purposes in making the study. These may be usefully clarified by seeking answers from yourself to the questions below. Incidentally, these or related questions could be posed about all other studies, including those recounted in Chapters 5 and 6.

1. Are you trying to make permanent something that you fear may otherwise be lost? If so, what is it?
2. With respect to the subject, do you have specific questions of your own to answer? If so, what are they?
3. Are you trying to create a memorial? If so, to whom?
4. Is your work an act of enterprise, i.e. do you hope to sell the product?
5. Are you preparing a thesis, i.e. an examination document?
6. Were you hired to write? If the answer is yes, what are the objectives of your hirers?

When you have got answers, you can usefully go on to consider what form you intend your product to take. It may differ in form and style according to how you answered the questions.

Having got your research material, it *seems* natural, in many instances, to attempt to create a story that adds it all up; a forward-going account, first to last, and to include in that, all the firm facts that have been discovered. This may make a sizeable essay or a book. But before you decide that this really is what you are about, do consider that there are other possible products to local research (see for example Chapter 10). After this, if an account of this kind is nevertheless to be the product you will prepare, do ask, even before you start work, who are to be the intended readers. And do try to be clear what it is that you intend those readers to get from the text. People writing theses are generally very well aware that they will be read by examiners, who have different requirements from ordinary people. Whoever it is who is going to read it, make sure that it is the sort of thing that they would need, though always at the same time being accurate and rigorous.

I am assuming in the remainder of this chapter that the product of research is indeed intended to be a progressive story. I am partly illustrating the account with some material of my own, offered in this form. However, as befits a book on method, there is also included a commentary – asides and notes about the journey or process by which any given account or story was arrived at. Naturally, as pointed out much earlier, the journey of the research may be backwards, even when the story is forwards. Readers are invited, as they read, to read again the questions posed earlier in this section, and conclude if they wish, what my answers to the same were, for the three topics described.

I should add that I do not necessarily believe that the purpose of an historical account is to include absolutely *all* available facts. That is often impractical, though it does depend on the scale of the product that is contemplated. In theses, large books or extended essays, more can be included than in accounts covering only a few pages. Whatever the intended scale, writers are always responsible for deciding what is important, grasping the crux of things as they see it, and having done so holding that up to the eye of the reader by a means of a judicious choice of exemplars, illustrations and extracts. Find the most important thing, and make sure you say it!

In accounts of this sort, the sources used to gain the necessary data, information or quotes should be cited. Each citation has to meet three needs:

1. The source must be unambiguously identified, perhaps using a piece number (see Chapter 4).
2. Its location must be stated.
3. The point in the text it supports must be made clear. Generally, I would recommend the use of numbered footnotes or a list of references.

The first two needs put together would permit readers to go to the same source if they wished.

MY OWN STUDIES

Of all the sorts of institutions that I might have studied, I have generally found myself coming back to those concerned with work and religion. In this chapter, three particular examples are offered, which between them illustrate some of the variety of possibilities, issues, sources and outcomes. Two are indeed concerned with religion, but in contrasting ways – a Church of England parish, St John, Burslem, Staffordshire, and a Baptist Chapel, at Castle Street, Caerleon. The third organisation is a workplace, Caerleon Forge and Tinplate Works, for many years a principal employer in that town. The works and the chapel, both now lost, were two institutions in close (though by no means exclusive) connection, over a long period.

THE PARISH OF ST JOHN BURSLEM

It is appropriate to start by considering what a parish is, since only when that is clear, can the question of studying its history be discussed. According to standard published accounts, a parish is a unit whose origin is ecclesiastical, an area superimposed upon an ancient township or vill. Sometimes the area contained several townships. Many parishes have evidently existed for many centuries. In towns and cities, steep population rise, especially in the nineteenth century, forced the formation of new parishes from subdivisions of the old. In large places, the sequential process of new parish formation is an interesting research subject, already much reported in published diocesan histories.

From the 1530s, parishes acquired statute civil duties, some of which persisted in various forms until the twentieth century. The duties concerned included both the registering of vital events and the making of provision for the local poor. Latterly however, they have returned to a more purely ecclesiastical role. In fact, parishes can be considered to have been placed in rather different roles at different dates.

Belonging to a parish has thus had different implications at different dates. Evidently though, a parish is not, and never has been, a club to which one could voluntarily belong. You can be born into it or you can move your residence into it. However, being there does not necessarily mean that you feel a member of anything. You may be an active member of the church congregation there, but these days that no longer depends upon you living in the parish. You can be from the geographical outside, yet participate in self-consciously local actions which employ that church as a strong point.

It is clearly useful to distinguish between research on the parish as an historical administrative unit and research on church life – the congregation, the community of the religious residing within it. The account which follows addresses my attempt to gain some information on the latter, as it was during the first third of the twentieth century in one particular parish.

Sources and starting points

Originally I became interested because of a family story. Most of my father's family were chapel people; however, one, it was said, was different. Father's uncle was 'Vicar of Burslem'. I had this story in my head for perhaps twenty years before I decided to act. Acting took the form of finding a current edition of Crockford's Directory of Clerics and searching for the name of the vicar of Burslem, Staffordshire. Vicar was not the proper term, I discovered; it was Rector of Burslem. Having found the name and address of the then rector I wrote a letter inquiring if he had any information on my collateral relative, the Revd Arthur Williams. I received a reply soon afterwards. The answer was 'Yes', and I was in luck. Serendipity had struck again. The rector had a young relative who had recently been one of my (medical) students in Sheffield. I had an invitation to Burslem.

I managed to pay a fleeting visit to the church, but I was not able to take up the rector's invitation until several years later, by which time he had retired, though the new incumbent had not yet taken post. Anyway the Revd Philip Smith was happy to return to Burslem with me, and he introduced me there to several older parishioners, long-time members of the congregation.

A matter of character

The church lives of individual ancient parishes do have distinctive characters that have been settled over a long period. Some have long taken a 'high church' stance, something reflected in the fitments of the building, details of the liturgy and the expectations of the congregation. Others shelter under the evangelical wing of the church. These differences of emphasis may have deep roots and be reflected even in the words used for various objects by both vicar and congregation. Burslem had an evangelical tradition. Coming to the parish as a complete stranger, viewing the building (or indeed the registers, commenced 1578), that tradition would not necessarily have been apparent to me. Much more may have been revealed had I attended service, and certainly was when I talked with members of the congregation.

When I had visited the location on the previous occasion, I had found St John's Church to be an ancient stone building standing in an extensive grassed yard, which contained a certain number of blackened monuments (Figure 9.1). At the edge of the yard stood the buildings of a large, rather forbidding school, which, I was later told, had a history closely linked to the parish church. Evidently until schemes of clearance and rehousing took shape, modest terraces of brick houses and groups of pottery kilns had crouched close around. In the past, the air must surely have been smoke-filled. The town still offered hints of its historic connection with the china industry, through which it must once have been bustling with life. I was told that the church school had at one time up to 800 pupils. The Burslem of today gave me the impression of a place from which wealth had passed.

When I entered St John's with the Revd Smith, I saw the furniture and fitments, including some objects placed as memorials to Arthur, my relative, and to his wife. He discussed with me the layout, the balcony and seating. Without his commentary my scanty knowledge could not have let me read an evangelical history into the interior. I would not have known that my great-uncle had called the altar 'the table'.

Some of the older parishioners to whom he introduced me remembered Arthur, one having been a choir boy when Arthur was near the end of his time in the late 1920s. He told me of the severe authority of the old rector and the school-like discipline in the choir of former days. I saw numerous photographs of occasions and of prominent parishioners of St John's, and also of social events at the old rectory. In the vestry and its safe were portraits and a collection of certificates signed by Arthur. There were minute books of the governors of the church school, accounts and church door notices, including that announcing the end of Arthur's rectorship in 1928.

If you are interested in the traditions and style of a parish where you have recently arrived, it makes sense to ask if there is any kind of published history. Many church buildings and a few parishes have recent booklets devoted to them; a few lucky ones have published memoirs by incumbents, devoted either to the parish itself or to the minister's experience of it. However, if it is the style and politic one is interested in, you may not find that in either a recent or an older published history. The book may be more about stones than people. You will need to start from the present time, and to approach the present incumbents. As well as commenting themselves, they may know where a former vicar or his widow lives, and they will have certainly seen documents written or signed by their predecessors, possibly going back eighty to a hundred years. They may know also of parishioners who remember their predecessors. To a large degree, access to the past hundred years of church life in the parish centres in the first instance upon the present incumbent. Incumbents are always major players, and will be central in what is style and policy.

Going on from there

Having established a body of information about St John's, I had several options for how to proceed. First, I could go further back, seeking the roots of the evangelical tradition there. Second, I could fill out the study of church life by searching for documentary information of events in the local papers or social material from the school records; I could also look for any parish magazine that there may have been. Finally, I could look for explanations of the personality of Arthur.

I was very much interested in the evangelical stance of the place, but how my relative had come to be rector there at all was a question that intrigued me. How did it fit with the social history of Burslem? In searching for relevant information, I was shown two personal diaries of long-time church members, large collections of family photographs, my relative's ordination prayer book, and published tracts prepared by his wife (Figure 9.2). It began to be clear that the parish had played a vital social role – both in education and in the relief of poverty. The diaries indicated that Arthur had arrived there via a sponsor he met in Wales, who was possibly himself connected with a person or persons acting on behalf of Burslem church. His wife also had Church of England family connections in mid-Wales. I began to understand how the evangelical character could be at least maintained by the wishes of sponsors and influential patrons. The way the church presented itself was readable in the illustrations of its officers as they appeared in the Burslem Imperial Bazaar magazine for 1900 (Figures 9.3 and 9.4). Arthur Williams had been a very special choice for a Church of England parish in late Victorian times: a former Baptist chapel boy, once a railway porter, who found himself able to accept fees for distributing charity bread. If his daughters displeased him, he made them kneel. He was a man who, by some means, had crossed a divide that separated those in authority from those who stood against it.

DISSENTING COMMUNITY

One can argue that the life of a parish resides in its people. In former years this was influenced and led by a societal core of wealthier, landed, perhaps even titled people. Thus the physical fabric, the church building, the yard and its monuments are unessential – the trimmings. In theory this might be so: if conviction and commitment are strong enough, and especially if the preacher is sufficiently inspiring (one might risk the word charismatic), the work of a church will continue, using any available space. In practice, though, an old church building does itself acquire a kind of living identity. Clergy and laity will refer to their ancient building almost as a live thing. There is much to debate in the matter of buildings, and some people will assert that leaky, draughty roofs and fine cut stones are far less use than, say, a warm wooden hut, but others will emphasise the poetry, the majesty, and hence the inspirational power of beautiful and much worn buildings. There is no doubt that in both religious and secular groups, buildings are often a crux, and in the case of most institutions, they are vastly important adjuncts to survival. When groups dissent from the establishment especially, success turns on the securing of a building.

CASTLE STREET BAPTIST CHAPEL, CAERLEON

My father went to chapel almost every Sunday evening. Although he was totally committed to it, he did not make me go. I realised later in my life

Figure 9.1 (top left)   St John's Church, Burslem, from an Edwardian postcard.
Figure 9.2 (top right)   Mrs Nina Williams, wife of the Rector of St John's, the Revd Arthur Williams. She wrote many tracts and songs.
Figure 9.3 (bottom left)   A useful documentary source: Burslem Imperial Bazaar catalogue, 1900.
Figure 9.4 (bottom right)   Messrs T. Beresford and R. Malkin, officers of St John's Church, 1900.

that it was the sort of chapel community that believed membership was about conscious adult choice. I left the town when I was 18, thus never reached the age when local men had usually sought membership. As a matter of principle, he would not have pressed me to attend. I learned later that the chapel community had always known me, but I had never known them. Father occasionally preached there, but he did not tell me. When he died, the occasion of his funeral drew chapel people from across the region and a huge congregation gathered, requiring use of all available space and sound to be piped to an adjoining building. It was that day that cemented my need to know how, and for how long, it had been.

Sources

Without knowing at first in any exact way what I sought, I made local inquiries about the existence of written records from Castle Street Chapel. I was in a phase in my learning when written records seemed the most natural and reliable source of information. I wrote several letters seeking books. It was a Baptist chapel, so among other authorities I wrote to the Baptist Historical Society in London. Only after some months of prompting, and being passed from person to person, did the then secretary remember that some books had been deposited at the National Library of Wales some nineteen years before. The library in turn was surprised at my enquiry, stating: 'It is unlikely. We have very few deposits of that sort of thing here.'

The books were there, however, and they proved to consist of seven volumes, commencing with what was known in those records as 'The Old Book', a kind of log book of events started in 1772, with a retrospect to 1755. The series continued through until after the Second World War. The record thus covered just about 200 years. The most recent of the records had a style somewhat reminiscent of committee minute books.

In the books were four different generations of membership lists. Generally, each incoming pastor started a new list of current members and added to it the new ones whom he baptised. The deposited membership books were a very large source and required very detailed study. The record given there included not only adult baptisms, but also arrivals from other chapels. Apparently, you could either become a member by being baptised there, or by being transferred in by letter. There were records of dismissions (transfers elsewhere), exclusions for bad behaviour, deaths, a variety of texts and quotes, and even some political comments.

In addition to the deposited books, I subsequently discovered one further book containing some subscription lists, some birth records, two pages of burial entries and a certificate relating to the founding of a chapel at another town. From all these books it was possible to piece together a variety of aspects of chapel life in different eras. Some of the results I shall report later in this chapter. Before continuing, it is worth saying that since I started studying these books about 1980, I have also had cause to look for and at the books of about a dozen other chapels. Their records vary a great deal in quantity, in the matters reported on and simply in survival. Some that I have sought have been reported variously as 'lost in a house fire at Bristol', 'handed in but no one knows where' or 'disappeared'. Some were found intact and at the PRO, another part mutilated but deposited at the CRO. The use of chapel records is a very chancy business. They have no form laid down by law; they can thus be in almost any shape. They may be found ordered or disordered, kept with rigour or with a querulous absent-mindedness. The books for Castle Street Chapel, Caerleon, are some of the very best I have seen.

In those membership lists I found the adult baptisms of my great-great-grandfather Rosser Williams, his bride-to-be, Amy Jones, Martha Morgan, his daughter-in-law, her father, Adam Morgan, and her mother, Elizabeth Jones. Much later I discovered Adam's mother, who was received from another chapel aged 81, in 1832. My grandmother's grandparents too, a family called Gray or Grey, were in the records. My father's family had been Baptists since the eighteenth century, and associated with Castle Street Chapel since at least 1800. My parents were married there. My father's funeral service was held in the building in 1974, perhaps the last major public event there.

Castle Street Chapel and its yard

One of the first things I did when I became interested was to go on location: I entered the chapel yard (Figure 9.5). I went not only to search for family graves but also to see the number of monuments, the surnames on them and how they lay relative to the building. In the yard, a private burial ground, I also discovered the outdoor font for adult baptism (Figure 9.6).

Some graves near the building were evidently family vaults and had railings and gates. At some stage a few stones had been moved and stood around the edge. The earliest stone that I found was to a Samuel Watkins who died in 1787. The inscriptions on the stones and on some monuments inside the building had a certain flavour, which gave clues as the personal value system espoused by members. The stones did not speak of God, or of faith, or even of love. They rarely mentioned station or profession. Instead, they held up faithfulness as the virtue most to be prized.

The yard backed on to a lane between itself and the River Usk, on which there had been cottages until about 1935. Along the lane had formerly run

Figure 9.5 Castle Street Chapel Yard in 1983, while still intact. Despite objections, the lower part was used to build executive dwellings in the early 1990s.

Figure 9.6 The baptistry in Castle Steet Chapel Yard, Caerleon, 1983. This was last used for adult baptism in 1923.

a tramway used for carrying tin plates to the wharf. The River Usk is tidal at this point with an average rise and fall of 35 ft; at full tide, standing in the chapel yard, one looked out over a wide stretch of water.

Inside the chapel there was a space with softwood pews and a balcony above, a pulpit of modest proportions and windows with a little simple coloured glass. The floor was of wood, uncovered and unpolished. Painted on plaster, facing the seated membership, was 'One church One faith One Lord'. On shelves at the back lay testaments and copies of *Redemption Songs, 1000 hymns and choruses*. There were marble wall memorials, including one to '*Thomas Evans 35 years faithful Pastor of this church*', died 1820. To the side was a kitchen and Sunday School room. Here were chairs, and a table, and large bibles for children to read.

Talking to the chapel members

About 1984 there were possibly twenty members of the chapel; it was to four of these that I talked. None was younger than 65. Some were much older than 80. My conversations with two of them have continued until quite recently, though it is now several years since the building was sold at auction. The things said to me I put together with my teenage experience and with what I had gained from listening to my father, who was a lifelong member. He spoke often of his father, who had been Sunday School Superintendent there. Perhaps the most significant new insight to emerge from the conversations with members was the realisation of the marked difference in the character of the chapel community at different dates. Twentieth-century members, while knowing their chapel had a long history, were none the less unclear about its more distant past.

How it started

The Old Book commences with a memoir, or as that text is described by its author, 'a few thinks'. At first he talks of a meeting house at nearby Ponthir. Then in his third paragraph the writer continues:

> About 17 years ago /'tis now March i772/ Mr John Jones a Gentleman from Denbighshire North Wales came to settle in this Town. He had been in London for several years, and there contracted some acquaintance with the Dissenters and used to attend their Ministry, tho' he was not a member himself, nor his Wife, a Gentlewoman from Notinghamshire. They met in London and married; and after their lot was cast providentially here: tho' to their great grief there was no meeting for them to go to but the above mentioned one, and that mostly in Welsh which language she was an utter stranger to. Sometime after Mr Samuel Watkins /who is now a Member with us, and also officiates as Deacon in our church/ came to live here. He was the first member that lived here.

Later he goes on to explain how Mr John Griffiths of Pontypool, his wife and son John came from Abercarn; Mr Griffiths built the new Tin Mill and Forge near Caerleon. Hamman Davis of Hatton Garden London came to look after the investment of his father's money in the Forge and Tin Mill and when he came

> his father and him were something uneasy for want of a proper Place of Worship, and proposed to purchase the Place where the Meeting House stands and pay for it – which he did.

Mr Davis was subsequently a trustee. The property purchased was an old barn and paddock, with a small cottage and stable. This was their first meetinghouse, their toehold in the world, which opened 19 October 1764, an occasion when the Revd Caleb Evans of Bristol, an eminent Particular Baptist visitor, preached to the text: '*and I will fill this house with glory saith the Lord of Hosts*'.

But the members had a long struggle in front of them. They were a society with a meeting house, which was not at all the same thing as a church. Rather than choose their own minister, they were to be served by various visiting preachers, but especially Mr Miles Harrhy of Penygarn Chapel Pontypool, the oldest Baptist cause in the area, founded in 1727. Caerleon's attempts to be constituted as a church were blocked over a period of years by Mr Harrhy on the grounds that their choices of pastor were unsuitable. (Revd Miles Harrhy was a famous preacher born in northern Monmouthshire about 1700. He was well able to generate vitriolic argument, especially on subjects like infant baptism.)

Eventually, in the face of much unpleasantness, but with the support of other churches, they agreed to break away and form a separate church, with Thomas Phillips of Maesyberllon, Brecknockshire as minister. He was inducted into the ministry by the laying on of hands, after which he stood and preached to them both in English and in Welsh.

There was a price for freedom: he was now made, as the memoir says, an 'object of malice' and '*the calumnies and reproaches etc etc cast upon him and all concerned during that time I would rather bury in Eternal Oblivion than stain this Paper with them.*' The members of the new church got dismission by letter from their existing churches. Ten were from Mr Harrhy's church at Penygarn, eight were from Bassaleg (west of Newport) and one from a more remote church at Llanwenarth near Abergavenny. The former Penygarn members included John Jenkins Snr and Jnr, tin plate makers, and Samuel Watkins, part owner of the Forge and Tin Works. They held their first meeting as a church on 13 November 1771. Prayers were begun by Nicholas Williams, a member, and Rachel Davis was the first new member to be baptised.

The holy streams

Although there is a written record of the vows of the 1771 members, there is no record of the words said at baptism. There are records of the blessing of local streams for use as baptismal sites. I imagine that the baptisms at Caerleon at that time occurred in the River Usk at low water. The use of particular streams or reens (reen is a local name for a drainage ditch) and mill ponds in adjacent parishes gave indication of the sphere of influence of the chapel, and how far people might travel to attend a meeting. Castle Street Chapel was not something just for the town. On the contrary, it acted as a centre drawing members and 'hearers' (people who attended but were unbaptised in that or an equivalent church), from a radius of at least 7 miles.

Growth of the chapel

Apart from a group of fourteen new members gained from another church in 1773, the usual rate of new baptisms in the early years was about four per annum. Due to deaths among original members, and departures, some due to trade recessions in the iron business, the last decades of the eighteenth century saw a small static membership. Among those lost to the Caerleon chapel was Revd Thomas Phillips, who wished to go to serve a destitute chapel near his original home in Swansea, Hamman Davis who died young, and eleven members who left to found a new chapel at Wern near Pontypool.

The membership level must have greatly worried the Revd Thomas Evans, who had been ordained in 1785; the situation was worsened in 1800 by a fierce quarrel among the membership. Like some other original members, John Jenkins Snr had already died; he had been buried at Caerleon Chapel in 1799. However, now his son and some others in a dispute of some kind about the conduct of the church, split off and joined with some other non-members to form a new mixed chapel with a total membership of twelve, at nearby Ponthir. Later that chapel became known as New Works, and more recently has been called Capel Seion (see also Chapter 5). It was close to where Jenkins developed his new tin mills, later called Pontheer Works.

But Thomas Evans saw his church through a tough period. In the latter years of his ministry, the local forge and rolling mill were attaining a new pitch of activity. Owned at the turn of the nineteenth century by the Butler family, who had strong Bristol connections, the site had become renowned as one of the country's most extensive – something that visitors to the county were recommended to see. New workmen were attracted, and the influx gathered pace (see Chapter 7). Chapel membership prospered. By the time that Revd Thomas Evans died in 1820, there was need of larger premises. He had seen the community through its hardest times and was viewed by the members with the greatest affection. He is referred to in writing, occasionally, as 'beloved Thomas Evans'.

With such membership growth it was easily possible to support the formation of new chapels elsewhere by groups of Caerleon members. One such was at Caerwent, another started in 1824 at Usk town. Each new chapel required a certificate under the Act known as 52 Georgii III, which was usually obtained from the bishop's registrar. Such new chapels did not of course necessarily survive, and the one listed at Usk in the 1851 religious census seems to have been a later foundation.

The expansion of industrial activity in the area was achieved partly by speculators from Bristol. Three wealthy Bristol families called Nash, Caffin and Warren interested themselves in Castle Street Chapel in the first decade of the nineteenth century, donating a leather-bound book, in which they entered the births of their own children. Also in this book, which is in the author's family, were recorded donations made for the expansion of the chapel building (1821 and 1824). At the first of these dates an outdoor font of stone, called by the members a baptistry, was built into the yard (Figure 9.6). Three people from Ultra Pontem – William Price, his wife, Elizabeth, and Jane Edmunds – were the first baptised in the new baptistry on 18 November 1821. The Revd Christmas Evans, that most colourful of orators, then resident at Llangefni, Anglesea, was invited to preach as a celebration of the chapel's growth.

By this time the membership was on friendly terms again with New Works chapel, and the Revd James Michael of New Works preached several times at Castle Street. Known as the 'Silver Bell of Wales', he turned a fine phrase. Referring to the death of his daughter, Anne, he is reputed to have said: '*Anne my beautiful daughter will lie in Ponthir churchyard until the sounding of the trumpets raises the dwellers of the dust*'. His personal daybook compiled in Welsh, is deposited at the National Library of Wales.

Rebuilding

Most of the money used to expand the building, and to put in a large balcony, came from tin plate production. Although Caerleon Works was by now thriving in the hands of a church-going family, the Fothergills, on this occasion it was not Caerleon Works which were the providers. Job and Edward Jenkins, brothers of John Jenkins Jnr and thus sons of the older John Jenkins, had a works at Pontnewydd a few miles nearer to Pontypool. They gave £100 each towards the rebuilding, the remainder being raised by subscription. The subscribers (see Figure 9.7) were from quite a wide area

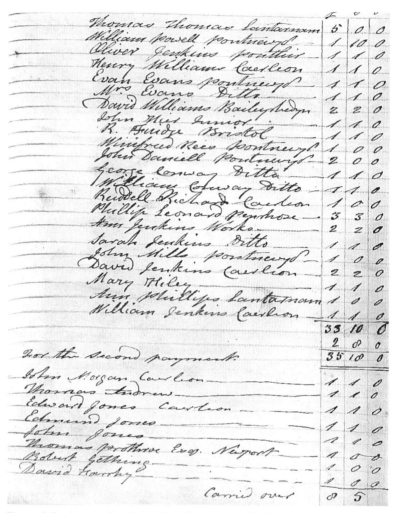

Figure 9.7   A part subscription list of people contributing to the 1821 rebuilding of Castle Street Chapel, Caerleon. Note the frequency of patronymic surnames and the Welsh locative surname Conway (*Conwy*). Some donors like Rudhall Richards feature also in the parish church records. Observe also the presence of the name of Thomas Protheroe Esq.

and some of them were anonymous, being recorded simply as 'A Friend'. The resulting building was that used until the closure of the chapel in the 1980s. It is worth reflecting that dissenting communities can survive only if they have premises they can be sure of: it is their rock of ages. Survival is best ensured by property ownership. The original purchasers had done at least as much for the Baptist cause at Caerleon, as did any later pastor.

The baptised membership at this time included not only numerous metal workers – forgemen, doublers, wiredrawers, shearers, and so on – but also families associated with the riverside and others from Ultra Pontem, who made a living by green wood trades. General woodmen, hurdlemakers and especially hoopmakers were quite numerous in the early nineteenth century, dry barrels being used to transport nails, butter and other items by canal. There is some evidence that the sons of fathers in these fading green wood trades became metal workers.

By the time of the Religious Census of Wales in 1851, Castle Street Chapel could claim attendances of 300 in the morning and 320 in the evening. Even allowing for some licence in the figures, these are significantly larger than those claimed by Caerleon parish church. The chapel congregation of course represented several parishes.

Castle Street Chapel also had a Sunday School. This was especially important locally, since the only day school available in the town was Caerleon Endowed School. This was a 'blue coat' Anglican charity foundation and most chapel children were excluded at that time. My great-grandfather Edmund Williams, a literate man, later a Deacon at Castle Street, learnt his letters entirely at the chapel, with the guidance of Mistress Sarah Morgan.

Times of insurrection

Towards the end of 1819, while Thomas Evans was infirm following a stroke, baptisms were effected by the Revd David Phillips. After Evans' death, he continued to minister through a period of expansion, and reading the records it comes a surprise to read of his sudden departure for North America in the spring of 1841. No memoir was left to explain the events that lead up to this. However, David Phillips was excluded from the chapel in his absence, by the action of the Revd James Michael of Capel Seion. A period of instability followed. The suggestions in the next paragraphs necessarily contain speculation.

Much of Monmouthshire was very politically alive in the period immediately prior to the Chartist Rising of November 1839. John Frost, the Newport Chartist, represented Newport, Caerleon and Pontypool at the Convention for the Charter. At least one major meeting of local Chartists was held at Caerleon and certainly a large open air meet took place on Christchurch Hill. There was undoubtedly much support for the Chartist cause in the area, though there is no firm evidence that any local men were involved in the riot on 4 November 1839. Caerleon tradesmen were among those issued with truncheons as special constables to put down the Chartist threat. John Frost knew Caerleon well, and indeed, in his greatest personal struggle against political corruption, his most significant opponent was Thomas Protheroe, clerk to the Caerleon Church Charity. In 1820, Frost accused the latter of raising a Grand Jury against him composed very largely of Caerleon tenants of the Caerleon Church Charity. At Frost's trial for high treason after the 1839 Newport uprising, one of the jurors was Matthew Cope, maltster, a member of a Caerleon family with a vault in the Castle Street Chapel yard; there were also five farmers from the Christchurch area included.

From all of this, it is not hard to believe that the people of the Caerleon area in general would have been deeply divided on the matter of Chartism. Furthermore, although Frost was a Congregationist, following the riot many members of the establishment held Baptist chapels among those morally responsible for the affair. Caerleon chapel certainly had some pro-Chartist elements. The burial record, for instance, includes a child aged 2 called 'William Frost Feargus O'Conor', buried in 1841.

Following the riot of 1839, some local dissenting ministers tried to exclude Chartist members. At least one of those local preachers found himself excluded instead. On which side the Revd David Phillips was in the affair, I do not know. It seems possible, however, that he left Caerleon over the divisions within the Castle Street membership concerning Chartism.

The golden age

The Baptist chapel at Caerleon had several remarkable men as pastors at different stages. In 1866 they appointed a young man whose name is now synonymous with that chapel in the minds of local people. Dewi Bevan Jones, a native of Llandyssul Cards, stayed sixty years. He personally baptised in the chapel yard well over four hundred members. During his ministry, the Sunday School flourished as did the social aspect of the chapel life. The hymns, now accompanied by music, warmed the hearts and minds. Trips in hired brakes were made to the nearby coast or to local fields for picnics. The chapel became integrated into the growing local political awareness. Dewi Bevan Jones became a local councillor, Liberal in persuasion, as was William Williams, his Sunday School Superintendent. By the time of the 1906 general election, several other members were active for the Liberals too. Through this work Bevan Jones' commitment to the concept of membership, loyalty and faithfulness still shone. According to oral testimony, in his closing years, the early 1920s, new members' baptisms were conducted in old clothes. Immersion in the baptistry was total. The Revd Bevan Jones, the water streaming from him, often with tears in his eyes, made each new member stand wet at the font side, before he came to them to give the hand of fellowship.

Evolution of the Baptist community

Castle Street Chapel was a church of the Particular Baptists. The latter had formed originally, not from the General Baptists, but as a 1633 offshoot of a group of London Independents. Particular Baptists were Calvinistic, believing in adult baptism and predestination. Here they differed much from the General Baptists, who were Arminian in origin. Raymond Brown's (1986) *The English Baptists of the 18th Century* gives an excellent account of the origins of Baptist sects. By the time that the Castle Street Chapel formed, most Particular Baptist churches had retreated from the High Calvinist ideals; Caerleon, though severe in its style, was not of the strict kind. A rather intolerant belief in predestination was combined with a more tolerant behavioural code. They were concerned with faithfulness to the brotherhood and the cause and with the struggle for a 'proper' life for ordinary people. Naturally, most members had spouses within the chapel.

Mostly through the medium of their deacons, the community punished their members' misdemeanours by exclusion. Almost always, though, they forgave them, even if sometimes forgiveness took several years. The only exceptions to forgiveness seem to have been made over abandonment of a wife and children, which constituted a *disgrace to religion* and hence a betrayal of the community as a whole in some way. However, there were exclusions in the first third of the nineteenth century for '*standing at what is called a christening in church*', for dancing in a pub, for fighting, for drunkenness, or holding a 'biddale', that is brewing ale and serving it on the Lord's Day. Drinkers, fighters and biddale callers were all reinstated as members after an interval of months. Regarding attendance at other churches, it is notable that they regarded the Independents at Ultra Pontem as their allies and friends, yet the Caerleon Wesleyan chapel was certainly no place in which to be seen.

During the long ministry of the Revd Dewi Bevan Jones, a gentle move towards evangelism was taking place; some members had their children baptised in the parish church, while many new members were former Anglicans. The impression given is one of warmth and energy. Handed-down oral accounts say that during the Revd Jones' preaching, members sometimes called out loudly 'Praise the Lord'. Illegitimacy did remain much frowned upon, however. There are verbal accounts of the public humiliation of unfortunate girls in the Edwardian period. The nineteenth-century written record shows, however, that unmarried mothers, after an interval, did become baptised as members, and sometimes later married other chapel members.

From 1919, returning soldiers wrought a change. The chapel was already political. Its concern with the life struggles of ordinary people had rather naturally caused members to take the political opportunities offered by increasing local democracy, from 1880 onwards. But returning soldiers were angry, and many chapels, which had been centres of gentlemanly Liberalism soon showed a sharp impatience for change. In some, as at Caerleon, where until recently aged members would still assert to me '*of course we are Liberals, really*', the Labour Party found a firm foothold, although this was not a secular political stand. Rather, it was a religious socialism. There was a rekindling of fires that had not burned since 1839. To explain, I can do no better than quote from a hymn book, which was in the hands of a few members in the 1920s. The *Socialist Sunday School Song Book* (Telford et al. 1925) contains words by William Morris, Edward Carpenter, Havelock Ellis and among many others, Joseph Whittaker, from whose words I quote, with the local emendations incorporated:

Lift up the peoples banner,
To trail not in the dust;
A myriad hands are ready
To guard the sacred trust;
With steps that never falter,
And hearts that grow more strong,
Till victory ends our warfare
We sternly march along.

Through ages of oppression,
We bore a heavy load,
While others reaped the harvest
From seeds the people sowed;
Down in the earth we burrowed,
Or fed the furnace heats;
We felled the mighty forests,
We built the mighty fleets.

But after bitter ages
Of hunger and despair,
The slave has snapped his fetters,
And bids his foes beware;
We will be slaves no longer,
The nations soon shall know
That all who live must labour,
And all who reap must sow.

So on we march to battle,
With souls that shall not rest
Until the world we live in
Is by the world possessed;
And filled with perfect manhood,
In beauty it shall move –
One heart, one home, one nation
Whose king and lord is love.

IRON FORGING AND TIN PLATE PRODUCTION AT CAERLEON

It should not be assumed from this long account of chapel life, and the use of the profits from tin plate, that all chapel goers were tin plate workers, or indeed that all tin plate workers went to chapel. Neither was true. Although undoubtedly, at the start, workers at the tin mills and forge were encouraged into the chapel, first as hearers then as members, things changed in the nineteenth century. Incomers associated with nineteenth-century expansion were often of English origin, although they were in many cases not first generation arrivals in Wales. The number of English surnames in the town increased rapidly (see Chapter 6). Many of these were not chapel-going people; indeed, even though children were christened in church, they were not necessarily church-going either. The Church of England records are one useful source in reconstructing the works history, however; they can be put together with some early records of Caerleon Works held at Newport Reference Library, and with census enumerators' books for the town. In attempting to reconstruct the industrial process, A.H. John's (1950) *The Industrial Development of South Wales 1750–1850* is helpful, as it gives early process details.

What the early records show

There are two particular advantages when studying Caerleon Works. First, for much of the time between 1760 and 1875 it was the town's major local employer; it is thus reasonable to assume that men in the appropriate trades mentioned in the parish registers, or on the census enumerators' books, worked at that site. Second, a set of records for the site has been deposited in Newport Reference Library. Neither asset is absolute: after 1835 some Caerleon men did work at the Cordes Dos Nail Works, while a few may have worked at Pontheer Works. Furthermore, the surviving books are not by any means a complete set. Despite these complications, the relative isolation of Caerleon Works as a site does allow one to make the assumption that most finers, tin men, rollers, shearers or hollowfiremen were employees at the Caerleon site.

The earliest forge and tinning works at Caerleon (1756–61) were a small affair, perhaps involving on the site, no more than a total of fifteen to twenty men. There was a charcoal furnace and nearby, a water-powered rolling mill, probably derived from a grist mill. Also present was a tinning shop. The surviving account books allow one to infer that at that time a set of rolls was worked by a team of three men. Indeed there were two such teams, the rollermen being named as Abraham Jenkins and Thomas Watkin. These acted as master craftsmen, who paid their own labourers and shearers. David Robert, the tinner, likewise had his own labourers.

John Griffiths, of Abercarn in Mynyddislwyn parish, and Samuel Watkins, founder of the chapel, had provided business capital, and the records reveal the monies that they were taking out of a profitable operation. John Jenkins Jnr was the principal craftsman, while John Snr (both Jenkinses were also chapel founders) was apparently supplying tinning expertise. From whence came the first skilled rollermen and shearers is not clear, but it seems inevitable that they should have been incomers from Abercarn or Pontypool.

Those early records give a vivid picture of the way that the works fitted into the local economy. At least fourteen different coal haulers are mentioned. Some brought coal from The Race near Pontypool, some from 'Gelly', possibly Gelligroes in the Sirhowy Valley. Bran for steeping, lard as a flux for tinning, and goose grease, all came courtesy of local farmers' wives; candles, hemp and nails came from Caerleon tradesmen.

Boxes of finished plates presumably went by boat to Bristol, but the offcuts of tin plate, black plate and bar iron were bought by blacksmiths and tin plate tradesmen of the locality. The latter made saucepans and other household and farm objects. Smiths in sixteen parishes are mentioned as buying the Forge's metal scraps. Black plate was sold to make ploughshares and to mend home hearths. The iron trimmings went in large part, though, to be rolled into ship bolts.

These same numerous activities are also evident in another set of surviving records for Caerleon Forge from the early 1780s. Here more rollermen, shearers, plate washers and labourers can be identified by name. At this time also, one George Conway was being paid for rolling plates. Later he founded his own works at Pontnewydd. The tin plate making business, like the Baptist chapel to which its founders were devoted, spawned satellites. This is not surprising: like the chapel, they were small, close, active human communities, built around strong personalities.

The nineteenth century

After 1813, references in St Cadoc's Church baptismal records to forge and tin plate workers abound. By now, Caerleon Works was owned by a church-going family, and John Jenkins Jnr had started up a new plant at nearby Ponthir. One of the first Caerleon rollermen mentioned in the St Cadoc's record is James Grey. He rolled black plate for tin dipping, while his brother Joseph was a ship bolt roller. Both men came from Mynyddislwyn in the next valley to the west, where there were early metal working sites at which the Butler family apparently had an interest. Accompanying these brothers were other Western Valley men and women, who found work as servants. Richard Cullis, another roller, came from the Forest of Dean in Gloucestershire. In the first part of the nintenth century, wire making was important at the Caerleon site and wiredrawers were often mentioned in the parish records, until a sudden cessation about 1826. This skill too was established in the eighteenth century at Mynyddislwyn.

In the nineteenth century the forging and rolling process at Caerleon was old fashioned; water wheels, of which there seem to have been three on site from early days, probably remained in use for driving rollers until the works went out of business in 1876 (see Chapter 6).

Until that crash, which was due perhaps to tougher conditions for exporting to the USA, the business had been protected by an expanding market, and old technology could persist. As well as water-powered rolling, iron refining with charcoal remained in use until mid-century. The first iron puddler referred to in the parish records is one in 1863, suggesting that the more modern iron puddling process was not adopted until about 1860, certainly rather late. It is possible (though unlikely) that some of the other men recorded on censuses as forgemen were puddlers. However, charcoal making is mentioned up to 1855. At least one of the puddlers, Rees Williams, was born at Nantyglo, the site of a large leading-edge iron making operation. He was thus another example of bought-in expertise.

The marriage and baptismal records of St Cadoc's Church allow one to roughly reconstruct the technical procedures in use at Caerleon Forge at different dates. As well as the earlier charcoal finers and forgemen, and the later puddlers, there are annealers, picklers and, towards the end, hollow-firemen. Census returns add further information. In those records, as in the baptismal lists, it is possible to note men rising through the hierarchy of the rolling mill. They were sometimes boy plate dividers (some aged 12 or 13), then doublers or shearers, before becoming rollermen – if they ever did, that is. Some men can be traced who got the top job, but who later stepped down again to shearer as age overtook them. This reminds one that a roller-man on the hot rolls was 'top man'. His job was an almost unsurpassed combination of weight, skill and danger.

The works reopened in 1884 under new management (see Chapter 6) and was apparently then refitted with steam-powered rollers, though one water wheel remained until the final closure in 1939.

Between the reign of the Butlers and the 1876 closure, local directories show that two families owned the business. Richard Fothergill's family were associated with the works from 1818 until mid-century. The Moggeridge family put their name on the company from then on, though they seem to have had a financial interest for some time before that happened. Local people persisted in calling the Caerleon Works 'Mr Fothergill's', whomsoever was the actual owner. Several local monumental inscriptions refer to Fothergill's Works. One local eighteenth-century stone only uses the word 'tinplate'.

Local tin plate in the twentieth century

Although the Pontheer Works of John Jenkins grew from the Caerleon Works, and was not far from it, the two remained in separate ownership. The Pontnewydd Works also remained apart; indeed further works were built in the same valley near the Pontnewydd Works, so that in the mid-nineteenth century there were at least five tin plate operations lying on the Avon Llwyd River, within a few miles of each other. Of these, one was still a major employer after the Second World War; even then, Caerleon had its rollermen.

Pontheer Works and Caerleon Works were the focus of the rivalry between two adjacent parishes – Llangattock and Llanfrechfa. Old residents can still tell tales of Cary Rees, the last of the rollermen at Pontheer, who it is said was preserved ('kippered') by the heat and hence entirely safe from unfortunate journeys in the after life. The then owners of Pontheer Works, who closed it in 1912, used to arrive formally to visit, wearing top hats. Accordingly, Caerleon men largely abandoned their old term 'uchins' (Welsh 'uch', meaning 'above') for Ponthir men, calling them latterly 'the tophatters'. Men of Caerleon town were known then as 'the flies' – apparently a reference to the use of one-horse carriages. Naturally, in this game, the men of Ultra Pontem had to resign themselves to being 'the Philistines'.

REFERENCES AND FURTHER READING

Atkinson, Revd J.C. (1891) *Forty Years in a Moorland Parish*. London and New York: Macmillan, 2nd edn [A vicar's account of parish life in north Yorkshire].

Brown, R. (1986) *The English Baptists of the 18th Century*. London: Baptist Historical Society [One of a series on English Baptists. This one covers the period 1689–1815].

Cordell, A. (1991) *The Rape of the Fair Country*. Boston, MA: Little, Brown & Co. (re-issue) [A novel, but one of the best ways of picturing life in the nineteenth-century iron trade in South Wales].

John, A.H. (1950) *The Industrial Development of South Wales 1750–1850: An Essay*. Cardiff: University of Wales Press.

Jones, D.J.V. (1986) *The Last Rising*. Oxford: Oxford University Press [One of the several published accounts of the Chartist uprising at Newport 1839].

McGeown, P. (1987) *Heat the Furnace Seven Times More*. London: Hutchinson [A treasure: autobiography of a twentieth-century furnace-man].

Nair, G. (1988) *Highley The Development of A Community 1550–1880*. Oxford: Basil Blackwell [A 'one parish' social history].

Plomer, W. (ed.) (1977) *Kilvert's Diary 1870–79*. Harmondsworth: Penguin [Truly a classic. Vicar's diary of his daily life in his several parishes].

Prince, Revd J.E. (1922) *The History and Topography of the Parish of Silkstone*. Penistone: Don Press [An example of a vicar's wide-ranging parish history].

Rees, D.B. (1975) *Chapels in the Valley*. Upton, Wirral: Ffynnon Press [Research on the social role of chapels in a Welsh valley].

Scrivenor, H. (1854) *History of the Iron Trade from the Earliest Records to the Current Period*. London: Longman, Brown, Green and Longmans. Reprinted Cedric Chivers Ltd (1968).

Steel, D.J. (1973) *Sources for Non-conformist Genealogy and Family History*. London: Society of Genealogists [Sane account of origin of sects, and of the variety of written sources].

Telford, M.B., Hopkinson, D.D. and Russell, A. (1925) *The Socialist Sunday School Song Book*. National Council of British Sunday School Unions.

Williams, D. (1969) *John Frost A Study in Chartism*. New York: Augustus Kelley [Previously published Cardiff (1939), it is both a monograph and a local history].

CHAPTER TEN

But What is it All For?

PRODUCTS AND PURPOSES

It will be apparent to the reader by now that the author thinks that the study of local history is important. If the author did not think it was important why else would he go to the trouble of offering in such detail opinions on how it should be done? Yet however enjoyable and important the doing of work is, all work is also intended to have some product; perhaps the importance of any work can be fully assessed only when both the value of doing and the utility of the product are recognised. There is here more than one possible sort of product. But what are they for? And are they worth the effort?

Possible products

How many local 'histories' do you see that are entitled *A History of X from its Beginnings to the Present Day* or, at least, which in spirit are offering such an account? A forward progressing story is what many of us think a history to be. These days, with the ready availability of desktop publishing software, there are many opportunities and much need for the creation of locally produced short, specialised local histories. Indeed it would be fair to say that there is great scope for them, since national compilations will not provide the required coverage. Furthermore, provided these small publications are given an ISBN (International Standard Book Number), which is a cheap and easy matter at one pound sterling a number, they will gain entry to the lists of books in print, and a place in the copyright libraries. They will then be accessible to all via libraries and bookshops.

However, there are other valuable ways of offering research results, and there are many other products of local research than traditional accounts of this kind. For instance, there is a demand for stories intended to educate – accounts for children. They help to cement identity with a place. For this the account may need the choice of characters and the creation and addition of drawings or coloured illustrations, maybe even quizzes or games.

Furthermore, poetry, ballads and plays for the theatre are true products of local research, with a local currency. Some of the same material can also be set up as musical or spoken voice productions on audio tape.

In Chapter 9, much of the main substance is a forward progressing story of how a particular iron works and a particular chapel were intertwined; a story of that sort would make a small locally produced book. But the account has other elements besides the story that I created. The account talks a little, for instance, of my path of study in the years that I was unearthing the detail. That path is an account of what I call 'process' – the ways things happened during the investigation. This way of reporting (and Chapters 5 and 6 are an even better examples of process accounts) allows the consumer much more opportunity to question both the content and the conclusions in the final written result. If I had done it differently, would I have had a different result? Were any different conclusions possible? Could the emphasis have been placed elsewhere? In a process account, readers can see the points on the research journey and may query them if they wish. Of course, research papers in journals are usually a part description of a research process and method, a part results and finally, a part concerning discussion and conclusions. This is the traditional professional product.

CREATING A LEGACY OF REFERENCE MATERIAL

Written texts are gifts both to present and future people. However, there are other gifts which may be offered, not direct to present readers, but to readers of the future, via other researchers. For example, an invaluable product of your work might be obtained by screening, extracting, combining and ordering the sources relating to a certain topic, thereby creating a specialised local archive. This could take the form of audio or video tapes, carrying interviews or commentaries, or perhaps of typed-up reference material presented as an indexed book. This sort of thing might have been done, for instance, using all the personal service material I derived in the study of the First World War service that I reported in Chapter 5. The product would be a book containing all the local men and women who gave First World War service, with a paragraph about each, and the information sources that were relevant for each person listed. The index of it would allow searching by name, unit, birth date, home address and very many other parameters, such as if wounded. This book, if placed in the Gwent

County Record Office, would I am sure be much appreciated by future generations of local and family historians of the county. The object, which would really be a database, could alternatively be deposited at the CRO on electronic disk, using database software, though there is uncertainty about the longer term fate of computer software and hardware, and particularly about the readability in the future of obsolete types of disks or tapes.

HYPERTEXTS

While it may be true that in your research you are able to define a narrow question or topic and ferret out information relating to it, often things do not entirely work out like that. It is not at all unusual for a question to broaden as you work on it, and for information to get included in the cull when it is not definitely connected to the original question. Research can move laterally as well as forward. Yet sometimes lateral information is very interesting information, either to you or to some other person.

Since matters do often unfold in this wandering, lateral way, it is often quite hard, or indeed rather false, to write a history in the form of a linear story, whether of the process of research or of the events themselves. One way to handle this, is to avoid writing a single linear account, but compile instead a series of islands of text, that might be read in many different orders. Some of the islands may also be illustrations such as photographs or maps. Further ones may be reference lists of people, dates, locations and so on. If each piece is given a number, then links between islands can be offered to the reader, by highlighting certain words with footnotes that contain the numbers of other islands for them to jump to if they choose.

This sort of structure has several practical advantages. A major one of them is the ease of adding new material, either in the form of new islands or by editing an old one. The latter will naturally not necessitate reworking a large body of text, since each island is likely to be a separate word processor file. The structure also permits the addition of new bridges at any time, as totally new angles to the work come into the mind of the writer.

As well as making hypertext on paper, it is possible to use marketed hypertext authoring software, such as *KnowledgePro, Guide* or *ToolBook*. The larger authoring packages permit individual islands to contain image sets, dictionaries or even video material.

WHAT IS THE PURPOSE OF LOCAL HISTORY?

There are plenty of people who have well-rounded views of what is important and what is not. Often judgements of value are made by appeal to such measuring questions as 'What can you use it for anyway?' and 'What income does it generate?' I have had my own involvement in this subject challenged with '*And is that a profitable way to spend your time?*' As far as local history is concerned, one can answer these sorts of questions by re-course to two different lines of argument: first, the humane, and second, the business-like.

The study of local history is important because of people's need to feel connected, to feel they have roots in a collective enterprise of living, to share an origin and to use common reference points. To steal the words of Simone Weil, we owe respect to a collectivity because it is food for human souls. The search for connection to roots – in the collective gene pool, the common experience and the remembered townscape – has become urgent for many, many people. Perhaps this ties in to the way that localness itself is being eroded. Not merely are buildings laid flat and hastily shovelled away, but streets themselves are wiped from the map. Small-scale struc-tures collapse. The corner shop is no more; the footpath is without mean-ing. Is anyone local? The school teacher lives in the next town. Now our neighbour works in Derby or Abu Dhabi. We drive a hundred miles to go to the theatre. Friends live invisibly in the Hypernet. Who of us can be sure that they have a neighbourhood? Yet all do need to belong, somewhere, with somebody. Local history is a way of finding connection, not only with genetic family, but also with a social group, certain environs, the facts and the myths that one can lay claim to. It can be the vehicle for rejoining with the descendants of emigrants in distant countries. This will be increasingly possible through computer bill boards and e-mail systems.

Further even than that, since all history has to have a life in the present as well as the past, it is satisfying that local studies are a means of making connections in the present, within the group that cares about the events, conditions, fabric and documentary residues of the past. On both these counts, local history is something far more than a mere entertainment or an indulgence, though entertaining it can be.

The attempt to achieve connection with the past has importance because, to a large extent, getting connected to the past is the same as becoming fully aware in the present. The way our society currently operates means that large numbers of people stop living in ways that connect them to events: to the weather, to the land, to the locality. They stop being practically respon-sible for their surroundings. Thus they may buy from a builder a new house patently built on a flood plain – the sort of site men and women have known for 2,000 years was a flood plain – yet when they are flooded, they expect the local council to be responsible for putting matters right. Through the medium of television, they see wars and yet remain unconnected; see all manner of skilful events without moving from their chairs; and are confused by doctored images, so that they can scarcely tell document from fantasy.

If you are unconnected, you will not be concerned when the local grave-yard is dug up and used for house building, or when the most historic part of your town is obliterated to make an underpass. Our ability to somehow 'live' the past is a key to a better handling of the present, and also to a more sympathetic treatment of the remaining artifacts of the past. The more you can get under the skin of the past, the more you can understand it as an experience, not only the richer it proves to be, but also the more chance you have of infecting others with your interest.

THE EDUCATIONAL AND CONSERVATIONAL DIMENSION OF LOCAL HISTORY

But the questions thrown at us at the start of the chapter can be answered also in a second way, that makes no appeal to matters of soul or conviction. There are good sound business reasons for being interested in local history. Much of the effort directed at bringing wealth to particular towns and cities turns upon attracting businesses and major financial investors. These days these have to bring enterprises that rely much on high technology, and hence on qualified staff who run complex and technical operations. Why should those people want to come and live in a town devoid of interest and beauty? They will want there to be old buildings to visit and examine, an interesting, unique past displayed, to be in a place with traditions to celebrate. There are important roles for local historians in providing the arguments for conservation, the substance for local literature, and the evidence that somebody cares.

To some extent a local historian's active role must be as teacher: to give encouragement to anyone else who asks questions, to promote genuine research activity, to make sure sound answers are offered in local newspapers or to local political figures on matters to do with the town's past. The role is about being enthusiastic as well as competent, and it is about welcoming the enthusiasm of others. Here is a story. I was in France. It was a summer evening, I was walking in the town of Albert, almost in the shadow of the famous madonna, when I met a young Welshman. He had come to France on a whim to try to answer for himself some questions. These questions had come to him very suddenly when he was reading a book about men from his locality, who were at the battle of Mametz Wood. The young man and I talked. He was relieved to find that I did not think him strange to be so driven by questions; that I did not laugh at him for taking a book out of his local library, and then with it, getting on the first available boat. I shall always remember the long summer dusk, the joy and intensity in his face, and his wonder at finding another person with whom to share the questions. All students have to be teachers sometimes, and it was my turn that evening.

LOCAL HISTORY CLASSES

It is probably true to say that evening and extramural classes are the way that local histories are usually taught and the medium through which much research and teaching of research method progresses. Without this sort of learner group, methods could not be taught and standards of scholarship set. One must understand that whatever the depth of personal involvement there is in local studies, intellectual rigour is still achievable. Those who assert this is not so would do well to consider how emotionally involved many physicists and chemists are with their subjects. In a local history class there are three categories of person: the teacher, whose role may be as expositor, but who is often more of a facilitator of the learning of others, and two sorts of class members. First, there are those who are born locally and tend to want to contribute because they remember the old locals and the usages of buildings. They enjoy making their contribution – cashing in the capital of the native. Second, there are the incomers, who typically want documents to help them understand the place they have arrived in, to rationalise, and to create a personal rootedness. When the class researches the place, it often reveals the current natives as descendants of earlier incomers. The two student groups in the class, natives and incomers, are thus revealed as echoes of strands in the past of the town itself and indeed of all towns.

It is more than possible that using contemporary and future technology, the products of networks of these study groups, spread across the country, might be harnessed to generate a version of national history, something hardly thinkable before the advent of personal computers and of the Internet. However, among the many barriers to a successful joining of the outputs of groups spread across the country must be the setting of agreed tasks, of mutual standards and of unified means of approach. It is also important to understand that many natives, especially, get into local history out of a love of what they see as the uniqueness of their own town or village. Yet compelling as the conviction of uniqueness is, almost certainly it is commonality that will prove most important in a national context. The general mechanisms and processes that are shared with other towns are the kernel of what networked research will be able to reveal.

BUT HOW, AND HOW FAR SHOULD WE GO?

I contend very strongly that all research is a search for the truth. It can sometimes be very hard to define the truth, but nevertheless it is fairly easy to comprehend a search for it. If we are not seriously pursuing the truth of the past in our locality, we are wasting both our time and our resources. The world may be better off with no record than with a false record. But having said that, it is necessary to ask how much of the truth do you want? Do you only want the bits that show your own origin in a good light? The aspects that are curious? Would you mostly look for what is baffling or wonderful? Or do you really want all of it? So much of the past is squalid, disgusting, horrifying even. Did you realise that it stank? Do you think on the violence, the overcrowding, the untreated illnesses? Maybe we all should. Certainly, it is untruthful to both oneself and to one's potential readership to pick and present the fragments that attract, or which are the exception.

But taking on board the past as it was is about thinking one's own self into the situation of former people; imagining as far as you can what it may have felt like. This can be very hard to do. After all, to do it, one has to be able to tell one's self frankly about one's own feelings. Does anyone reading this know what it is like to have to beg, or have only rags to wear? Do we all understand how convenient it is to have aspirins, and a cream for athlete's foot? I believe that the best way into understanding the reality of past time is via your own family. Invest effort in understanding the upbringing of your parents, their schooling and life experience. (In those things lie very many of your own attitudes too.) By closely studying them, you can get a view of their society and their time. From your parents you can proceed on to your grandparents. Get their every life detail that you can. Build a picture of the conditions they lived in; the attitudes they grew up with, the issues of their time. What views were passed to them by their parents? These things are your best way into an understanding of how it was.

But this still does not answer the question of how far in factual detail and in understanding of others' lives we may go. Are we entitled to ask *anything at all*? Is any of it private, in grandfather's life, or in that of his neighbours, or of his workmates? Perhaps the answer to this depends on how we intend to use any information that we gain. Twice in the course of interviewing village people, I have had murders recounted to me. Both included specific details. Then I was told about a man who was believed to have starved his wife, and another who used to shut his wife in a cupboard. I have had many accounts of alcoholism and family violence. I did not insist on having any of this information. On the contrary, in some cases I did not ask, but I was given it. Many people will give information very freely, to the depth at which they think you can cope. But what may I do with it? Is it better that I know, and have built from it and from other information, a truer picture of that particular rural society? Or should they have suppressed it? I think the former, provided that I conserve all confidentiality. Really, provided you behave respectfully, to both living and dead, and use your information responsibly and honestly, the depth to which you go truth seeking will not be limited by others. It will depend only upon yourself, and on your understanding of yourself. The limits to experiential understanding lie within the bounds of one's own self-knowledge.

Index

Items in italic are surnames. Place names are in roman type, as are the names of identified individuals.

271